Spirit Matters

Spirit Matters

The Transcendent in Modern Japanese Literature

Philip Gabriel

University of Hawai'i Press
Honolulu

© 2006 University of Hawai'i Press
All rights reserved
Printed in the United States of America
11 10 09 08 07 06   6 5 4 3 2 1

LIBRARY OF CONGRESS CATALOGING-IN-PUBLICATION DATA

Gabriel, Philip.
Spirit matters : the transcendent in modern Japanese literature /
by Philip Gabriel.
  p. cm.
Includes bibliographical references and index.
ISBN-13: 978-0-8248-2974-2 (hardover : alk. paper)
ISBN-10: 0-8248-2974-3 (hardcover : alk. paper)
  1. Japanese literature—Showa period, 1926–1989—History
and criticism. 2. Japanese literature—Heisei period, 1989—
History and criticism. 3. Religion and literature. I. Title.
PL726.65.G23 2006
895.6'09382—dc22

                                    2005032153

University of Hawai'i Press books are printed on acid-free
paper and meet the guidelines for permanence and durability
of the Council on Library Resources.

Designed by University of Hawai'i Press production staff

Printed by The Maple-Vail Book Manufacturing Group

To my family, Junko and Mika

Contents

Acknowledgments

First of all, I wish to thank Murakami Haruki and Ōe Kenzaburō for allowing me to translate their works, in particular Murakami's *South of the Border, West of the Sun; The Place That Was Promised; Sputnik Sweetheart;* and *Kafka on the Shore;* and Ōe's *Somersault.* Their work has stimulated me to think beyond the boundaries in which the present book was originally conceived and has helped me better understand the intersection of translation and scholarship. I greatly appreciate their kindness in responding to questions and the trust they placed in me in allowing me to translate their work.

I am also thankful to my colleagues in the Department of East Asian Studies at the University of Arizona. In an era of budget shortfalls and tight economies, they have been unfailingly upbeat and cheerful and have always provided a congenial space in which to write this book. I am particularly grateful to Professors Timothy Vance, Li Dian, and Noel Pinnington for their friendship and support. I am thankful to Pamela Kelley and Jenn Harada of the University of Hawai'i Press, my copy editor, Nancy Woodington, my indexer, Kathy Barber, and to the two anonymous reviewers, whose comments helped me rethink many points.

I also wish to acknowledge the support I have received from my mentor, Professor Asai Kiyoshi. I treasure his kindness and encouragement of my career, and they leave me in a rare state for an academic—speechless.

Introduction

For many years I was enamored of the type of literature that goes by the name "postmodernist." I wrote my first book on the novelist Shimao Toshio, but I dreamed of someday doing a study of Japanese postmodern writers, a work that would examine the writings of Shimada Masahiko, Takahashi Genichirō, Kobayashi Kyōji, Ogino Anna, Tsutsui Yasutaka, and others.[1] To this end I translated Shimada's novel *Yumetsukai* (as *Dream Messenger*), wrote essays on Shimada and Takahashi, read extensively in postmodern theory, and taught seminars on Japan and the postmodern. In a word, I was thoroughly fascinated by these writers' lightning wit, their verbal inventiveness, their iconoclastic outlook on writing, the challenges they threw up to the literary establishment and to received beliefs about what constituted literature. Who could not fall for a story entitled "Yukiguni no odoriko" (The snow country dancer), which playfully brought together characters from two of Kawabata Yasunari's best-known stories?[2] Or a novel about baseball in which pitcher and catcher engaged in extended debates on Leibnitz's theory of the monad and how it perfectly describes the art of pitching?[3] I envisioned a study that would, despite the linguistic barriers, convey something of the wit and verbal play of the original texts, and place these Japanese writers squarely in the mainstream (if indeed one can use this term here) of world postmodern literature.

As sometimes happens, though, the romance soured. My reaction was perhaps not as dramatic as that in A. S. Byatt's novel *The Biographer's Tale*, where the protagonist one day gives up his studies in postmodern literary theory for a pursuit of the concrete ("I must have *things*," he muses), but as time went by I found myself increasingly in agreement with Fredric Jameson's assessment of much of the artistic product of the postmodern as "depth-

1

less."[4] However one wishes to interpret the term and its application to post-modern literature for me it came down to a combined intellectual and emotional reaction: an honest assessment of my reading experience of Japanese postmodern literature left me feeling hollow. In my article on Shimada's writings I concluded that his work revealed a "slippery stance" toward his subject matter that demonstrated an "ethical moment," a "continued resistance to fixed identity."[5] While this type of writing may reveal a clever artistic approach that is enormously entertaining, I found I wanted something more. When I examined my own feelings about literature—why I was drawn to the field, and to Japanese literature in particular—I realized that, if not a total lack of "slipperiness" and a fixed-in-stone identity, at the very least I hoped for an attempt to address, not to defer or to deflect, some of the major issues of life. I wanted to end my reading experience (dealing with texts in a foreign language constitutes an extraordinary investment of time and mental energy) with a sense that the writer had honestly struggled with meaningful areas of life, and had even dared to provide some answers. This is not to imply that postmodern writing does not grapple at times with the meaningful; in a back-handed way its slipperiness underscores the whole question of meaning. What I was looking for, though, was more of a frontal assault on ordinary yet important questions, perhaps even universal ones.

The questions I have always found the most compelling are the spiritual. In postmodern literature spiritual questions are more likely to be deflected into parody. One thinks, for instance, of Takahashi's discussion of God and baseball; the ending of Shimada's *Dream Messenger,* a parody of Genesis; Kobayashi's character who creates his own deity of unbridled consumption. I wanted to examine to what extent, and in what ways, contemporary Japanese novelists have dealt with a variety of spiritual questions, including the existence of a soul or inner being, of an afterlife, of a god or spiritual forces beyond the everyday; and the possibilities of the supernatural and the miraculous. It is important here that a Western-oriented view of the spiritual not intrude too much on an examination of the spiritual in Japanese literature, except where there is some justification for its doing so, as with a discussion of the works of professedly Christian Japanese writers. Much thought must be given to the context before terms such as *kami, tamashii,* and *tsumi,* for example, are translated as "God," "soul," and "sin." One must be sensitive to the ways in which contemporary Japanese writers are often writing in a complex spiritual environment that includes traces of many traditions—Shinto-ism, folk beliefs, and various sects of Buddhism—but which also, most strikingly in the work of Ōe Kenzaburō, is informed by the study of other spiritual traditions, such as Christianity, Judaism, and New Age spirituality.

The more I looked into these issues, the more I realized (not an original insight, to be sure) how apt a vehicle literature is for their examination. As Murakami Haruki notes in his study of members of the Aum Shinrikyō cult, the role of the novelist and that of the spiritual seeker are not dissimilar; both delve deeply into the unseen realms of the self—in spiritual terms, what might be called the soul, though in Murakami's terms, something closer to the unconscious. Both literature and the spiritual, too, deal with unseen worlds, in faith and belief in the non-material, the invisible, what exists not in verifiable form but in the individual's heart, mind, and imagination.

Japanese literature has a long history of dealing with aspects of the spiritual. Indeed Japan's earliest surviving narratives, those that form the eighth-century A.D. *Kojiki,* depict the creation of Japan itself as a sacred act of a pantheon of deities *(kami).* This mythology was revived in the militaristic 1930s and 1940s as part of a "spiritual mobilization" in support of Japan's colonialist agenda, and it informed much of the literary production of that period.[6] In the late Heian period (794–1186) classic prose narrative, *The Tale of Genji* (ca. 1001–1014), Murasaki Shikibu depicts in dramatic fashion the existence of spirit possession *(mono no ke)* and "spirits of the living" *(ikiryō)* that defy the limits of time and space to possess others.[7] Spirits of the living turned to spirits of the dead in medieval Noh drama, which largely dealt with the revelations of ghosts as they struggle to break free of worldly attachments. Ghost tales were current in Edo period literature as well, as in Ueda Akinari's collection *Ugetsu monogatari;* and the continuing influence of Zen Buddhism on the visual and literary arts found expression in, most famously, the poetry of Matsuo Bashō, whose poems have been called "the product of his intuitive and profoundly mystical response to life and nature."[8] The late nineteenth and early twentieth centuries saw a new element in the mix: the significant interest of many emerging writers in the spiritual possibilities of Christianity. As Karatani Kōjin notes, "an encounter with Christianity, however ephemeral, was the point of departure for many Meiji writers," and he links this encounter to the development of the "practice of confession," which is the impetus for the rise of the prominent genre of the confessional "I-novel."[9] Many writers soon turned away from Christian beliefs; for Shiga Naoya, for example, Christianity was partly the impetus to "rediscover his own literary and spiritual roots," and led to his development of what Roy Starrs has dubbed Shiga's "Zen aesthetic."

With the possible exception of some studies of the novelist Endō Shūsaku, as well as studies of Shiga and Kawabata, the connection between literature and the spiritual in the field of modern Japanese literary studies in English has largely been left untouched.[10] It is as if there is an unspoken agreement among scholars that, with the spiritual "vacuum" following the Second World War and the rise of Japan as the premiere consumerist, materialist—and in many ways postmodern—society, literature that reflects any spiritual elements is largely peripheral. Clearly, though, in the realm of the "new religions" and their successors, the "new new religions," spiritual pursuits in one form or another continue to occupy a substantial segment of the Japanese population.[11] And in literature, too, a view of the Japanese reading public as unconcerned with the spiritual is belied by the continued influence of such writers as Miyazawa Kenji and Kawabata, whose writings are permeated with a native (i.e., Buddhist/Shinto) Japanese spiritual aesthetic; by the enormous popularity of such openly Christian writers as Endō, Sono Ayako, and Miura Ayako since the 1950s and 1960s; by the popularity of such works as the bestselling nonfiction book *Tariki: Embracing Despair, Discovering Peace,* by the novelist Itsuki Hiroyuki, about his explorations into Buddhism; and by the New Age–influenced narratives of the pop novelist Yoshimoto Banana.

What really brought the present book together, however, was the literary reaction to the Aum Shinrikyō terrorist attacks on the Tokyo subways in 1995. I was asked to translate both Murakami Haruki's 1998 *Yakusoku sareta basho de* (translated as *The Place That Was Promised*), a collection of interviews with eight Aum members that followed the bestselling book *Underground* (interviews with survivors of the attack), and Ōe Kenzaburō's 1999 novel *Chūgaeri* (translated as *Somersault* [2003]), which deals in fictional form with the leadership of an Aum-like cult. After September 11, 2001, these translation projects flowered into an interest in exploring connections between terrorism and literature, which in turn led me to consider in broader terms the ways in which religious belief and spirituality have been portrayed in contemporary Japanese literature. A second research interest I had been pursuing was an exploration of Christian writers in Japan (Shimao Toshio, after all, being considered one of the leading Catholic writers), and I decided at this point to weave together the two strands of my research, combining the literary reaction to Aum with an examination of fiction by Japanese Christian writers in an attempt at a broader look at spirituality and literature. The choice of Miura Ayako and Sono Ayako seemed obvious, since, with Endō, they have long been leading figures in Japanese Christian literature, and yet have been virtually unexplored in English scholarship. This aspect of the study I found particularly appealing, as it allowed me, among other things, to examine the themes of self-sacrifice and martyrdom, which have long fascinated me (an interest spurred on by my earlier exploration of Shimao's own *tokkōtai* (kamikaze) experience and his later interest in the martyrdom of Father Kolbe at

Auschwitz). It has also allowed me to take the first steps toward an exploration of "popular" or "mass" literature in Japan (e.g., the works of Miura
Ayako). Through this study I have begun as well to address the question of
why—in the case of such novels as *Hyōten* and *Shiokari tōge*—fiction with a
fairly open Christian message could be enormously popular in a nation where
this message is the voice of such a tiny minority. It is comparable to, say, having a Jain or a Sikh in the United States write a novel about their religious
beliefs and then having that novel become a blockbuster. This may be an
exaggeration—Christianity has a history in Japan reaching back to the late
sixteenth century, and there have been many indigenous Christian movements—but the fact remains that a writer like Miura Ayako has had astounding success with novels underscoring a theology that is still largely unfamiliar
to the general populace. How did these openly devout writers balance the
sometimes conflicting demands of their personal faith and their literature?

The choice of texts I have made here covers a wide range of writing, from
enormously popular fiction (*Hyōten, Shiokari tōge,* the novels of Murakami),
to more problematic, "serious" fiction *(Somersault),* to nonfiction medita-
tions about martyrdom and miracles (Sono's *Kiseki*) and about the dynamics of religious cults (Murakami's interviews with members of Aum). The
works discussed in *Spirit Matters* are generally presented in chronological
order of publication, from the novel *Hyōten* to Ōe's *Somersault,* and cover
the period from the Tokyo Olympics (1964) to the end of the millennium.[12]

Chapter 1 explores Miura Ayako's *Hyōten* (translated as *Freezing Point*)
series: the 1964–1965 novel *Hyōten* and its sequel, the 1970–1971 *Zoku hyōten (Freezing Point II)*. These works, along with Miura's *Shiokari tōge,* are
among the best-known Christian novels in Japan. *Hyōten,* Miura's first work,
which catapulted her to literary fame, centers on the nature of sin, in particular the notion of original sin. In a lengthy, convoluted series of plot twists,
involving murder, adultery, deception, and mistaken identities, Miura brings
her three main characters (husband, wife, and adopted daughter) to varying
degrees of spiritual awakening regarding their own sinful nature. In the
process, however, Miura diverts attention from the basic theological implications of original sin, leaving the reader with the impression that sin is less
a basic state of being for fallen humans than a case-by-case inherited trait.
Further, in *Hyōten* Miura leaves her characters with little sense of where to
go next, a strange turn of events for a writer who sees her literature as an
avowedly evangelical enterprise. One must take into account the fact that, as
the first novel of a devout Christian trying to carve out a career as a novelist,
Hyōten decidedly tones down the Christian ideas at its core in order to oper-
ate as a successful—even formulaic at times—popular serialized novel. It is

only in the sequel, *Zoku hyōten*, that Miura, by this time an established literary figure, returns to complete the story begun in *Hyōten*, more openly presenting a tale of sin and forgiveness in accord with the tenets of her faith. A comparison of these two novels, then, leads to a productive consideration of the constraints—self-imposed or otherwise—under which writers of pronounced faith in Japan, in particular Christian writers, must work. Interestingly, when *Hyōten* was translated into English (a co-translation by a Japanese and an American missionary), the missing message in many passages, the hidden Christian element, as it were, is restored for a Western audience that might not fully appreciate the tension between Christian faith and literature in Japan.

In chapter 2 I turn to the question of self-sacrifice and miracles, in particular how these are treated in Sono Ayako's 1977 nonfiction study *Kiseki* (Miracles), and Miura's 1968 novel *Shiokari tōge* (translated as *Shiokari Pass*). Self-sacrifice and martydom are the very cornerstones of the Christian experience, and here Sono and Miura explore, respectively, the story of a foreign Christian martyr, Father Kolbe of Auschwitz, and that of the much less well-known Japanese one, Nagano Masao, a humble railroad employee in Hokkaido. As the title of her book indicates, Sono approaches the topic from a Catholic perspective, as concerned with the miracles associated with Kolbe as she is with the sacrifice itself. She brings a refreshingly questioning attitude toward the whole subject, beginning her book with an exploration of her long-term doubts about the possibility of the miraculous in the modern day, and ending it with a meditation on her own, idiosyncratic view of the concept of "eternal life," viewing it less as a gift from God than as a gift between people. In between, in a work situated somewhere between a travelogue and a meditative essay, Sono comes face to face with the quiet yet overwhelming reality of the faith lives of ordinary European Catholics; Father Kolbe is, in the end, but an extreme example of the kind of piety she finds at every turn, and the greatest miracle of all, she concludes, is faith itself. Unlike the often problematic situation for Japanese Christians, always a tiny minority in a country that, if not always hostile to their faith, is at the very least puzzled or indifferent, Sono discovers how, in the lives of European believers, the transcendent and the ordinary are equal strands of the very fabric of life.

Shiokari Pass is Miura's imaginative recreation of the life of an ordinary railway worker known, until the success of her novel, only to a small number of people in her hometown of Asahikawa in Hokkaido. Nagano Masao (Nagano Nobuo in her version) was a young railway worker who organized Christian youth organizations among his fellow workers, and who gave his life in 1909 to stop a runaway train by throwing himself under the wheels. In

Miura's rendition of his life, Nobuo undergoes a gradual and often tortured spiritual awakening, traveling from youthful antagonism toward Christianity, to adolescent curiosity, to mature faith. Much more than her *Hyōten* series, *Shiokari Pass* is Miura's theological and novelistic magnum opus. It provides readers with a more complete and nuanced understanding of the Christian teachings that motivate her literature. The novel also presents a view of the often radical nature of Christianity in Japan, the way it runs counter to much of the accepted ideology of modern Japan, including the centrality of the family/state. As to the issue of self-sacrifice and martyrdom, Miura, even more than Sono, downplays the drama of her protagonist's sacrifice, portraying it as a normal outgrowth of one person's faith.

Chapters 3 and 4, which come closer to the present, might well be subtitled "Literary Reactions to Aum." Chapter 3 focuses on the work of Japan's leading novelist, Murakami Haruki, beginning with the 1998 nonfiction work *Yakusoku sareta basho de,* which makes up the second half of the English book *Underground.* After interviewing some sixty survivors of the Aum Shinrikyō gas attack in the Tokyo subway on March 20, 1995, Murakami next turned to in-depth interviews with eight ordinary members of the Aum cult. Dubbing Aum a kind of unknown "black box," Murakami sees his task as "try[ing] to pry open that black box to catch a glimpse of what it contained."[13] In doing so he uncovers a surprisingly complex spiritual hunger in many younger Japanese, and delves into such issues as the inner dynamics of cults, connections between violence and religious fervor, and the tensions between the individual ego and its suppression by the more "enlightened." Perhaps most strikingly, Murakami sees the world of cults and the world outside (closed-circuit versus open-circuit worlds, as he later puts it) as engaged in a struggle of competing "narratives." He writes that it is the work of novelists and other writers to produce narratives that both account for the spiritual thirst so evident among the young—the search for something beyond the gleaming materialism of contemporary Japan—and counter the destructive, apocalyptic visions of a cult like Aum. This is exactly the project Murakami is engaged in in his post-Aum fiction. Here I contrast two earlier works— *Hardboiled Wonderland and the End of the World* and *South of the Border, West of the Sun*—with his latest post-Aum novels, *Sputnik Sweetheart* and *Kafka on the Shore.* While all his works portray disaffected, alienated young people searching deep within themselves, people who have many affinities with those who joined Aum, and also a kind of parallel "this world/other world" division of reality, in the earlier works Murakami depicts the "other world" as ultimately dark and threatening, as a place of no return. In his post-Aum fiction, in an attempt to counter the Aum narrative, Murakami begins to reveal a different vision, one of a mysterious soul-searching, where contact with the "other world" can lead to personal restoration of a profound kind that ultimately brings people back, transformed, into *this* world.

Chapter 4 analyzes Ōe Kenzaburō's own literary reaction to Aum, the 1999 novel *Chūgaeri*. Ōe's literature, which deals increasingly with spiritual issues through the 1980s and early 1990s, reaches its culmination in *Somersault*, to date his most extended exploration of faith and the dangers of religious zealotry. The novel follows the fortunes of a religious cult split asunder by the apostasy of its two leaders (Patron and Guide) and is Ōe's attempt, in his words, both to penetrate the mind-set of young people who join an Aum-like cult and to trace a scenario wherein followers—and leaders—are forced to confront the relationship between humans and the transcendent following a renunciation of faith. As the novel makes explicit, while directly motivated by Aum and the events of 1995, *Somersault* raises painful questions for all postwar Japanese, drawing parallels between the apostasy of Patron and Guide and the dilemma this created for their followers, and the Shōwa Emperor's own "renunciation of divinity" and the ensuing spiritual void.

Somersault is a complex novel weaving together poetry, philosophy, and theology, an attempt at the "new style" of writing Ōe proclaimed as his goal following his own renunciation of novel writing in 1994 (ironically just before he won the Nobel Prize). Ōe devotes one entire chapter, for instance, to a discussion of the poetry of the Welshman R. S. Thomas, a chapter that underscores Thomas' embrace of the *via negativa* (i.e., that God is known only through traces and by absence), a stance that Ōe's novel takes to a more extreme conclusion, namely, that ultimately humans confirm their relationship to God only by, paradoxically, denying God. A second text Ōe explores is the biblical book of Jonah. Here Ōe focuses not only on the apocalyptic visions of destruction the book contains, but also on the potential for a dynamic relationship between humans and God, of human beings engaged in a dialogue with God, pitting their "imagination" against God's lack thereof. As a response to Aum, *Somersault* posits its own counter-narrative, depicting a tortured leader attempting to contain the violence inherent in his apocalyptic narrative.

Though having its genesis in two separate projects—a study of Japanese Christian writers and one of literary reactions to Aum—this book reveals, I believe, a productive dialogue between the two types of writers. The Jungian idea of the unconscious as the "source of religious experience," that salvation comes only from exploration of the "dirtiest and most mundane part of our being," which is present in Christian writers like Endō, certainly finds echoes in Murakami's work, particularly in *Kafka on the Shore*—itself Murakami's most extended meditation on the healing found in plumbing the inner self, the "other side."[14] It is Kafka's doppelgänger, Crow, who insists that salvation is found only by letting go of the anger and hurt inside. By discovering the power of forgiveness, he holds, one is saved. In a scene reminiscent of Yōko's forgiveness of her mother in *Freezing Point II*, after an extended journey to the depths of his unconscious, that is exactly what Kafka does.

There are, however, critical differences. In Yōko's case, at the climax of *Freezing Point II* she feels a "will of something beyond human beings . . . there was indeed a God who could right now truly forgive human sin" (367). For Murakami, forgiveness is found not in an appeal to some higher power but at a human level: unlike Yōko, Kafka does not ask God for forgiveness— he asks his mother. This is not to say that Murakami rejects the notion of a "will beyond human beings": the pervasive presence of evil in the novel is certainly set out at times as such a will, but the restorative "other side" is portrayed as an internal journey through the labyrinth of the unconscious mind —what some might call the soul—more than as an encounter with a transcendent being. One may argue that this is, in Endō and Jung, a religious experience, but the possibility of its leading to something beyond the plane of mundane existence is uncertain. Kafka is, indeed, reborn into a "new world" in the final lines, though the boundaries of this new world (unlike those of Yōko's) are left to the reader's imagination.

Likewise, the centrality of self-sacrifice in Sono's *Miracles* and Miura's *Shiokari Pass*, and the very possibility of miracles in the modern day, are taken up in *Somersault* in the notion of the character Kizu's miraculous cure and Patron's fiery self-immolation. Ōe's take on self-sacrifice and miracles, however, is more ambiguous than that in Sono's *Miracles*. This is not to suggest that Sono has a clear-cut response to these topics; the appeal of her work lies precisely in her questioning nature, in the tension between her faith, her doubts about the possibility of miracles, and whether any ultimate good was brought about by Father Kolbe's sacrifice. *Miracles*, then, is no simple catechism of faith but a very human, very appealing struggle with belief. Still, for Sono—unlike Ōe and Murakami—the appeal is always to a God who can, in some way, actually *connect* with the lives of people. The real miracle is the miracle of faith, manifested in the lives of devotion of ordinary followers; this "transcends the realities of human life."[15] Likewise, though Kolbe's life and inner motivation remain hidden ("the only ones able to understand Kolbe's sacrifice are God and the Father himself"), ultimately his sacrifice is done to complete the bond between one man and the Almighty.[16]

What about miracles and self-sacrifice in *Somersault*? In Patron's world readers end up with a "real but silent" God, with humans responding to inner spiritual needs, knowing that their "deeds of the soul" will not necessarily bring them nearer to God. Kizu's "miracle" is, in the end, left totally undecipherable. He is cured by Patron's power—yet he once again contracts cancer and dies. Susan Napier writes of the trilogy preceding this novel, *Moeagaru midori no ki* (The flaming green tree) that "Ōe gives us a vision of the outside world as revitalized by the sacrifice of a body," but what exactly in *Somersault* has been "revitalized"? Ōe's notion of "repetition with slippage," discussed toward the end of *Somersault,* is helpful here as shorthand for the worldview the novel leads to. Patron bases his fiery suicide on the idea from Ephesians that the "old man" must step aside to make way for the "new man." While the biblical idea is of Christ—the "new man"—reconciling once *for all time*— man to God through his sacrifice, Patron's sacrifice is of a different sort, revitalizing the younger generation only *temporarily.* In Ōe's fictional world, repetition with slippage equates to one generation's continuing to struggle with the same issues as the previous one, as today's new person becomes tomorrow's old, with often little sense of progress toward some ultimate spiritual understanding. Given the young character Gii's predilection for mixing violence and religion, one can almost hear Patron sighing, in whatever afterlife he is in, that nobody learns from the past. Patron appears to introduce the notion of a kind of linear, forward spiritual progress in the idea of the antichrist—the necessity of an antichrist (or many antichrists) as herald of "end times"—but this is problematic. The only way to bring about an ultimate encounter with God, it seems, is to *deny* him. Ōe's world is one in which one who believes in a god must deny him in order to confirm his existence. It is a world of *via negativa* taken to extremes. The denial of God leads, as in Patron's somersault, both to a paradoxical renewed understanding of God's existence and to the inability ever really to *know* him. In Ōe's world, this may be as good as it gets.

The present work only begins to examine the relationship between spirituality and modern Japanese literature. It is my hope, however, that the range of works covered in this book gives a good indication of the ways in which a variety of contemporary Japanese writers of the last half century have revealed that spirit does, indeed, continue to matter.

The Frozen Soul

Sin and Forgiveness in Miura Ayako's *Freezing Point*

On the first of January, 1963, the Asahi newspaper company announced a series of five prizes to commemorate the eighty-fifth and seventy-fifth anniversaries of, respectively, its Osaka and Tokyo offices, including a prize for the best serialized novel.[1] Though such a prize was certainly not unknown (the practice dates back to 1904), what captured the attention of the literary world was the fact that the competition was open to both amateurs and professionals, and that it offered an astounding amount of prize money for the winner, ten million yen.[2] The selection committee received 731 novels, of which they chose an even dozen for review. Finally, on July 10, 1964, the winner was announced: *Hyōten (Freezing Point)*, a book by Miura Ayako, an unknown Christian writer from Asahikawa in Hokkaido.[3] Overnight Miura went from greengrocer's wife to literary star. After winning, she was requested to trim her lengthy manuscript to accommodate the requirements of daily newspaper columns. The novel was then serialized in 338 installments in the morning edition of *Asahi Shimbun*, running from December 9, 1964, to November 14, 1965.[4]

Unprecedented excitement preceded *Freezing Point*'s appearance in print, for following the announcement that the novel's theme was *genzai* (original sin)—a term so unfamiliar to most Japanese that a note was added on how to pronounce it—the definition of "original sin" became a hot topic nationally. This national discussion only intensified, naturally enough, as the novel was serialized, leading to a so-called *Freezing Point* boom.[5] Perhaps inevitably, this popular work on a serious topic became caught up in the long-standing debate over the distinction between "pure," or "serious," literature and "popular" literature. With its familiar plot elements—the love affair of a woman of the privileged class, the mistreatment of a stepchild, and the revelation of the secret of the protagonist's birth—and its accessible style, *Freezing Point* appealed to a broad audience.[6] At the same time, the novel clearly went beyond the bounds of mere entertainment, a point recognized by critics from the start. Sako Junichirō, for instance, contrasted *Freezing Point*'s significant—and to most Japanese unfamiliar—theme with the paucity of meaningful themes in contemporary serious fiction, while Etō Jun saw the novel as a challenge to the *bundan,* the literary establishment that supported "pure" literature.[7]

Certainly *Freezing Point* and its sequel *Zoku hyōten (Freezing Point II)* have been and remain enormously popular. In Japan they are arguably among the most widely read novels of the past three decades.[8] The novels are not only still available, but after Miura's recent death, bookstores in Japan devoted special displays to these two works. In the two decades following the publication of *Freezing Point* a number of television, film, and stage versions of the story were also shown to wide audiences. Not long after the novel finished serialization, the first TV drama version was shown, on NET (the forerunner of Asahi Television) in thirteen episodes, from January to April 1966, with the final episode reaching an astonishing audience rating of 42 percent. *Freezing Point II* was likewise shown as a TV drama on that channel, first in 1971 and again in 1989, when Asahi TV made it a special drama to commemorate the twenty-fifth anniversary of the station. The rival network TBS televised versions of the novel in 1971 and again in 1981, when the drama was run in short daily installments. As Asai Kiyoshi notes, these TV versions of *Freezing Point* helped change the image of the so-called home drama from that of a typically warm *(honobono)* story to that of something drier *(karakuchi),* at a time when the daily serialized newspaper novel was losing ground to the television drama. And finally, successful film and stage versions of *Freezing Point* were produced in 1966.[9]

In its original serialized format *Freezing Point* immediately followed Niwa Fumio's serial novel *Inochi narikeri.* Miura had earnestly studied Niwa's handbook on writing newspaper novels, *Shinbun shōsetsu sahō* (Rules for newspaper novels), before submitting her own novel to the competition.[10] In his handbook Niwa formulates four rules for writing successful newspaper novels: (1) that the work be written in short units of about fifteen characters *(ji)* per sentence; (2) that it emphasize action and dialogue over psychology; (3) that it stay with the same scene for four or five daily installments; and (4) that it introduce a limited number of characters. While generally remaining faithful to points 1 and 3, about short sentences and developed scenes, as Asai notes, Miura completely ignored rule 4, while coming up with her own unique way to circumvent rule 2.[11] The mostly unobtrusive narrator of the novel does refrain from lengthy descriptions of the characters' psychology, but readers learn about their inner world through a sort of parallel text set up in the numerous—and at times interruptive—parenthetical statements that dot the novel. To give one example from early in the novel, when Dr. Murai comes to discuss something with his boss (the husband of the woman with whom he is infatuated), Dr. Tsujiguchi Keizō, we read the following:

> "Chief, there's something I need to discuss with you . . ."
> "Something to discuss?" Keizō said casually, suppressing his rising displeasure. Murai had been working at the hospital for two years now, yet never once had he come to discuss anything personal.
> (What could he mean by discuss something?)
> Keizō felt uneasy somehow.
> "It would be better to talk in my office, so why don't we go there?" Keizō said and walked on ahead.
> "But aren't you busy?"
> Murai came beside Keizō. He stood five centimeters taller than Keizō.
> "No, not really. It's no problem at all," Keizō replied quite calmly.
> (Why can't I say something unpleasant to this unpleasant guy?)[12]

In the published translation of *Freezing Point,* this and all other parenthetical statements have been reworked into third person narratorial comments, as in the following translation of the final two lines of the above: "'No, not especially. Have something on your mind?' Keizō's gentle tone surprised him and he wondered to himself why he couldn't be completely abrupt with such a devious fellow."[13] While this change in the translation from first to third person, from direct to more indirect approach to the character's thoughts, may make for smoother English, it all but eliminates an aspect of great importance to Miura as a Christian writer, namely, the contrasting outer and inner worlds of her characters and the critical importance of exploring the inner one. Despite working in a medium that, as Niwa insists, emphasizes action over psychology, Miura's world is one in which these parenthetical statements are not mere asides, but the essence of the characters and the story.

Much of this arises from Miura's religious and philosophical base: her devout Christian faith. Later, in *Shiokari tōge,* Miura raises a foundation issue of Christianity—the importance of sacrificial love. Likewise, her maiden work, *Freezing Point,* was motivated by her strong religious beliefs. In her autobiographical trilogy Miura recounts how she and her husband prayed deeply before and after the composition of the novel.[14] Before she began writing the novel, she prayed, "If this work is pleasing to God's heart, then please let me write it. If it sullies the body of the Lord, then I pray that I not be allowed to write it." And when the novel was completed, she and her husband "gave heartfelt thanks to God" and prayed that the novel be allowed to see the light of day "only if it is pleasing to Him."[15]

Such piety, however, did not come easily to Miura. As a young schoolteacher she was a confirmed "hater of Christianity," someone who thought that Christians "put on airs" and were "arrogant in looking down on nonbelievers."[16] The shock of Japan's defeat in World War Two and the subsequent Occupation period order to black out sections of existing school textbooks made her quit her job in disgust, and she was filled with an "emptiness" and fear of ever believing anything. A dark period of illness followed, during which she battled lung and spinal tuberculosis for thirteen years. One poem she wrote expresses these feelings well: "Take two times the maximum dosage, and you'll die, they say / I remember these words as, again today, night comes on." Reading this, one is not surprised to learn that she attempted suicide during this time. As with many people who come to Christianity late in life, though, it was through the love and devotion of a friend who was a believer that she was led to baptism. Through her faith she made her way out of this dark and depressing time of her life. Of her baptism and faith, Miura writes: "After my baptism I most definitely changed. A light came on in my heart and I was happier than I'd ever been. And this happiness has not changed one bit in the twenty-some years since then, as I continue to want to keep telling this [the Gospel] so that as many people as possible can know the love of Christ."[17]

What of the relationship between her faith and her writing? Kubota Gyō-ichi sees her writing as a "literature of love and confession . . . rooted in her spirit of thankfulness for chance encounters." For her part, Miura makes no bones about the fact that her literature is, in the final analysis, subordinate to her faith. "Directly or indirectly I write to transmit the good news of Jesus Christ. Whether the work is literary or not, I write standing on this foundation of faith." As Kubota notes, this clear religious stance makes Miura unique in the Japanese literary world. While examples of earlier writers' putting their work to the service of extra-literary beliefs can certainly be found (the left-wing writers of the so-called Proletarian School of the 1920s and early 1930s, who subordinated literature to radical political ideals, for instance), no Japanese writer before Miura so openly declared that the point of writing is to transmit the Gospel. In the years following her maiden work, Kubota writes, her dozens of books in many genres, all testaments to her faith, established her as a unique "missionary writer" (fukuin no dendō sakka), attracting great numbers of readers who may have had little initial interest in the faith undergirding her work.[18]

Freezing Point, though, is a far cry from being some dry religious tract by a writer determined to transmit Christian beliefs at the expense of an appealing story. As I have indicated above, the novel was, and remains, enormously popular, and Miura's genius lies in the way she packages a religious theme in a familiar and attractive narrative.[19] In fact, by doing so, she sacrifices a fuller understanding of her ostensible theme—original sin—in favor of creating a story that appeals to a wider audience. This tension in her maiden work between popular novel and religious theme is tipped in favor of the popular. Only in the sequel to *Freezing Point,* written after the success of the novel *Shiokari tōge* (translated in 1974 as *Shiokari Pass*), when Miura had established herself fully as a novelist, did she return to the characters and themes of her first work and overcome its doctrinal shortcomings.

Freezing Point is set in a suburb of the Hokkaido city of Asahikawa, Miura's own hometown. A variety of characters appear in the novel, but the main actors are Dr. Tsujiguchi Keizō, his wife Natsue, their daughter Ruriko, their son Tōru, and their adopted daughter Yōko, as well as Dr. Murai Yasuo, an ophthalmologist on the staff of the Tsujiguchi Hospital, Dr. Takaki Yūjirō, a close friend of Keizō's, Fujio Tatsuko, a friend of Natsue's, and Saishi Tsuchio, a laborer who commits the crime that propels most of the action in the novel. The novel begins on a hot summer day, July 21, 1946, in the Tsujiguchi household, where Natsue, a stunningly beautiful twenty-six-year-old woman, bored with her life as the wife of the workaholic head of a hospital, is flirting with one of her husband's young staff doctors, Dr. Murai. Murai has gradually been falling in love with Natsue since she began seeing him for treatment of a minor eye condition. In the opening chapter the reader learns that Natsue has recommended a girl for Murai to wed, a move that he finds cruel in view of his passionate feelings for her. For her part, Natsue realizes that her recommendation for Murai sprang from a need to test his feelings for her and to force him into a declaration of these feelings. This is done in the typically restrained fashion favored by Japanese melodramas. Although the story is ostensibly set in motion by Natsue's infidelity, there is, technically, no affair between the two, a clear sign that Miura considers the inner world more important than the outer (the focus is on "lust in one's heart," and the body is secondary). The "lovers" make do with oblique references, burning glances, and minimal physical contact. As Murai lays his hands on Natsue's shoulders, they are interrupted by her three-year-old daughter, Ruriko.[20] In her innocence, Ruriko mistakes Murai's embrace for an attack on her mother and tries to defend her. To get rid of her, Natsue, who is on the brink of giving in to Murai's advances, commands her to go outside and play. After Ruriko leaves, Murai finally dares to kiss Natsue on the cheek, but she is coy and he misreads her attitude as refusal. Miffed, Murai leaves, and Keizō, her husband, returns unexpectedly.

The early pages of the novel are filled with foreshadowings of tragedy.[21] In a flashback to Murai's treatment of Natsue's eye condition, he finds the piece of ash that's been irritating her eye and declares it to be the "culprit" (*hannin*, literally, "criminal") (1: 6). Much more obviously, as Natsue sits down to play the piano after Murai leaves: "Her white fingers ran across the keys, playing a Chopin 'Fantasia Impromptu.' Steadily her playing grew more intense. Natsue played on, eyes closed beneath her long eyelashes, a drunkenness to her playing. Natsue knew nothing about what was happening to young Ruriko at that very moment. With a loud snap one of the piano strings suddenly broke. An ominous feeling" (1: 14–15). Soon afterward, remembering Ruriko's cry that she will "tell Daddy" if Murai hurts her mother, a chill runs through Natsue (1: 16). Finally, Tōru is discussing a war movie he has seen, and he asks his father about enemies and death. Tōru remarks, "Death is terrible. But it's okay if our enemies die, right? But, Daddy—who are our enemies?" (1: 20). This in turn leads Keizō to remember the biblical injunction, love your enemies, taught to him by his mentor, Dr. Tsugawa, Natsue's father. It is a teaching, Dr. Tsugawa says, that is extremely hard to follow.

Keizō realizes that something suspicious has gone on between Natsue and Murai. Here his enemy (and this first chapter is itself entitled "Enemies") is Murai, whom he curses for wrecking his marital happiness. But he soon learns that, tragically, he has another enemy, one who has brought death to his house.

Ruriko does not return home, and a frantic search is undertaken for her. Finally her dead body is discovered in a nearby riverbed. Ruriko was kidnapped by a passing day laborer, Saishi, and when she began to struggle, Saishi strangled her. Saishi never makes an appearance, though, because he has hanged himself while in police custody. But his background comes out—his impoverished life of hard labor, the recent death of his wife, his infant daughter. And Keizō, rather than hating him, directs his hatred toward Natsue and Murai, whose passion for each other led, indirectly, to Ruriko's death.

After Natsue struggles with depression following her daughter's death, she and Murai have a second encounter that leaves a telltale kiss mark on her neck; noticing this, Keizō turns insanely jealous and contemplates both suicide and killing Natsue. When Natsue, however, who is unable to have any more children, tells him she wants to adopt a baby girl to assuage her loneliness, Keizō hatches the cruel scheme of adopting Saishi's infant daughter and having Natsue unwittingly raise the daughter of her own daughter's murderer. Thus is born Keizō's revenge and the dark secret of the novel. Dr. Takaki, Keizō's long-time friend, at first opposes this adoption, but Keizō convinces him his motives are pure, pledging to love the child. In yet another example of the web of deceit that makes up the world of the Tsujiguchi family, Natsue and Keizō go off to Sapporo to collect the baby. They agree to have Natsue stay there for an extended period and put out the word that she has given birth to the child and that it is their own baby. Natsue wants to name the baby Ruriko after her dead child, but they finally agree on Yōko. Keizō feels his two missions in life now are to "keep the secret of her birth, and love Yōko" (1: 192), but the first makes him feel he suffers more than Natsue, while the second he finds emotionally hard to accomplish. He prevaricates when it comes to adding Yōko's name to the family register and officially making her his daughter, and is repulsed by the idea of holding or touching her.

The narrative leaps ahead seven years. Natsue discovers her husband's diary, which reveals both Yōko's true identity as the daughter of Ruriko's killer and the depths of Keizō's loathing for Natsue for her "betrayal" of him with Murai. Natsue at first is in denial about this discovery, but then decides to exact her own revenge on Keizō by not giving him the satisfaction of knowing what she's learned and by raising Yōko in the coldest way possible. She decides to bide her time and wait until she can truly betray Keizō and make him suffer. When Yōko returns home from school, Natsue attempts to strangle her, stopping only when, in one of the numerous parenthetical inner monologues, she realizes, "(What in the world am I doing? This child is without sin.)" (1: 245). Natsue makes Yōko promise not to reveal this incident to Keizō, adding another layer of deception.

After a long absence to treat his tuberculosis, Murai returns to work at Keizō's hospital, and Natsue's only concern becomes making herself attractive to Murai so that he will notice her again—and she can hurt Keizō where he is most vulnerable. Natsue also begins a campaign to undercut and humiliate Yōko wherever possible. Tōru, Yōko's older stepbrother, meanwhile becomes more attached to Yōko with each day, and secretly hopes she is an adopted child, so he can someday marry her. He confronts Keizō with the rumors that Yōko is adopted, but Keizō insists that she is not.

Tatsuko, Natsue's friend and dance instructor, to whose studio Yōko escapes when she finds home oppressive, is often the outsider who is the voice of reason in the novel. She is the first to notice that the Tsujiguchi family is headed toward a crisis and, reviewing her own life and seeing it as shallow, voices one theme of the novel: "There must be a deeper wisdom in this world" (1: 308). Soon after this there are glimmers of a growing maturity in Keizō, as he regrets his actions and feels his plan of revenge may backfire. Yet he still blames Natsue's actions with Murai for their marital and family problems. Circumstances, however, soon push him to a better understanding of this "deeper wisdom."

Keizō sets off on a business trip to Honshu, and a typhoon capsizes his ferry. As he and the other passengers struggle to survive, a foreign missionary offers his life jacket to a young woman whose own is ripped: "You are younger than I am," he says, "It will be the young people who will build Japan" (1: 362). The boat sinks, and after a terrifying struggle with death, Keizō barely makes it to shore (the missionary does not survive). Back home, Natsue prays for Keizō's safety, her concern for her husband wiping away, at least for the moment, any hatred and desire for revenge. Keizō, recuperating in the hospital, has a revelation of sorts about his present life and the life he wants to live from now on. He realizes that everyone who died in the accident wanted to live just as much as he did, and that his survival was due less to good fortune than to others' sacrifice (1: 367). While filled with a new sense of the severity and weight of life, Keizō also has a profound sense of a new role for himself as a loving husband, father, and friend. "I want to love Natsue, love Tōru, love Yōko, and be friends with Murai" he thinks to himself (1: 368, notably *not* in a parenthetical statement).[22]

To some extent Keizō does seem a changed man after the accident. He purchases and reads a Bible, noting the story of Joseph and Mary and the strong bond of trust between them, so absent from his own relationship with Natsue. Likewise, he is finally able to hold young Yōko on his lap and to act more like a loving father to her. Meanwhile, Murai is scheduled to be married, and the Tsujiguchi family are to act as go-betweens. Natsue's anger toward her husband has been blunted by the traumatic ferry accident, and she thinks about how Murai was merely a convenient stimulus to distract her from the boredom of her marriage.

The story now is further complicated by a new character, Yukako, a young woman who works for Keizō at the hospital. Although in love with Keizō, she ends up sleeping with Murai, whom she then begins to hate so much that she runs away from the town. Natsue's antipathy for Yōko, meanwhile, has increased, and she goes out of her way to torment her stepdaughter.

One of the major confrontations of the second half of the novel comes when, four years after learning the secret of Yōko's identity, Natsue reveals her knowledge to Keizō. Keizō berates her for her betrayal of him and for her failure as a mother in watching over Ruriko, while Natsue counters that she never betrayed him in the way he imagined. Keizō wonders whether he's been suffering all these years for nothing, whether Natsue is telling the truth about herself and Murai. Natsue tells him she never did anything as awful as he has done in forcing her to raise Yōko. Tōru, who has overheard their conversation, lashes out at his parents and tells them that he will someday marry Yōko. After this, this previously well-mannered young boy becomes uncooperative and refuses to take tests at school. With the family relationships in shreds, Keizō realizes that his revenge has backfired and that he is now suffering as much as anyone. Yōko, the story tells us, "is the one beacon of light in this dark Tsujiguchi family" (2: 132), a real change from the beginning, when she was seen as the one dark secret in an otherwise bright and happy family.

The story leaps ahead another four years. Tōru is in college now, studying to become a doctor, while Yōko has been chosen to give the valedictory speech at her high school graduation. In a typically cruel move, Natsue switches Yōko's speech for a blank sheet of paper. Yet Yōko manages to give a heartfelt extemporaneous speech at the ceremony. This makes Natsue hate her even more, while Yōko, who is warm and compassionate, is unable to hate Natsue in return: she tries to see the situation from Natsue's viewpoint, speculating that Natsue must hate her because of her parentage.

As a new character enters, Kitahara, Tōru's classmate from college, the relationships between the characters become even more complex. Yōko feels close to Kitahara because he, too, lost his real mother; Natsue is attracted to him partly because of her innate flirtatiousness and partly to block any relationship he might have with Yōko; Tōru continues to pine for Yōko and wants to marry her (while hoping that, if that does not happen, at least his friend Kitahara will have her). Hovering in the background is Keizō, who has gone through several incidents where, in Lolita-like fashion, he admits to himself his own attraction to Yōko. Keizō wants at all costs to keep Yōko and Tōru from falling in love, and wants Yōko to live with Tatsuko to keep the two of them further apart.

In the pages that follow, much more of Yōko's inner world is revealed. Kitahara, a philosophical young man, urges her to consider the bigger picture, how there is a "will greater than human beings" that acts on human life. Yōko considers the greater reason that brought her to this house and pledges to take full responsibility for her own life, not letting circumstances dictate her direction. The reader learns of her loneliness, her feeling that no one really loves her, and her desperate desire to be loved.

Keizō and Yōko travel to a famous Ainu graveyard and discuss death. Keizō comments on life as fleeting, and his own life as in vain. This presages later events and also reopens the issue of Keizō's spiritual progress. Over the years he's read the Bible off and on, contemplating his past actions in light of the instruction to love your enemy. In one memorable scene he stands at the door of a church, but ends up not going inside, concluding, "(It's written that *For God so loves the world,* but does God really love people?) I'm far too ugly to be loved by God, Keizō told himself" (2: 254).

Meanwhile, Natsue, ever scheming, plans to reveal the truth about Yōko's birth to Kitahara so that he will leave her. She sees herself and her family as victims, and Yōko's as victimizers, but Keizō insists it's time to forget about Yōko's parents and to recognize that she herself is blameless. In a scene reminiscent of Murai's and Natsue's original passion, which leads to Ruriko's death, here, at the end of the novel, Kitahara visits Natsue, who is greatly attracted to him, and the novel reaches its climax, Yōko's suicide attempt. Natsue, ever spiteful, tells Yōko and Kitahara the secret of Yōko's birth. Kitahara reacts sympathetically (he touches Yōko for the first time, hugging her), but Yōko is shocked.

Yōko wanders out into the snow, takes poison, and collapses. Tōru discovers her farewell letter, and Keizō goes into action to save her life. As they gather around Yōko, who is in a coma, Keizō's doctor friend Takaki, who has long had a smoldering desire for Natsue, reveals the real truth about Yōko's birth: she is not the daughter of Ruriko's murderer. Because Takaki felt sorry for the position Keizō was putting Natsue in, he substituted an illegitimate baby born of the adulterous affair of a married woman, Mitsui Keiko, and her student boarder, Nakagawa Mitsuo. One layer of deception after another has been peeled back, revealing this final truth—but to what end? As they all hover near Yōko (including the now tearfully contrite Natsue), Keizō thinks, "(Even close friends can't see to the depths of another's heart. But what if we were to face God? . . .) Takaki and I didn't know that, after all, we would end up having to face God" (2: 358). He goes on to think, "If only I had forgiven Natsue from the beginning, none of this would have happened" (2: 360).

The novel ends on a hopeful yet somber note, as Keizō and Takaki recognize that Yōko might pull through after all. As the nurse gives her a shot of penicillin to prevent pneumonia,

> Keizō was startled. As the needle went into her, for the first time Yōko's face grimaced in pain.
> (She might make it!)
> Keizō checked her pulse. It was weak, but regular. Takaki also quickly reached out and checked her pulse. A faint smile rose to his lips. Keizō and Takaki looked at each other, and nodded quietly.

Keizō, with a prayerful look, gazed down at Yōko's pale face.

The glass door rattled. He noticed now the wind racing through the woods. Another storm may very well be on the horizon. (2: 363–364)

Though peopled with a number of memorable minor characters, the drama of *Freezing Point* revolves principally around Natsue, Keizō, and Yōko. From Miura's Christian perspective these three characters represent varying degrees of awakening to sin, to God's presence, and to the possibility of grace. Natsue is the least awakened, while Keizō wavers in the middle, and Yōko, by the powerful climax, has attained the greatest degree of awareness of sin. Miura uses these characters and their compelling drama to depict a range of ordinary people's understanding of the sinful human condition as defined by Christian belief, but the view of sin presented is incomplete.

The novel begins *in medias res,* with little indication why Natsue, a supposedly happily married woman wedded to a successful, attractive doctor and living a life of relative luxury, should wish to dally with other men. Her degree of intimacy with Murai strikes the modern reader as laughably tame and quaint in comparison to more recent Japanese literary depictions of human sexual behavior (Ōe's *Somersault,* for instance). But it is also an indication of how very calculating and in control Natsue always wishes to be in her relations with men—and indeed with everyone. With next to no history of her early married life, and certainly no indication that she has been mistreated, the reader is puzzled at first as to how to react to Natsue. The physical depiction of Natsue as overpoweringly beautiful, following the formula of popular literary romances, is easily decipherable: it indicates that she is, while perhaps not without flaws, ultimately the heroine the reader should admire. Miura, though, is playing with the conventions of the popular novel here again, as with the discrepancy between dialogue and thoughts, indicating a dichotomy between *outer* and *inner.* In standard popular romances, outer beauty reflects inner moral virtue, but in Natsue this seems, disturbingly, not to be so.

Although the reader may not be favorably predisposed toward Natsue, Miura early on relates incidents that evoke sympathy for her, first and foremost the tragic loss of Ruriko. As they discover Ruriko's dead body, Natsue reacts with understandable horror: "'She's been murdered?' Natsue shouted out and began to pitch forward. Murai reached out and caught her, keeping her from falling. 'I hate Dr. Murai! I hate Mommy, too!' Ruriko's final words rang in her mind" (1: 41–42). In her shock and grief, Natsue soon begins to hallucinate, calling out to Ruriko in the garden, insisting that she sees her playing there (1: 37). Keizō immediately takes her to see a psychiatrist, who diagnoses schizophrenia and prescribes electroshock treatment.

The swiftness with which women in the 1940s and 1950s were diagnosed as mentally disturbed and given such radical treatment as electroshock therapy has been examined elsewhere.[23] In modern Japanese literature a similar, though more involved, scene is found in Shimao Toshio's *Shi no toge* (serialized from 1960 to 1977), a lengthy novel based on the mental illness of his wife, Miho. In both cases the reader cannot help but sympathize with the hapless woman, swept into the clutches of a male-dominated medical establishment quick to prescribe painful and radical treatment—as long as the patient is female.

Despite these incidents, sympathy for Natsue soon fades when one sees how Miura has positioned her as a self-centered and often despicable person, who, as far as Yōko is concerned, is a *beautiful*, not an ugly, "wicked stepmother." Only twice in the novel, really, does her hard heart melt, both times when she fears she has again lost a family member: when Keizō is thought to be lost at sea, and when Yōko hovers between life and death following her suicide attempt. As Natsue listens to the radio broadcast of the list of passengers on the sunken ship, she is greatly relieved not to hear Keizō's name among them: "She found her hands pressed together as in prayer. She couldn't understand why she'd ever planned to betray Keizō" (1: 353). Not long before, all she had been able to think about was having an affair with Murai to get revenge on Keizō. But the incident only temporarily distracts Natsue from her plans, and she soon reverts to being the egotistical woman the reader has come to know and despise.

During the final scene in the novel, as Yōko lies in a coma, Natsue uncharacteristically bursts out sobbing, asking Yōko for forgiveness. But her thoughts belie any true sense of repentance: "Pondering how, though Yōko turned out not to be the child of a criminal, she had hated her all this time, Natsue felt both she and Yōko were quite wretched" (2: 359). Natsue feels sorry for Yōko for having been the victim of a deception and sees her now as an ally against Keizō, someone she might even enlist to help her carry out her revenge. She does not repent of her own coldhearted behavior toward Yōko over the years—it was just an unfortunate misunderstanding. Again, any awareness of her own inadequacies and sin is short-circuited; she is still the calculating Natsue of old.

Repeatedly throughout *Freezing Point* Natsue steadfastly refuses to grow and develop beyond the conniving, calculating woman she is at the start. Miura underscores this lack of development by repeating, toward the end of the novel, the motif with which the novel begins. Just as Natsue's flirtation with Murai leads to Ruriko's death, so too does Natsue's calculating flirtation with Kitahara, Yōko's boyfriend, help lead to Yōko's near-death. In both cases Natsue's desire to have all men bow before her beauty is more important to her than the life of her child. Those who think that Yōko's suicide attempt will transform Natsue have only to read the sequel to *Freezing Point* to know better. Natsue is a static character. She alone of the three refuses to acknowledge her sinful nature and remains blind to any awareness of God, sin, and the possibilities of grace.

Keizō, however, is a much more complex and appealing character, one who lives a life largely based on hatred and revenge, yet who increasingly suffers for his actions and seeks a way out of that suffering. Unlike Natsue, by the end of the novel he has begun to awaken to the nature of sin and to turn toward God. In his college days, Keizō had read the Bible and had adopted as his motto the biblical injunction to love your enemy. Keizō clings to this teaching, which crops up over and over in the novel, yet lives a life of hatred toward the one person he should love above all, his wife. Discovering the kiss mark left on his wife's neck by Murai, he flies into a rage and plots the revenge that drives the novel. The following scene portrays Keizō's inner struggle. He is compelled by his hatred while acknowledging the depths to which he has fallen.

> What will happen when someday Natsue finds out she's unknowingly been raising a criminal's child? . . . Imagine how mortified she'll be when she discovers she's been raising as her own child the child of the criminal who murdered Ruriko. . . . I gave "Love thy enemy" a try. I might have suffered even more than Natsue, since I was the one who knew the truth about Yōko. . . .
>
> Keizō could imagine how astonished, saddened, and mortified Natsue would be when that day came.
>
> He felt fearful as he realized the dark pit that had opened up at the bottom of his heart. How could he be acting this way toward the one he should love the most—his wife? That awful thought welled up from the dark pit deep inside him. . . . He understood that this bottomless pit was in him, in Natsue, in all humans. (2: 121–122)

This recognition that his actions spring from the "bottomless pit" of man's mind comes even earlier in the story, soon after Ruriko's murder. One might find it odd that Keizō's hatred is not directed more at her killer, Saishi; but Keizō sees *himself* as a potential murderer, for when he was seventeen or eighteen he groped an eight-year-old girl. Later on, whenever he saw the girl, "He wished she would suddenly die of some illness. He even hoped he could kill her, if he could do it in secret":

> (How am I different from Saishi?)
>   (He might have even been a better person than I am, since he didn't have any lust.)
>   (I might very well have choked that girl to death if she had cried out.)
>   Keizō hung his head. (1: 93–94)

Throughout the novel Keizō's thoughts stray toward other women; he, as much as Natsue, has an inclination to be unfaithful. In one scene, for instance, as he begins to doze off, he dreams of other attractive women he knows—his wife's friend Tatsuko and the young office worker at his hospital, Yukako, who has an intense crush on him (1: 172). More disturbing are Keizō's lustful thoughts toward his adopted daughter, Yōko. Having been for many years unwilling to hold Yōko or even touch her, soon after his boat accident he vows to be a better father. One day he holds her on his lap. As he plays with her, evil thoughts race through his mind, with him "now feeling he could understand the psychology" of such "perverts" (chikan) (2: 16):

> As soon as Keizō became aware of this [his inner inclinations] he quickly put Yōko down from his lap.
>   "You're too heavy, Yōko," he said.
>   (If Yōko really were my own flesh and blood, I would never imagine such a thing.) He realized what a thoroughly despicable human being he was. (2: 16–17)

Natsue is driven by pride and boredom more than by lust to pursue Murai. Keizō is by far the more prone to lustful, even taboo, sexual desires. Natsue may be a bit of a cradle robber in pursuing Kitahara, who is young enough to be her son, but her actions cannot compare to Keizō's pedophiliac tendencies. Keizō torments Natsue for indulging in a watered-down version of his own dark desires. Unlike Natsue, though, he is far from oblivious to the contradictions he lives with; each instance of sinful thoughts leads to an agonized inner struggle, a further recognition of his sinful nature. Missing from this equation, Miura implies, is God. Recognition of one's sinfulness is but the first step; reliance on God's forgiveness and salvation is the second. Keizō is keenly aware of sin, but is unsure where to turn, and for much of the novel suffers alone. He has made the first step; he falters on the second.

The Tsujiguchi family faces three crises in the course of the novel: first, Ruriko's murder, last, Yōko's suicide attempt, and in the middle, the ferry accident from which Keizō barely escapes with his life. Indeed, the accident is not only a major dramatic episode, but a turning point for Keizō in his spiritual search, because of the missionary's selfless action. While recuperating in the hospital after being rescued, Keizō remembers the man's sacrifice:

> The thought made Keizō see his own life in awe-inspiring terms. It was hard to survive when so many hundreds perished, yet he was greatly moved.
> (Everyone wanted to live.)
> . . . Life lay harsh and heavy on him now. . . .
> (Was that missionary rescued?). . . . the missionary's purpose in life, and his own, seemed like two very different things. (1: 366–367)

Miura develops this theme of self-sacrifice further in *Shiokari tōge* (see chapter 2, below). Here, though, the sacrifice and selflessness of others, and his own brush with death, bring Keizō to a turning point in his life, a reconsideration of its purpose, especially with regard to his treatment of Natsue and Yōko.

He recalls the words of a patient of his who had recently passed away: "After all, a man can only live once"; likewise he is struck by the ephemerality of the "snow insects" in the air (the source of the title of this particular chapter): "Happiness and peace are like these tiny insects," he thinks (2: 7), remembering a poem by the same patient:

> I am but a being
> Adrift between heaven and earth.
> Night, as I face an operation. (2: 7)

This recalls Miura's poem about her own illness, before she converted to Christianity, as she faced numerous painful operations and contemplated suicide. Here she employs a poem to underscore the gravity with which Keizō now looks at life; his growing awareness that he has been adrift; and the fact that we are given only one chance on this earth. The challenge, as he will see it for the rest of the novel, is somehow to close the gap between the missionary's loving, sacrificing behavior and his own self-centeredness. Keizō's undergraduate interest in the Bible soon revives. He picks up a Bible in a bookstore and begins reading Matthew. Ever mindful of Natsue's infidelity and his subsequent treatment of her, he is immediately struck by the story of Joseph and

Mary, particularly the way in which Joseph, when he found out Mary was pregnant out of wedlock "had in mind to divorce her quietly," but then, when commanded to marry her, obeyed God's call.

Immediately afterward, though, Keizō falls back into his old resentful, suspicious attitude toward his wife, and much of the rest of the novel tracks his halting progress on the path to spiritual enlightenment. Keizō comes to many realizations along the way: that true love is the giving of one's life for others, as the missionary did; that his revenge is backfiring, for he is the one suffering most; that spiritual sustenance is at least as important to human life as physical well-being. This final point is brought home to him when a patient of his suddenly commits suicide, leaving behind a note that says there is no place for him in the world. Keizō, who has been increasingly questioning his own role as physician, understands that, although he was able to cure the man's physical illness, he could not reach his sick soul (2: 206). Someone else is needed for this task—and for curing his own troubled heart.

After much hesitation he decides to attend church, impelled by feelings of guilt over what he has done to make Natsue suffer and by his own powerlessness to stop attacking her in his heart. Further, from reading Proverbs he understands the extent of infidelity in human history, how husbands are much more likely to commit adultery than wives, and how, in essence, he is far from alone in his suffering. In the end, though, he never makes it into the church. He is brought up short on the steps outside by the church's sign, with the famous quotation from John 3:16: "For God so loved the world that he gave his one and only son. . . ." Keizō thinks, "(It says God loved the world, but does he really love people?) I'm far too dirty to be loved by God, Keizō thought to himself" (2: 254).

It is fascinating, and instructive, to watch how Miura systematically takes Keizō through a slow but earnest spiritual journey. Christian readers (probably few of Miura's) can almost predict what comes next, for Keizō's progress is something with which many seekers can identify: the gradual, often nonlinear movement from self-centered vengefulness to awareness of one's own sin and of the possibilities of God's forgiveness, with all the attendant doubts and questions that contemplating these issues bring. In what is probably the most important page in the novel, Keizō voices the crux of the theological issue that Miura wants to present. After another erotic dream about the now grown and beautiful Yōko, Keizō thinks of how frightening a person he is to have such a dream:

> (Even in dreams, the person there is me. All the thoughts and actions in dreams still come out of me.)

Keizō felt strongly how very deeply sinful he was. Still, though, he found it strange how he could be so lenient about himself compared to anyone else.

(If someone else were to do what I did and, loathing his wife's infidelity, make her raise someone like Yōko, I know I would denounce him. If I were to have a short affair, I wouldn't then be angry with myself, would I? Yet I can never forgive my wife's affair. Why is this? What is wrong for my wife to do should also be wrong for me.)

People get upset even if others don't answer correctly, or respond to others the way they should, but why do we forgive ourselves? Keizō was amazed at how self-centered [*jiko chūshin*] human beings are.

(What is self-centeredness? Isn't it the root of sin?) (2: 277)

The notion of egotism, or self-centeredness, lying at the heart of sin is, of course, nothing new, indeed is at the core of Christian theology. For Miura, bringing her characters—or at least some of them—to an initial awareness of the nature of sin is what *Freezing Point* is all about. In *Hikari aru uchi ni* (While in the light [1971]) Miura reviews these very points in a chapter entitled "What Is Sin?" People measure themselves and others by two different yardsticks *(shakudo)*, she writes, a double standard that is a "manifestation of our self-centeredness." [24] (She gives as a classic example of this the story of David and the prophet Nathan in 2 Samuel 12.) Not only does this allow us, like Keizō, to judge others more harshly than ourselves; it compels us to make others our accomplices, to lower them to our level so that they join us in slandering and backstabbing others. Miura notes that people often tell her they don't like Christianity "because it treats people as sinners." Her response to this—and recall her own twenty-year-long battle with grave illness—is, "If I'm sick, I want to be told I am." [25] Those familiar with medical practice in Japan will note here that, even today, terminally ill patients are often not told the extent of their illness. Instead, they are allowed to suffer in ignorance. Miura has three categories of sin: sin against the law, sin against morality, and original sin. We are all, she writes, self-centered rather than God-centered, which is original sin. Sin is turning one's back on God, and turning away from knowledge of this act further compounds sin. Indeed, she concludes, "The greatest sin is not being able to recognize sin as sin" *(tsumi o tsumi to kanjienai koto ga saidai no tsumi na no da).* [26]

In Keizō's step-by-step progress toward spiritual awakening, he could be expected to make the leap from awareness of the nature of sin as self-centeredness to a turning toward God. This is what happens, but only tentatively. Despite his stumbling, haphazard attempts to approach God through the Bible and through church, as with so many real-life Christian converts it is a crisis in the family, here Yōko's suicide attempt, that compels him toward the final stage of spiritual growth. As Yōko lies in a coma and Keizō attends to her, he makes three discoveries: that God knows all, that we will be judged for our sins, and that we should forgive others so that we may be forgiven. Keizō thinks, "[We] didn't know we were standing before God"; we can "fool people," even ourselves, but not God"; and, "If I had only forgiven Natsue in the beginning, none of this would have happened" (2: 358, 359, 360). Keizō does not make the crucial leap of calling on God for forgiveness, though he is edging toward this. This final notion of forgiveness, however, has a central role in the sequel to *Freezing Point.*[27]

Finally, then, there is the third person of Miura's trinity, Natsue and Keizō's adopted daughter, Yōko. If Natsue is totally self-centered and oblivious to sin, and Keizō slowly awakening to sin, Yōko is so pure, beautiful, and righteous that she cannot possibly be sinful. Yet it is she who feels the weight of sin come crashing down on her so terribly that the only way out is death. In an essay written soon after publication of the novel, Miura writes that she wanted to make Yōko a good, unblemished girl *(zeni no katamari no yō na shōjo),* one who comes to realize the existence of sin. She succeeded brilliantly in this portrayal.[28]

If there is a true hero in the public's mind in *Freezing Point,* it is Yōko. (Significantly, though, since Yōko is either not present or a mere infant, through much of the first half of the novel she is not an actual player in the drama.) Much of the drama in the novel involves the conflict between Natsue and Yōko. The reader may have some initial sympathy for Natsue, but this is soon dispelled in the face of her horrendous treatment of her adopted daughter. Natsue is beautiful and bad, in other words, while Yōko is beautiful and good. Though the novel never deteriorates to the level of Cinderella, Miura does play the wicked stepmother/pure adopted daughter dualism to the hilt, relating a series of events in which Natsue tries to get even with Keizō by foiling Yōko and making her miserable at every step. In one memorable scene at a school play, for instance, Yōko is forced to wear red clothes when everyone else wears white because Natsue deliberately ignores her request for a white costume. It is as if Natsue wishes to announce Yōko's sin (the fact that she is a murderer's daughter) to the world—the symbolism of red as sin and white as purity has a history in Japan as well—and in fact it is at this performance that the first rumors about Yōko's being adopted begin to surface.[29] In another scene, Natsue refuses to give Yōko lunch money, and eventually Yōko takes a job delivering milk. This not only demonstrates Yōko's self-reliance and toughness at a young age, but, when she insists on making her rounds in a severe snowstorm because there are babies who need the milk, her compassion as well. And at Yōko's graduation, as already mentioned, Natsue switches her prepared valedictory speech with blank paper, forcing Yōko to improvise, which she does brilliantly, smiling in the face of adversity.

Such harsh treatment by the only mother she's ever known understandably leads Yōko to feel unwanted and unloved, and belying her almost unbelievably happy exterior, one gradually discovers a more brooding, unhappy girl. Reading her favorite novel, *Wuthering Heights* (she identifies with the adopted Heathcliff), she asks, "Is there anyone in the world to love me?" (2: 155) This melancholy question is soon answered by Kitahara in his love for her. Kitahara raises the question of the "will of something greater than man" that guides human beings, a notion that Yōko takes to heart. She concludes that she was brought into the Tsujiguchi household for some purpose—by a will greater than any accident of birth or desire of her adoptive parents (2: 189). Yōko combines this budding recognition of a supernatural will *(ōinaru mono no ishi)*, tragically, with a lack of understanding of the nature of original sin. She believes that she can remain sinless and unsullied in any circumstances: "I'm a human, not a river," she declares. "Dirty things poured over me won't make me dirty" (2: 199). She wants to keep herself pure and take responsibility for her life herself, rather than admitting that she is a sinner and entrusting herself to God. Though a totally admirable person (in fact, some might argue, a character so good she sometimes borders on the saintly), Yōko is blind to her human nature, which, just like Natsue's and Keizō's, is sinful.

Miura soon offers a view of Yōko's darker side. When she sees a photograph of Kitahara and another girl, Yōko flies into a jealous rage and burns his letters. The incident mimics the earlier Natsue-Keizō drama; sounding very much like her stepfather, Yōko realizes she cannot forgive Kitahara for "betraying" her, when she never betrayed him (2: 280–281). Clearly this supposedly pure person has the same mean-spirited reactions as Keizō and Natsue: anger and jealousy, feelings of betrayal, and a lack of forgiveness. One major difference between Yōko and the others, however, is that, when confronted with the mistake she has made (as the girl in the photo is Kitahara's sister), Yōko unhesitatingly writes to him to ask his forgiveness. Like Keizō, though, her understanding of forgiveness is limited to forgiveness from other people. She does not think to seek forgiveness from God.

The climax of the novel, and certainly the most disturbing aspect of it, is Yōko's suicide attempt. Why, of all these scheming, lying characters, is it the gentlest and kindest one who tries to take her own life? In a long farewell note, Yōko sympathizes with Natsue for having had to raise her, knowing whose daughter she was, and she writes at length about the discovery of her own sin. "I, too," she writes, "have the possibility of being a murderer, like my father . . . I've discovered myself as someone who has inside her the possibility of sin, and I've lost all hope in life" (2: 342). She has tried to live up to her name, Yōko, which means "light," and be a light to all around her, but now, she writes, she has found inside her heart a freezing point (the *hyōten* of the title), that she is "the child of a sinner." For the first time in her life she awakens, she says, to the "depth of her sin" (2: 343), and she feels she cannot live with this knowledge.

The novel presents three kinds of sinners: the sinner who is unaware of sin (Natsue); the self-reflective, suffering sinner who seeks, but cannot discover, the final step toward redemption (Keizō); and the sinner who is fully conscious of sin, but seeks to die to escape from and atone for it (Yōko). In a novel whose explicit theme is original sin, it is remarkable that all three of Miura's main characters end up with an incomplete understanding of the nature of such sin. Natsue asks Yōko to forgive her only *after* Takaki reveals that Yōko is *not* the daughter of a murderer after all; Yōko, not knowing this, attempts suicide precisely because she believes that she is *indeed* the daughter of a murderer. In this peculiar view, inherited sin (the sins of the fathers) is important only if one's parent has actually committed some horrible crime. When Yōko's father turns out *not* to be a murderer, then everything is fine, all is forgiven, and she has no reason to feel guilty or to need forgiveness. This short-circuits, however, what Christian theology means by original sin. As Paul's famous passage in Romans puts it, "All have sinned and fall short of the glory of God" (Romans 3:23). Yōko sees herself as the "child of a sinner," but Miura fails to drive home the point of her own theology: Yōko is no different from anyone else, for *all* are children of sinners. As one commentator on Romans puts it, we are all "member[s] of an apostate race."[30] In its presentation of original sin, *Freezing Point* itself falls short.

In John Irving's novel *Son of the Circus,* a young Jesuit missionary remarks to his Protestant friend, "To us—to us Catholics, I mean—you Protestants appear, at times, to overemphasize the human propensity toward evil."[31] For Catholics, and even more so for non-Christians, the Protestant theology that underlies Miura's writing—summed up in the phrase "total depravity"—is often a misunderstood concept. One theological scholar sums up the Protestant case this way: "The essential nature of man is good, since it is created by God, but his existential nature, his being in the world, is corrupted . . . sin is rightly seen as a deviation from human nature. It signifies the unnature of man, the abnormal which has now become normal. The *imago Dei,* the reflection of the being of God in man, is defaced, but it is not destroyed. Man is still responsible before God, though his freedom has been considerably impaired."[32] Original sin, of course, comes from the Fall as depicted in Genesis, a story that, as Reinhold Niebuhr remarks, "must be taken seriously, but not literally."[33] As Donald Bloesch writes, "Original sin is not a biological taint but a spiritual contagion . . . yet it does not become rooted in man until he assents to it and allows it to dominate his whole being"; the cause of the human predicament is "being caught up in a rebellion against the Creator, one that was already in effect at the beginning of the race."[34]

If, as the *Freezing Point* "boom" maintains, the novel introduced the concept of original sin to a Japanese audience generally unschooled in the idea, the novel must be faulted in two areas. First, it fails to clarify the notion of original sin as part of *everyone*'s existential nature. The reader, in other words, does not, from the text, grasp what is generally meant by "original sin." The closest approach is in the final pages of the novel, as Keizō and the others attend to the unconscious Yōko:

"No, no matter whose child she was born as, she might very well have ended up like this." Takaki said this, remembering the note she'd left that he'd just read.

"I wonder about that," Kitahara replied uncertainly.

"I think so. Someone like her with such a strong sense of sin would probably end up thinking the same thing no matter whose child she was."

"But if Natsue had not said such terrible things to her, I don't think she would have done this," Kitahara said angrily.

"Perhaps, but Yōko's the kind of person who would someday have the same sense of sin," Takaki said, looking at Keizō.

(Perhaps that's true. [Keizō thought] I'm concerned about sins that are committed, but Yōko agonized over the fundamentals of sin [*tsumi no konpon*]. If she knew she was born of adultery, she would surely suffer, and even if there were no problems at all in her background, she might still be the same sort of person who suffers.)

Keizō realized he had never suffered to the extent she had. (2: 361)

Here, then, Yōko is presented as a special case, one of a rare breed who suffers from an excess awareness of sin—not an awareness of original sin as a spiritual contagion *all* have contracted. It is these fundamentals of sin that *Freezing Point* never fully embraces. In the published translation of the novel (co-translated by an American missionary who "polish[ed] it up for publication")[35] Keizō's final thoughts above are rendered very differently: "Keizō made no reply but mused, 'Perhaps, but there are two kinds of sin here. One related to breaking God's law, which all mankind is guilty of. She felt shame about her father's actions which she was not guilty of. Like those who practice adultery and those born of it—both are bound to suffer.'"[36] This highly interpretive rendering reveals two opposite movements. On the one hand, the translator naturalizes the text, converting *tsumi,* which Miura surely uses to mean "sin" in the Christian sense, to "shame"; on the other hand, the translator attempts to compensate for the idea that is missing from the novel— that all mankind is guilty. Still, though, even this attempt to articulate a sense of the nature of original sin by saying what Miura "meant to say" is incomplete, for it is not the breaking of God's law that constitutes original sin, but the "existential nature" of humanity.

The second failing of *Freezing Point* stems from the first. While Christians' understanding of the nature of sin would lead them to repent (in the sense of turning back toward God and asking for forgiveness), in Miura's novel there is only Keizō's vague notion that all will be judged by God and cannot fool God. And of course, except for the repeated injunction to love one's enemy, Jesus and the ultimate forgiveness he represents are absent from this "Christian" novel.

This may be judging Miura too harshly. As Flannery O'Connor puts it, "The problem of the novelist who wishes to write about a man's encounter with this God is how he shall make the experience—which is both natural and supernatural—understandable, and credible, to his reader. In any age this would be a problem, but in our own, it is a well-nigh insurmountable problem."[37] O'Connor reminds readers that the novelist is a teller of stories, not a "philosopher or theologian."[38] As Miura herself wrote about the novel, she wanted to show how these characters, who were ordinary people in terms of their views of morality, could not be happy because of "their self-centered lives and . . . their not being ashamed before God."[39] The Tsujiguchi family members are thus best seen as negative examples. Keizō and Natsue represent "people who don't fear God" and live with the tragic consequences. Yōko, basing her life on the belief that she is absolutely right, in the end commits the "great sin of [attempted] suicide." "Yōko, too," Miura comments, "didn't turn to God. By understanding these characters I wanted people to know another way—one of good will and a spirit of belief in God."[40] In these more modest goals she has mostly succeeded, and despite its shortcomings, its incomplete development of the relation of humanity and sin and humanity and God, *Freezing Point* remains a landmark in the history of Japanese spiritual fiction.

Considering its enormous popularity, and the way the novel ends without a resolution (does Yōko live or die?) a sequel was, in retrospect, inevitable.[41] Readers' reactions to the suspended ending were immediate and impassioned; after the serialization, Miura recalls receiving many letters and telegrams from readers pleading with her not to let Yōko die,[42] and one can well imagine the pressures on her from both her readers and her publisher to continue the story. But she must have had internal motivation to continue as well. A 1967 article points out the strategic sense it made to downplay the theme of original sin in the novel; if the story had dealt with original sin in a strict, moralistic way, the novel would have failed as a newspaper novel, goes the argument, for it would have lacked the two most basic characteristics of popular fiction: that it be easy to understand and entertaining.[43]

Miura thus succeeded in creating a successful work of popular fiction by toning down her faith, making it more easily digestible for non-believers. But for a writer of such strong convictions there was both artistic and religious dissatisfaction with the way *Freezing Point* only began to scratch the surface of her belief, as well as how certain articles of faith were left open to misinterpretation. She herself pronounced the novel a failure, saying, however, "I'm very happy so many people read the book, but my inability as a writer meant readers couldn't fully understand what I wanted to convey, namely, the Christian idea of original sin."[44] Questions left hanging at the end of the novel also had to be addressed. Now that these characters (at least Yōko and Keizō) have begun to acknowledge sin and God's presence in their lives, where do they go next? How do they pursue a relationship with God further? How can they be saved? Hints of what is to come lie in Keizō's comments on forgiveness at the end of *Freezing Point,* and Christian readers should not be surprised to find that the awareness of sin leads to the search for forgiveness. As Miura herself commented after publishing the sequel: "Yōko awoke to sin, despaired, and tried to kill herself. That's how *Freezing Point* ended. That being the case, after she was saved, Yōko should naturally struggle with sin, and consider how sin can be forgiven. I felt I had to write to the point where Yōko attains true forgiveness of sin. And so I began writing [the sequel]."[45]

And indeed, as Harada Yōichi notes, if the theme of *Freezing Point* is original sin, the sequel, *Zoku hyōten* (hereafter *Freezing Point II*) is concerned

with the "forgiveness of sin" *(tsumi no yurushi).*[46] Four and a half years after
the original novel was completed, Miura began serializing *Freezing Point II.*
The sequel ran from May 12, 1970, until May 10, 1971.

As *Freezing Point II* begins, Yōko, recovering from her suicide attempt,
learns the truth about her background from Keizō. She is a changed person,
colder and more distant, who burns with disgust at the adultery of her real
mother, Keiko, and Keiko's abandonment of her. Kitahara and Tōru realize
that they are both in love with Yōko, and for the rest of the novel they engage
in a friendly rivalry over her. Yōko begins to have great compassion for other
abandoned children, visiting and later working at a children's home. She is
more interested in what happened to Saishi's daughter than in meeting her
real mother.

Takaki's mother dies suddenly, and when Keiko appears at her wake,
Tōru, who had visited her neighborhood, met one of her sons, and is always
interested in finding out more about her, introduces himself. In a hotel lobby
they have a long talk during which Tōru reveals Yōko's situation to Keiko.
Keiko is stunned. She tells him how terrible she feels for having abandoned
her. Keiko wants to learn more about Yōko in order to put her own life back
on the right track, but Yōko refuses to meet the woman whose immorality has
"laid a dark shadow on [her] heart." A further connection between Tōru and
Keiko's family occurs when Tōru and Yōko attend a concert in Sapporo,
where they meet Kitahara and a friend of his, Aizawa Junko, who befriends
Yōko. After the concert, Tōru is seeing Yōko off at the station when Keiko's
elder son appears and asks him about her because of her resemblance to his
mother.

Several touching and memorable scenes follow. Natsue and Yōko finally
reconcile, at long last forgiving each other, after which Yōko takes a long visit
to see her maternal grandfather, Natsue's father, who imparts to her his philosophy of life, underscoring the idea that what we give to others is our most
important legacy. Back home, Yōko has a visit from Kitahara, the first since
the suicide attempt, and they, too, forgive each other for the hurt they've
caused. Yōko talks about about how cold she knows she has been to everyone
and says she just wants to be friends for the time being. The first volume ends
as Keizō analyzes his own life. He concludes that he doesn't want to fight with
Natsue anymore and that they are both equally lonely.

The second volume begins at Hokkaido University, where Yōko is now
enrolled. Yōko, who is deliberately living a self-disciplined, ascetic life, feels
that she'll never love again and that she's lost her will to live. Keiko's elder
son, Tatsuya, who has been looking for her, introduces himself, and they
become friends. (Yōko is aware that he is her half-brother, but Tatsuya is not.

He is attracted to her for her resemblance to Keiko, whom he deeply admires and loves.) Tatsuya becomes a third rival for Yōko's affections, and he and Kitahara become jealous of each other. When Tatsuya brings his brother, Kiyoshi, to meet Yōko, Kiyoshi sees the resemblance between Yōko and Keiko and speculates that Yōko might be Tatsuya's twin, separated at birth. This increases Yōko's anger at Keiko for the pain she has caused by her adultery.

Kitahara's friend Junko has meantime fallen in love with Tōru, who has eyes only for Yōko. In a letter to Keizō, Junko reveals that she was adopted by the Aizawa family at the age of four, but that her real father's name was Saishi. Junko hated her real father but overcame her hatred after going to church and learning of Christ's atonement for all human sins. Yōko contrasts her hardheartedness with Junko's forgiveness. The scene shifts, and Keiko suddenly shows up at Natsue's door to tell her that Tatsuya suspects Yōko is related to him. Two new secrets are born: Yōko's identity, which must be kept from Tatsuya and the rest of his family, and the identity of Junko's father. But when Junko visits Yōko's home, she soon learns who her father was. As Junko, Yōko, Keizō, and Natsue are walking in the area where Ruriko had been murdered two decades before, Natsue, who knows nothing of Junko's background, mentions Saishi and Ruriko's murder. Junko faints at the news, collapsing in the same riverbed where Ruriko had died at her father's hands.

Keizō soon begins attending church regularly, finally coming to understand the nature of sin and the unfairness of his judgment of Natsue. In a business trip with his friend Takaki to Kyoto, Keizō also experiences a further awakening to the preciousness of life and the need for forgiveness. Natsue wants Tōru and Yōko to marry, but Keizō opposes this. Tatsuya meets Tōru, learns who he is, and begins to suspect Yōko's real identity. Then Tatsuya forces Yōko into his car to take her to meet Keiko, and Kitahara chases after them in a snowstorm. Finally Kitahara confronts Tatsuya, demanding that he let Yōko go, but Tatsuya speeds off, running over Kitahara's leg and injuring it so badly that it must be amputated. After the accident Keizō reveals the depth of his spiritual understanding as he discusses the nature of love and forgiveness with Natsue and with Yōko, both of whom resist forgiving others. Natsue can't forgive Tatsuya, while Yōko can't forgive Keiko.

A letter arrives for Keizō and Natsue from Mitsui Yakichi, Keiko's husband, revealing that he has known all along about Keiko's infidelity and her having borne an illegitimate child while he was at war in China. Because of the atrocities he committed himself during the war, Yakichi writes, he has never felt justified in blaming her. Yōko, meanwhile, has decided she loves Kitahara more than she does Tōru, and Tōru declares he will leave Japan to study abroad because of his grief at losing Yōko. Before Yōko and Kitahara can decide anything about their future, though, Keiko and Yōko meet briefly. Yōko is cold and unforgiving toward her mother. Kitahara tells Yōko to go see the ice floes, to contemplate nature, and to meditate on her true feelings for him. In the final section of the novel, Yōko does just that and comes to a great spiritual awakening. She believes in God and in Christ's atonement, and she forgives her mother. The story ends with Yōko, in tears, dialing Keiko's phone number to tell her that she forgives her.

Freezing Point II is the Christian novel that Miura had failed to write four years earlier. In this sequel she explores in much greater depth the ideas of original sin and forgiveness. The book reaches a memorable climax when Yōko—resistant to the end to forgiving her mother—witnesses a kind of miracle that leads her to ask for forgiveness and to become a believer. In the years since the original *Freezing Point,* Miura had established herself firmly as a novelist, publishing five major works, including *Shiokari tōge.* She could now complete the story with a more overt Christian message than was possible for her in *Freezing Point.* Confident in her reputation as a writer, Miura was able to tell the story she had only hinted at before.

Like *Freezing Point, Freezing Point II* focuses on the spiritual struggles of Keizō and Yōko (Natsue is even more static than before, a character the reader comes mostly to loathe), but it also includes a number of moving stories about secondary characters that help to impel the two main protagonists forward spiritually. Aizawa Junko, who in an all-too-convenient turn of events turns out to be the murderer Saishi's daughter, is an instructive counterpart to Yōko. Junko's hatred of her father for abandoning her closely parallels Yōko's similar feelings for Keiko, yet Junko has overcome her anger and forgiven Saishi through knowing Christ's atonement (2: 152). One wonders how Junko would have reacted had she known earlier that her father was a murderer (the news causes her to faint), but Miura's subsequent depiction of her shows the strength that her faith gives her to overcome this shocking news. She has a firm grasp of the concept of original sin, and no accident of parentage can make her more sinful. *And* she knows she is forgiven. Junko's conversion becomes a model for Yōko's at the end of the novel.

Tatsuko, Natsue's friend, has also had a difficult life. Her hard-won spiritual understanding and accommodation, though not Christian, incorporate Christian elements. More than any other character, Tatsuko is the cool voice of reason throughout both novels. She is the one who recognizes first that the seemingly happy Tsujiguchi family has a dark stratum running below the surface, and she also dispenses important wisdom. (According to one survey she is the character most readers sympathized with most.)[47] One day, for example, as Murai and Natsue visit her in her home, Natsue notices a church outside:

> "What is that cross? A church?" [Natsue]
> Under the cloudy sky a cross of a tall building was visible directly in back.
> "It's a church all right." [Tatsuko]
> "Nothing to do with me, then." [Murai]
> "Someone like Dr. Murai should go, don't you think? Right, Natsue?" Natsue smiled awkwardly.
> "No, Tatsuko, there's no god to save a profligate like me." [Murai]
> "What a trite remark. [Tatsuko speaking] They say, though, that the profligates and villains are the easiest to save. If you really think you're wicked, then you can't hold your head up in front of God. That's the easiest [person to save]. The ones that are the hardest are the people who feel—in front of both men and God—that they haven't done a single thing wrong." (2: 54)

Later, speaking with Yōko, Tatsuko discusses her anger over the death of her lover, a political dissident, in jail. After his death, anger was what kept her going, she says, and thoughts of taking revenge on his killers in the manner of the heroic stories of the forty-seven loyal samurai and the Sōga brothers:

> "But how do you feel now?" [Yōko asks]
> "Once I read in a novel these words: 'Don't seek revenge yourself. I am the one who will take revenge. I will mete out a reward.' I was really taken aback by this. I didn't really understand it, but those words struck me as the truth. And strangely enough I felt a burden lifted from me. I figured instead of my taking revenge, a far more impartial judgment will take place. And I started to think that only he who can truly judge can truly grant forgiveness, and will truly take vengeance." (2: 190–191)

Mitsui Keiko, Yōko's birth mother, suffers lifelong for her wartime adultery, for abandoning Yōko, and for deceiving her husband and family. Speaking with Keizō, she remarks, "People who have betrayed others, and those who have not, lead different lives." Though Keizō counters with the argument that all have sinned through lust in the heart, Keiko argues that having sinful thoughts and acting on them are very different things, and that "one sin leads to another" (2: 44–45). At the end of the novel, in the kind of description at which Japanese literature excels (summing up a person's emotional state by describing how he/she appears from *behind*), Yōko, after meeting Keiko for the first time and not saying a word to her, watches as she leaves: "She could see Keiko, in her green overcoat. Keiko didn't hail a taxi, but trudged down the snowy road, her head bowed. She walked a few steps, and stumbled. Keiko stood there, and looked as if she were gazing up at the sky. Then she looked down again and continued walking away" (2: 361). All of Keiko's suffering (there is no "statute of limitations on one's conscience," she states [1: 265]), compounded now that her daughter won't forgive her or even talk with her, is summed up in this plaintive scene of a woman bowed down by care.

Keiko's husband, Mitsui Yakichi, appears only briefly in the novel, but he makes a dramatic entrance at the end with his startling letter to Keizō and Natsue. Though Yakichi was a soldier in China when Keiko had the affair that produced Yōko, he knew all along the secret that Keiko tried to keep from him. Not only did he know of her infidelity, but he had also forgiven her in his heart long ago, even welcoming the birth of the illegitimate child. Only now does he confess his own sins to Keiko, and, through this letter, to the Tsujigichi family. His sins are the atrocities in which he participated in China. Most horridly, he cannot wipe out the memory of ripping open the stomach of a pregnant Chinese woman: "After I was repatriated, I couldn't hold my own child in my arms for a while. There was no way I, who had murdered an innocent person, whose hands were stained in blood, could blithely hold my pure, innocent child" (2: 333). Hearing from a nurse about Keiko's having given birth to a baby girl, Yakichi, unbeknownst to Keiko, investigates the whole affair. He concludes that the birth of the baby, the new life to replace the one he killed, somehow lightens his own burden of sin, and that his wife's infidelity is a just punishment for his cruel actions.

The stories of these minor characters forcefully demonstrate that one cannot opt out of sin and suffering. It is part of the human condition and the question is how to deal with it. Junko shows the importance of Christ's atonement. Tatsuko describes the futility of human hate and revenge, as judgment—and forgiveness—come ultimately only from God. Keiko shows the compounding of sin and the necessity for confession. Yakichi's story reveals both the universality of sin and the blessing that comes from forgiving others.

These stories punctuate and support the main concern of *Freezing Point II*, namely the spiritual awakening of Keizō and Yōko. Early on, Keizō understands that what he wants most is forgiveness for what he has done to Yōko and to Natsue. Tatsuko asks him if forgiveness is something humans can do themselves (1: 52). In an interesting conversation with Yōko about dreams, Keizō, who is usually a step or two ahead of Yōko in his spiritual quest, refutes her idea that dreams—the 80 percent hidden from our conscious mind—reveal a cruel, fearful self alone. He argues that this "unknown quantity" within us shows we should have "hope" *(kibō)* (1: 92–93). The idea of hope also comes up in a conversation he has with Natsue and Murai about death, heaven, and hell. Murai characteristically laughs this off as *kodomo damashi* (a trick only a child would fall for), arguing that one cannot know anything about death or any afterlife, but Keizō is serious. He argues that the universal fear of death is the one issue doctors like themselves *must* consider. Human life cannot, he feels, merely produce a pile of ashes and bones. He upholds here, as throughout the novel, an increasingly informed supernatural viewpoint that contrasts sharply with the materialistic views of characters like Natsue and Murai (1: 151–154).

Attentive readers of the *Freezing Point* novels will by this point have noted an important structural change in the novel, that is, the gradual disappearance of Miura's parenthetical statements dividing characters' inner and outer realms. This division is expressed in several ways: through parenthetical inner thoughts, in the discussion of dreams as revealing a hidden self, and in natural imagery. In one haunting instance of this last point, Yōko, on an outing to a deep mountain lake with her friends, thinks about how this deep lake has a forest on its bottom, and how, she was told, any dead bodies would get caught up in the sunken trees and never float to the surface:

> All of a sudden she imagined the skeletons of many dead bodies lying below the surface of this beautiful lake.
> (It may look beautiful, but . . .)
> There might not be anything one could declare truly beautiful. And the same thing might be said about the lives of human beings. (2: 128–129)

The strategic use of the parenthetical statement here—a rarity by now—serves to emphasize a major movement throughout the novel: the way in which the truth of man's sinful nature *is* coming to light, the way the bodies *are* floating to the surface.

As in *Freezing Point*, in *Freezing Point II* this floating to the surface is, in Keizō's case, steady and gradual. In Yōko's, however, at the end at least, it is more sudden and dramatic. After meeting Yukako one day and being confronted by Natsue, who is upset he did not tell her about the meeting right away, Keizō again is struck by the way people use a double standard to measure their own actions and those of others. "Even if there had been something between me and Yukako tonight," he thinks, "if I were pressed about it, I'm sure I would have turned defiant and said 'What are you accusing me of!?'" People, he notes, "no matter what sort of evil thing they do, are not honest enough to take responsibility for their deeds" (1: 287). Earlier, when speaking with Natsue about Keiko's adultery, he struggles to understand why he can sympathize with Keiko despite her adultery, but cannot forgive Natsue. The reason, of course, is that Natsue's infidelity affects him more directly; and like all human beings, he is out to protect himself at all costs. Using the term "error" *(kashitsu)* instead of "sin" here, Keizō concludes that we "more easily forgive ourselves than any others" (1: 120).

At one point Keizō and Yōko discuss human freedom, with Yōko wondering why, especially in this postwar age of "freedom," humans are not truly free. Keizō, who has been reading the Bible regularly, remarks:

> "People were originally created free, however, they say." Keizō said this as he recalled the story of Adam and Eve in the Bible.
> "Then why did they become unfree?"
> "I'm not really sure, but being unfree was not man's original condition. Well, I guess we could say [lack of freedom] is proof of being a sinner." (1: 293–294)

Keizō, of course, has hit on one of the major themes of Christian belief. In our sinful state we are under the illusion of being free, whereas, paradoxically, true freedom comes only in submission to the will of God. There is no return to humanity's "original condition" without God's intervention. As one theologian puts it, left to his own devices, man may "yearn for the good, but he is incapable of pursuing the good."[48]

As he wrestles throughout the novel with the issue of forgiveness, Keizō struggles to find truths that are (Miura would insist) right under his nose. Now that he has realized the Christian truths about the nature of man, sin, freedom, and forgiveness, Keizō is confronted by the ultimate, practical question every seeker at some point reaches: I know this, but *now what?* As he reads Junko's letter discussing how she eventually forgave her real father—through faith in Christ's atonement—and how her adoptive father, Aizawa, took her in because no one else would, Keizō contemplates both what a terribly "sinful couple" he and Natsue are and his own base motives for adopting Yōko. More than anything he wants to apologize to Yōko and Natsue. He asks, "What should I do to be forgiven? . . . Really, what should I do to be forgiven?" (2: 153). The answer is right in front of him in Junko's letter. Readers should not be too harsh on Keizō, or on any of these characters, however, for the slow, painful, tortuous path they take to spiritual awakening. Miura's genius lies in outlining, in a detailed, evolving manner—for an audience who, for the most part, is skeptical of any literary proselytizing—the way in which an ordinary person comes to understand extraordinary truths.

Junko's hint that attending church might help strikes a chord with Keizō. In one of the most openly Christian passages in the novel, ten years after he first hesitated at the church door, he's finally able to push it open and attend worship services. What does take place is the usual Protestant service— hymns, Scripture reading, prayer of confession, sermon, and so on—but in a nation where less than one percent of the population is Christian, this scene may have a voyeuristic claim on the readers' attention as a glimpse into what takes place behind the doors of a little-understood religion. The Scripture reading is Luke 18:10–14, the parable of the Pharisee and the tax collector:

> Two men went up to the temple to pray, one a Pharisee and the other a tax collector. The Pharisee stood up and prayed about himself: "God, I thank you that I am not like other men—robbers, evildoers, adulterers—or even like this tax collector. I fast twice a week and give a tenth of all I get."
>
> But the tax collector stood at a distance. He would not even look up to heaven, but beat his breast and said, "God, have mercy on me, a sinner."
>
> I tell you that this man, rather than the other, went home justified before God. For everyone who exalts himself will be humbled, and he who humbles himself will be exalted.

This is followed by testimony from a young woman about Yōko's age, who talks about her job at a nursing home, and how she came to realize that she was not serving the elderly patients out of love for them, but, like the Pharisee, out of a desire to be praised and to be seen to be doing good. She quotes from 1 Corinthians 13:3 (part of Paul's famous sermon on love): "If I give all I possess to the poor and surrender my body to the flames, but have not love, I gain nothing." Keizō is struck by this, convinced that all he's accomplished in his life until now is meaningless, and by the pastor's words, which seem directed right at him: "There is probably no other thought more deeply rooted than the desire a person has to think he is correct" (2: 227), and by the pastor's explanation that, although we try to base our sense of righteousness on ourselves, "There is no other way than to return to the righteousness based on the Bible" (2: 229).

Keizō is deeply moved by all these words; the whole chapter is an epiphany for him in answering the question Where do I turn now? In a deeper way than ever, Keizō re-evaluates his marriage and his treatment of Natsue and

Yōko, seeing as never before that his treatment of others is based not on love, but on egotism, and understanding where guidance to a better life can be found. As the novel plays out, Keizō more than ever takes on the role of spiritual adviser and sounding board for Natsue and Yōko, two women still deep in the throes of unforgiveness and anger. After Kitahara is injured, for instance, Natsue disputes God's existence, claiming that a benevolent God would never allow such a terrible thing to happen. Keizō, sympathetic to Kitahara, allows that "God's will is not something people can easily comprehend" (2: 323). And in a conversation with Natsue and Yōko about love, Keizō raises the Christian view of love:

> "Of course there are all sorts of love. Instinctual love of a parent and child, what is commonly called erotic love, and love between friends. But the type of love that human beings should really examine is essentially a matter of the will."
>
> "So there is a kind of love beyond just being in love?" [Natsue]
>
> "I think so."
>
> "I don't like that at all. That's not love. Love isn't such a complicated thing."
>
> "But it *is* complicated. You should read a book on the subject. It's a very tough thing, to love. True love means giving up that which is most precious to you."
>
> "By most important you mean money or clothes or something like that."
>
> "So life to you, Natsue, is number two in importance?"
>
> "Apart from life, is what I'm saying."
>
> "Being able to give up one's life for another, that's what love is."
>
> (2: 330)

This passage near the end of the novel is interesting for the contrast it draws between Natsue, who has learned very little over the years, and the spiritually awakened Keizō, now the voice of Christian reason. Some might argue that in the original Japanese, with Keizō's use of the tentative *da sō da* (or so they say) he is reporting knowledge external to him rather than a thoroughly internalized belief. But over the course of *Freezing Point II*, however, steadily and ploddingly at times, Keizō has demonstrated remarkable spiritual growth.[49]

Yōko's spiritual awakening is equally painful and halting, though it culminates in a dramatic way that sets it apart from Keizō's. Yōko reconciles with Natsue and Kitahara, but sensing that her immoral birth has "laid a dark shadow" on her heart (1: 214), she struggles to forgive Keiko. Immediately following her tearful reconciliation with Natsue, Yōko travels to see her adoptive maternal grandfather in Chigasaki, outside Tokyo. Her grandfather, from whom the secrets of Yōko's birth and of her suicide attempt have been kept, reveals that he nevertheless knows all about these. He begs Yōko's forgiveness for his daughter's cruelty to her, for his not having raised her to be a better mother; this once again sets Yōko thinking about her own lack of forgiveness: "I have to become the kind of person who can sincerely apologize" (1: 319). The grandfather, though not a Christian, preaches to her in a way that reaches her heart. She is particularly struck by the notion that what remains after our death is what we give to others. Determined now to be more giving, she feels the dark shadow inside her giving way to a "ray of light," and that night she dreams of a star drawing ever closer to her (1: 320–321).

Yet Yōko still struggles with being a child of adultery, and she tells Tōru that "dying is far easier than living" (2: 138). Later, however, in a lengthy meditation on forgiveness precipitated by Junko's letter, Yōko truly grapples with what forgiveness entails. Impressed by Junko's words about Christ's atonement *(shokuzai)*, she confides to her diary that though she doesn't understand this, "I can well imagine the profound meaning, and reality, contained in this word" (2: 158). But she can't see herself forgiving as Junko has done: "At any rate, Junko was able to forgive her father, a murderer. If she can do that, I should be able to forgive my mother. I really should be able to. But I cannot. Why am I unable to do what Junko has done?" (2: 158). Yōko is further impressed by Keizō's reaction: he feels he should apologize deeply to Junko, for if it were not for his and Natsue's inattentiveness to Ruriko, Saishi would never have become a murderer: "But I have no desire to forgive, or to apologize to my . . . mother. There's nothing I need to apologize to her for. At the same time, though, I hear a voice asking whether or not that's really true. What could that possibly be?" (2: 160). The main stumbling block for Yōko is that human forgiveness does not erase the consequences of a sinful act. Junko may forgive her father, for instance, but Ruriko is still dead, and "murdered people don't come back to life" (2: 161). Yōko is comforted, however, by the fact that she took on Natsue's hatred—when she assumed that Yōko was Saishi's daughter—in place of Junko. Miura's message here, of course, leads back to the notion of atonement. Though Yōko is edging ever closer to the Christian message, at this point she is still unable to connect the dots. Later on, though, she does understand the need for a radical change in her spiritual life. As Kitahara confesses the depth of his love for her,

> Yōko thought, if she didn't find a solid way to live [*kakutaru ikikata*], she would never find true happiness. Junko had already shown her the

direction to live, but Yōko had not yet made a fundamental change in her life. Only when her spiritual life is fundamentally transformed would she be able to solve the issue of her hatred for Keiko. Looking at Kitahara, Yōko thought that as long as she was not transformed, she wouldn't be truly happy no matter who she married. (2: 293)

Yōko's transformation finally comes with the poetic, and dramatic, climax of the novel. Traveling to the northern Hokkaido town of Abashiri at Kitahara's suggestion (he makes a yearly pilgrimage there to view from afar his mother's grave on an island in Soviet territory), Yōko takes a taxi ride to see the sights, then returns to contemplate the massive ice floes offshore. Much in the landscape suggests loneliness and human alienation. One landmark is a lighthouse in which a lighthouse keeper whose lover died has lived alone for fifteen years, often cut off from other humans for half the year. Yōko also passes by the infamous Abashiri Prison and ponders the fate of the inmates, locked away for decades to atone for their sins. "But," she wonders, "is sin something to be atoned for?" (2: 356).

She recalls that that morning, as she left Asahikawa, Keizō gave her a Bible to take with her, urging her to read John 8:1–11. This is the episode in which an adulterous woman is brought before Jesus by "teachers of the law and the Pharisees." As Jesus tells them, "If any of you is without sin, let him be the first to throw a stone at her." Yōko remembers her first meeting with Keiko, Keiko's plea for forgiveness, and her own heartless reaction, and now wonders, as she stares out at the ice floes, whether her heart is as frigid and unyielding as the ice before her. The ice image, of course, is inevitable in a novel with this title, but unlike the "freezing point" of the original novel, which seems abrupt and unmotivated, here the interplay of nature and Yōko's emotional state is fully developed and powerful. When you think you alone are correct and others are wrong, Yōko thinks, you end up with a heart as cold as the scene before her:

> (Original sin!)
> Yōko suddenly recalled this term she had heard from Keizō.
> With this massive, unyielding ice field before her, Yōko felt she understood for first time the ugliness concealed in her heart.
> Jesus alone was qualified to throw the stone, but he didn't throw one at the adulterous woman. Instead he warmly forgave her. Yōko couldn't help but remember that.
> (But why? . . .)

> Why did Jesus forgive her? Because even at the cost of our human life sin cannot be fundamentally atoned for? Certainly there is no way to deal with sin other than through forgiveness. (2: 362–363)

Yōko recalls the words she wrote in her suicide note years three years before ("I want something that has the power to decisively forgive sin"), and now understands that one can never expect human forgiveness to be complete: even though one forgives, one never knows when "hate will raise its head" (2: 363).

The last few pages of the novel present an extraordinarily moving scene. As Yōko gazes at the dark gray sheet of ice ("perhaps a true representation of our lives"), she suddenly notices red on the ice, the ice burning "fires on the plain" (*nobi,* the same term as in the title of Ōoka Shōhei's war novel). She stands dumbfounded at the red spreading over the ice and suddenly feels a "strange ray of light shining in her heart." The red spreads like drops of blood seeping into the ice, and she suddenly imagines it as "Blood from heaven!" "In that instant Yōko is struck by the deep feeling that she was witnessing— before her very eyes—the blood Christ shed on the cross" (2: 366). Here Yōko reaches the spiritual awakening that has eluded her:

> She couldn't help but feel the will of something beyond human beings.
> (Human beings are so very small.)
> Watching the brilliant flames, Yōko thought there was indeed a God who could right now truly forgive human sin. Junko had told her that only through the sacred life of God's son could sin be atoned for, and now Yōko could believe that was true. Someone who could, silently, accept a cold-hearted person like herself. Why didn't I believe this up till now? (2: 367)

Yōko cries out in her heart to Keiko to forgive her, and picks up the phone to tell her of her own forgiveness. For much of her life the dark secret in an outwardly happy family, Yōko can now finally live up to her name and be a light in her family and to others. As Philip Yancey notes, "We are bound to people we cannot forgive."[50] In Yōko's case, she has been bound to her birth mother through her unforgiveness; only now that she forgives will she be set free. This setting free, though, does not imply independence, but rather a greater level of interdependence and love. Echoing the words of Yōko's grandfather about the centrality of giving, Henri J. M. Nouwen writes, "We are called not to own but to serve each other."[51] Miura has shown us clearly, and with great conviction, the birth of a loving, serving heart.

Many have noted the use of nature in the two novels, especially in the wintry scenes that conclude each—Yōko unconscious in the snow after taking an overdose, and here in Abashiri as she reaches spiritual awakening. Kuroko Kazuo argues that in the suicide scene at the end of *Freezing Point,* "the nature that surrounds [Yōko] works as a kind of affinity [*shinwaryoku*] that can transform even an abnormal act like the taking of one's life into 'healing.'" [52] As Asai Kiyoshi notes, though, Miura is likely to use nature in unconventional ways. From the first pages of *Freezing Point,* for instance, Miura flouts the conventions of the newspaper novel in regard to nature: instead of having the seasons in the story parallel the seasons in which it is serialized, Miura began her series, which was serialized starting in the winter, in the hottest part of summer. This suggests, as does her use of the parenthetical inner monologue, that Miura is, from the outset, concerned with a reality beyond the immediate and the material. [53] More to the point, Kuroko's "nature as great healer" point of view is one that Miura would reject. Nature, in the form of the impressive ice floes Yōko ponders at the end, does play a role, but as Harada Yōichi points out, the image of the ice floe on fire is not an actual, visible phenomenon (see Chapter 2 below for a discussion of miracles), for visible phenomena lack the power to change people's lives: "It is in reality perceived by the mind's eye that we find the transformation of the self." [54] To put it another way, quoting Yancey again, forgiveness "transcends the relentless law of nature." [55] Forgiveness and healing are not found in natural law, Miura would argue, but rather in a law that transcends this world and yet, in certain moments, descends to lap at our frozen hearts with tongues of flame.

Asai Kiyoshi notes that in *Freezing Point II* "the author has stepped away from being the narrator of a story and reveals the decision to proceed down the path of evangelistic literature." [56] While *Freezing Point* does begin to raise spiritual questions, these issues are more intimations than fully developed ideas; only with the sequel does Miura make her spiritual stance clear. Attentive non-Christian readers of the sequel should be quite able to summarize some of the basic tenets of Christianity, as well as have an acquaintance with some of the better-known biblical passages. *Freezing Point II,* though, is no dry catechism in disguise, for it is as entertaining and approachable as its predecessor. Yet it raises in interesting ways the whole question of the possibilities of "evangelical literature," especially in a country such as Japan, where Christian literature is very much a minority literature. As Flannery O'Connor writes, the "sorry religious novel comes about when the writer supposes that because of his belief, he is somehow dispensed from the obligation to penetrate concrete reality."[57] Miura has not sidestepped this obligation, penetrating the concrete reality of the human heart and minding well O'Connor's conclusion that "drama usually bases itself on the bedrock of original sin, whether the writer thinks in theological terms or not."[58]

Harada Yōichi, attempting to place Miura's work in the exalted company of such writers of "pure" literature as Natsume Sōseki, Akutagawa Ryūnosuke, and Dazai Osamu, writes that Sōseki shows us the undependability of love and the absence of hope for salvation, Akutagawa the egotistical nature of humans, and Dazai how people are "no longer human." All three are "diagnosing humankind's illness but not providing a prescription for how we should live." Only Miura, he writes, provides such a prescription, creating through her fiction a literature of hope and a *sukui no bungaku*—a "literature of salvation."[59]

CHAPTER TWO

The Seed Must Fall

Two Tales of Self-Sacrifice

S ono Ayako (1931–), after Endō Shūsaku Japan's leading Catholic novelist, is also known as one of its most peripatetic. Her journeys have taken her to all corners of the globe, to Southeast Asia, Europe, India, both Americas, and the Middle East, and have inspired a steady succession of works with themes on a wide variety of topics—the Arab world *(Arabu no kokoro)*, the story of Japanese migrants to the Americas *(Rio Grande)*, and the life of Jesus *(Sono hito no na wa Yoshua)*; she has also written on such varied topics as life in a nunnery, the construction of electric power stations, war crimes, and, in the first of her translated works, *Kami no yogureta te* (lit., "God's soiled hand," translated as *Watcher from the Shore)*, abortion.[1]

Within this prodigious literary output is a minor classic, *Kiseki (Miracles)*, again the product of a foreign journey, this one a trip to Poland and Italy following her attendance at an international PEN meeting in Dublin in 1971. *Miracles*, published serially from 1972 to 1973 in the journal *Catholic Graph* (and as a single volume in 1973), is a nonfiction piece of reportage tracing the career of Father Maximilian Kolbe, the so-called Saint of Auschwitz, and of miracles attributed to his intervention. Fascinated by the story of Kolbe's self-sacrifice since she first heard of it, a "tremendous shock," in her words (251),[2] the timing of her reporting was also motivated by the beatification ceremony for Kolbe, held at the Vatican on October 17, 1971, which Sono attended and describes in the book. Kolbe was canonized in October 1982.[3] In addition to *Miracles*, Sono also published a short piece, "Ochiba no koe" (The voice of the falling leaves [1973]), a reprise of her longer work and further evidence of her fascination with the story of Kolbe.

Miracles is an exploration, from Sono's Catholic viewpoint, of the nature of and possibility for miracles. It is also a meditation on the nature of self-sacrifice, and in this regard shares themes with a work by her Protestant counterpart Miura Ayako (the other of the "two Ayakos"), the 1968 novel *Shiokari tōge*. While Sono's work is a nonfiction exploration of a famous foreign martyr, Miura's is a fictionalization of the life of a much less well-known Japanese martyr, a simple railway worker who gave his life to save others. The two works ask some basic, yet compelling, spiritual questions: What are the spiritual effects—both on the person involved and on others—of self-sacrifice? Is the miraculous possible in our day and age? And what are the possibilities of faith's being a real part of ordinary, everyday life?

Miracles begins with "A Very Individualistic Preface" (Kiwamete kojinteki na maegaki) that questions the relevance of saints to the modern day: "The feeling I've had from a long time ago concerning the image of saints is like that of a tapestry, ornate and glittery, that over time has become worn and desiccated. . . . [As I read more about them] this impression grew stronger. These were, after all, stories, and I just couldn't picture saints as living, real people" (7). Sono briefly reviews (for her Japanese readers, the vast majority of whom would not be aware of this) how saints are designated, how miracles must take place to be considered valid, how they often involve cures, and how these must be verified by a panel of disinterested physicians. Remembering asking a Catholic friend as a young girl about this process, she recalls how they felt they were "talking about a sublime mystery we shouldn't touch on" (8), again underscoring the notion of saints, and by extension miracles, as something far removed from ordinary modern life.

Sono briefly reviews her own spiritual life as a young woman going through World War Two, how Japan, an "indestructible divine nation" was supposed to be saved by the miraculous intervention of a "divine wind" *(kamikaze)*, and yet ended up suffering an "extremely rational, predictable" defeat (8). In postwar Japan, she found, believing in the God of Christianity was often a personal embarrassment, something that subjected her to ridicule. A nation that had expected miracles now wanted nothing to do with any deity, and Sono, an admittedly "weak" believer, herself had an irresponsible, fatalistic attitude toward God (9).

Alternatives to her lukewarm attitude, however, were offered by devout believers she encountered both during and after the war. While Japan's defeat brought on an abrupt and drastic change in values (what Ōe Kenzaburō describes as a kind of somersault [see chapter 4 below]), the Catholic nuns she knew were unaffected: "In this time when Japan was defeated, when people were in total confusion, all values and moral views were changing, and people no longer believed in anything they believed in before, I saw with my own eyes how the lives of these women, focused totally on 'God,' did not waver in the slightest" (8). One particular nun, a Sister Odelia who continued to run a children's home despite financial and personnel crises, impressed her with an attitude of total confidence that "God would provide." Yet Sono, though sympathetic to these views, does not go so far as to expect miracles: "Even so, in the final analysis I did not believe that God would provide an answer in the form of a miracle" (10). Again, as with the subject of saints, Sono's skepticism dominates some of the standard elements of her own faith.

The only time she seriously considered the subject of miracles as a young woman was when a thirty-five-year-old friend of hers succumbed to chronic kidney disease. Thinking for the first time of praying for a miracle, and of asking her dying friend N to pray similarly, she imagines he would only laugh at her: "Recommending to N that he pray for a miracle would probably only make him ask, 'So, the jig is up for me, eh?'" (12). Here Sono detects a major difference between the way Westerners and Japanese approach death. The families of people dying in the West are more concerned with spiritual well-being than with physical death, making sure that the dying person confesses, receives the last rites, and is spiritually prepared for what is to come. Just as Westerners face death straight on in their dying moments, she writes, so too do they their entire lives. In contrast to this, "for Japanese death is always inauspicious *(engi de mo nai),*" something one does not want even to consider; hence the custom of sprinkling salt over those returning home from a funeral as a kind of incantation *(omajinai),* so that neither "death itself [nor] the idea of death will enter the home" (12–13). Sono concludes: "Somehow I couldn't make N confront death before he died. Before I was a Christian, I was an average Japanese. I never found the opportunity to tell N to pray for a miracle. Neither did I pray for him myself, believing in a miracle" (13). N died, and Sono writes, "Ever since, I was sure I'm a person who had nothing to do with miracles. For literary reasons I was strongly drawn to biblical stories of miracles, but I clearly distinguished between those and the boring, coldly logical present day, when miracles weren't about to occur." "But," she continues, "I no longer can say that" (13).

This dramatic turnaround in her attitude toward miracles came from her discovery of the story of Maximilian Kolbe. After Dietrich Bonhoeffer, the Lutheran minister executed for his role in an assassination attempt on Hitler, Kolbe is the best-known martyr to emerge from World War Two. Sono first hears about Kolbe from a certain Father S, who discusses the upcoming beatification and the miracles that support it. Sono, convinced she has "nothing to do with miracles," is suspicious of these and decides to visit the people

who have experienced miracles of healing through Kolbe's intervention—
Francis Ranier in Rome, Angelina Testoni in Sardinia, and Franciszek Gajowniczek, a man whose life Kolbe saved in Auschwitz.[4] Sono, highly skeptical of
these miracles and the witnesses who support them (in addition to the
attending physicians, ten witnesses are required for an incident to be deemed
a genuine miracle) writes: "If Father S could only know what ran through my
deepest thoughts at that moment, he surely would have been disgusted with
the incorrigible nature of those who write novels. . . . I'd long ago given up on
just believing things as they were. The excuse I used was that you can't believe
unless you doubt" (15–16).

Summing up her findings about Kolbe before she details her journey,
Sono writes that his life directs a "demanding question" to the "thirsting
hearts of modern people": What does it mean to love another? Kolbe asks,
"'Would you die in place of an unfortunate person?' 'Would you be able, in
the midst of hatred and pain, to wait for God's will to bring forth a wave of
his grace?'" (19). Because such Christian terminology as "God's will" and
"grace" is beyond most of her readers, she shifts the terminology to that of
aesthetics:

> Sometimes, when I touch on Father Kolbe in lectures I give, I say this in a
> small voice: "For those who don't believe in God, I'd like to speak of his
> death as a type of aesthetics. That even if you're killed, you save another.
> For him this was a kind of pure aesthetic. Unless he accomplished this, his
> life would not be beautiful, which is why he followed this aesthetic. . . .
> Sometimes I think this: if we subscribe to this kind of dangerous aesthetics,
> we will surely lose. Sometimes this will mean we actually destroy ourselves.
> When Father Kolbe was not chosen as one of the ten to die, he should have
> just thought *great!* and been happy about it. He didn't have to speak out
> and say he'd die in place of another. But his aesthetics wouldn't have
> allowed that. Unless we have such an extremely dangerous aesthetics,
> though, we might not be able to have truly lived in this world." (19–20)

A number of biographies and shorter writings on Kolbe are available, and
Sono makes use of most of them in tracing his life.[5] Born in a Polish village
on January 8, 1894, Kolbe, named Raymond at birth, took the name Maximilian after his ordination. "A boisterous, intractable child," in André Frossard's account, Kolbe as a boy prayed steadily to the Virgin Mary to help him
overcome his temper, which his mother deplored. One day, when Kolbe was
ten, his mother saw him crying and asked what was the matter:

With tears in his eyes, he told me [Kolbe's mother narrated], "When you
cried, 'What will become of you?' I prayed often to the Madonna to tell
me what I would become. One day in church I begged her again, and she
appeared to me, holding two crowns, the one white, the other red. The
white meant that I would stay pure, the red that I would be a martyr. She
asked me if I wanted them. I replied, 'Yes, I do want them.' Then the
Madonna looked tenderly at me, and she disappeared."[6]

Throughout his career as priest (he was ordained in 1918) and scholar (Kolbe
held two doctorates, in philosophy and theology), this childhood vision
remained the touchstone of his life, the notion always that the purity of his
life would, in the end, lead to martyrdom (57–58). After studying in Rome,
he and six colleagues founded the Militia Immaculatae (the Knights of the
Immaculate), dedicated to "conquering the world for God through love and
devotion to Mary, the only fully human being, he explained, who had never
deviated from soldering her will to God's."[7] Kolbe returned to Poland to
teach church history at a seminary in Cracow, then founded a thriving mon-
astery and several religious publications, including *The Knight of the Immaculate*, which reached a monthly circulation of 800,000.[8] Sono writes of his
early "revolutionary fervor" that, because of political repression in Poland,
was transformed into religious devotion. Kolbe became a religious activist,
founding, for example, a society to oppose Freemasonry, and his sometimes
overzealous nature brought him into conflict with less outgoing, more con-
servative monks (72–74).

There is also a connection between Kolbe and Japan, for he was a missionary to Nagasaki from 1930 through 1936. Sono, solicitous of her Japanese
readers, leaves discussion of this fact till the final pages of *Miracles*. Interviewing Japanese priests who knew and worked with Kolbe in Nagasaki, she
traces the extreme poverty in which he lived, his burning desire to publish
his Catholic journals in foreign languages, the advanced tuberculosis from
which he suffered, and his overriding devotion to the Virgin. Warned that he
wouldn't live long because of his tuberculosis, Kolbe replied, "I'll die pretty
soon, so I'd better work now while I can." And one Japanese priest recalls
how Kolbe's greeting to everyone was the exhortation, "Maria!" Understanding Kolbe's relationship to the Virgin Mary, Sono notes, is the open sesame
to his inner world (222–224).

No biographies would ever have been written about Kolbe, though, if it
were not for an incident that took place at Auschwitz on August 1, 1941. Like
thousands of priests in Poland, Kolbe had been rounded up early in 1941 and
condemned to the horrors of the concentration camps; unlike many, though,

his Germanic family name and fluency in that language offered him the possibility of escape through taking German citizenship. He refused this offer, though, and was sent to the camps. At Auschwitz prisoners were told upon arrival, "Jews . . . have the right to live no longer than two weeks. Priests one month. The rest of you three months."[9] Those who could not stand the inhuman conditions were always able to commit suicide by throwing themselves against the electric fence surrounding the camp. Holocaust survivors have documented the horrors of the camps extensively; Auschwitz was particularly infamous. Every Monday morning, for instance, between twenty and twenty-five men from Kolbe's work group were randomly executed. One German officer boasted of "personally executing 25,000 prisoners with a shot to the head."[10] Beatings, starvation, and of course mass executions in the gas chambers were also part of the hellish day-to-day existence of the inmates. (Sono cites an average of 12,000 per day killed in the gas chambers.)[11]

Survivors have testified that Kolbe was true to his devotion and piety during his entire stay at Auschwitz, praying with the sick and the dying, sharing his meager rations with the starving ("slipping bread into their pockets so that they wouldn't feel embarrassed"),[12] and secretly holding Mass despite the danger of doing so. On July 31, 1941, a prisoner from Kolbe's cell block managed to escape while working outside the camp. The next morning the almost 600 prisoners in Block 14, the one Kolbe was in, were assembled outside:

> All the SS wanted was to know where the escaped prisoner had gone, and surely someone had to know something. As the heat of the day intensified, minute by minute, prisoners began dropping and—since it was strictly forbidden to break ranks—lay crumpled just where they fell. . . . One by one they kept on dropping from exhaustion and heatstroke.
>
> Finally, toward evening, Kommandant Hoss's second-in-command, Deputy Commander Fritsch . . . walked out onto the parade ground. . . . Everyone could see that Fritsch was visibly perturbed; the prisoner, he informed the *polnische Schweine*, had not been found. Ten men would therefore be picked at random and sent to Block 11—the pit—where they would be stripped naked and starved to death in reprisal for the one who had yet to be found.[13]

One of the ten men chosen, a forty-year-old Polish sergeant named Franciszek Gajowniczek, broke down and cried out in anguish at the certainty of never seeing his wife and children again. At this point Kolbe stepped forward and offered to take Gajowniczek's place. As one eyewitness puts it, as Kolbe requested, in German, that he be allowed to die in the other's stead, Fritsch, at first furious at this breach of camp rules (it is surprising that Kolbe was not shot on the spot) gave in to Kolbe's argument that he was an old, sickly man—he was only seven years older than Gajowniczek—and allowed him to take the man's place.

The men were thrown into the dark underground cell; one by one they died from lack of water or food. The jailers reported that Kolbe alone remained lucid, singing hymns and praying with the other condemned men in this cell much like an "underground church," in Sono's words (95). As Paul Mariani writes,

> And each day, when the guards, accompanied by the Polish prisoner who acted as interpreter, entered the cell, Father Kolbe would be standing or kneeling there in prayer. When he gazed at his tormentors, one witness testified, his eyes burned with such liquid intensity that he was ordered to look at the ground. No wonder Kolbe's name quickly made the rounds, even among the SS. Here was a man of courage, an *Übermensch*, a singular priest, more than one guard is reported to have said. Some of the guards, according to the reports of reliable eyewitnesses, suffered psychic trauma. No one, they said, should be able to act as this priest had acted.[14]

By the end of two weeks, however, only Kolbe remained alive and fully conscious. The Nazis, eager to use the cell for another batch of prisoners, finally dispatched him with a shot of carbolic acid to the arm that "blew out his heart." The date was August 14, coincidentally the "eve of Mary's assumption, body and spirit, into heaven."[15]

Before he went into the starvation chamber Kolbe was once berated by an SS officer for still clinging to his faith. Kolbe's response was simple: "Yes. I believe" (98). What fascinates Sono is the possibility of belief in the face of sustained, organized evil. The cruelty of the Nazis, she writes, though on the surface apparently a systematic denial of God, an attempt on their part to supersede God, paradoxically proves the existence of God.[16]

> Sadism has to have elements beyond the mere tormenting of people by other people. In other words, precisely because of the pleasure derived by the thought that by tormenting human beings one is wounding God, sadism is linked to the pleasure that lies deep within humans. Putting it this way may lead to misunderstandings, but without the existence of God a dark passion like sadism would never exist. Or to put it another way, without an awareness of God it is impossible to either write about or understand sadism. (101)

Again, she writes that for "Japanese, who have no concept of God," no true understanding of sadism can be reached. Events like the death camps "essentially shouldn't be something I feel connected to" (102).

Sono, of course, *does* feel connected to these events—her Christian faith now outweighing, as earlier it did not, her "Japaneseness"—and *Miracles* underscores the whole emotional range of reactions she has to her journey through Europe. The most moving of all her experiences, both to her and to the reader, is her visit to Auschwitz, which is also documented in the related short piece "Ochiba no koe." There she descends to the underground cell in which Kolbe died, passing by, most memorably, row upon row of the I.D. photographs of individual victims of the death camp that line the walls: "I could almost hear them all yelling out to me, 'You're a writer. If you're a writer, write about my life! Write about how I felt when I died! Do writers only write about the famous? Can't you write about the nameless ones who die like worms?'" [17] In the deliberate death by starvation and dehydration that Kolbe suffered, Sono sees, again, the sadistic delight in defying God: "The people who planned all this were aware they were crushing God. God's face gradually turned pale, dried up, was destroyed, and here for the first time they were seized by the pleasure of man's victory." [18] But in this sadistic torture, Sono sees the agonies of an earlier death reflected as well.

> Hunger isn't the main concern. They grew terribly thirsty. A process in which, it is said, "Their blood would boil, sending explosions in the brain, finally leading to madness." This method of torture was already suggested in the Bible. When he was crucified Christ didn't complain of hunger, but of thirst. A soldier responded, giving him vinegar to drink. That was still fairly lenient. These Polish pigs can drink their own urine. [19]

In *Miracles* Sono writes that, after this visit to Auschwitz, she loses her appetite and can't sleep. To take her mind off the experience, she reads—and quotes—a lengthy poem by the Indian poet Rabindranath Tagore. This lyrical depiction of young love seems utterly incongruous, but Sono tells us that it is precisely the ordinary in this poem that she seeks as the only antidote to the extraordinary cruelties of the death camp. This may be Sono's answer to charges of how literature can be possible after Auschwitz, but it also becomes clear that she seeks in Kolbe's death a restoration of the ordinary, at least on the level of one man: on the day following her visit to Auschwitz she visits the man he saved, Gajowniczek. "Tagore's poem is a poem of youth," she writes, "and I wonder if the ordinary [*heibon na*] life in the latter half of [the poem] had been left to Gajowniczek" (102–107).

In her visit to Gajowniczek, though, she learns some shocking news: though he survived the camp (one of only two survivors from an original group of 1,700), Gajowniczek returned after the war to find that his two sons had died in a Soviet air raid. Sono is stunned by the news, and by the fact that Gajowniczek, bereft of his sons, wished he had never survived the war. She writes, "So that's what the world is like, I muttered to myself like some immature twenty-year-old. Kolbe's enduring two weeks without water, being tortured to death bit by bit, was not enough, in the end, to protect the happiness even of one single family" (117):

> The notion of a God, a kind of papier-mâché God, who always rewards those who do good things, is an idea thought up by the stupid people of this world. It looks like God just gives people a mission. To Maximilian Kolbe it was to find an answer to the question of what could be gained when people place others in extreme circumstances. And for the Gajowniczek family the mission was to use their entire life to aid the work of Father Kolbe. The mission has absolutely nothing to do with happiness. If forced to put it into words, one could say that only at the moment when one awakens to this mission does one experience, like a flame igniting, a sense of happiness, which at any rate is a miserable sort of happiness.[20]

The easy linkage between "good intentions and love" and happy results found in "TV dramas and novels" leads to stories that "warm people's hearts," but ultimately "deceive . . . neither purifying our hearts, nor giving us hope" (117).

Here Sono turns again to the notion mentioned earlier, of Kolbe's death as a form of self-actualization, of Kolbe following the dictates of a personal aesthetic redefined as a sense of mission from God. She flips the question around, asking what would have happened to Kolbe if he had *not* stepped forward on that fateful day, and concludes that Kolbe was compelled to act:

> Even if no one else thought so, as long as he had lived, aware that he had abandoned that person [Gajowniczek], he surely would have thought that death was his fault. Kolbe was aware at that moment of a spiritual death that transcends mere physical survival. . . . For Father Kolbe nothing good could have come from surviving in that way. That's it—Kolbe died according to the dictates of personal "taste" [*shumi*]. Surely some will be angered at this way of putting it, calling it sheer imprudence. (118–119)

What Sono means by "taste" amounts to a question of the transformative power of personal will in light of the model of Christ. Sono turns, surprisingly, to the work of the Czech Marxist philosopher Vitezslav Gardavsky here for guidance, specifically to his book *God Is Not Yet Dead*. Gardavsky argues that the miracles of Jesus were "radical answers to an urgent summons," revolutionary steps to transform people by taking them where they had never been before, overcoming an inherent human alienation. Gardavsky argues for the guiding role of love, not as a fixed moral structure, but as a matter of the will, and for Jesus' revealing the possibilities for humans themselves to produce miracles (119–120): "So Jesus' preaching does not tell us to love everybody. He doesn't tell us what to do in every single situation. All he asks of us is that we should enter into the situation wholeheartedly. And his own actions show us that it really is possible: man is capable of performing miracles" (122).[21] This is, Gardavsky writes, the only way truly to understand existence, and at the same time truly to exist. Sono concludes from this, "Father Kolbe didn't die for the Gajowniczek family. He threw away his life in order to *exist*" (122).

But to exist for what? In Kolbe's case, as Sono makes clear—if not here, certainly elsewhere in the book—it was not for some materialist existence or alienation that he sacrificed himself, nor for a secular aesthetic or an aesthetic of death in the manner of, say, Mishima Yukio. His act was, instead, to some modern eyes, antiquated devotion and service to an invisible God. (One of those dusty tapestries comes alive.) Here, of course, Kolbe parts company with Gardavsky, whose materialist ethic envisions radical transformation brought on by the focused will of individuals acting in the here and now. Surely Kolbe's act was radical, the result of a focused will, and acted in the real world. But the questions of motivation and belief remain. For an atheist like Gardavsky, there is no higher power in which to believe, whereas all evidence points to Kolbe's acting in light of an unswerving faith in a divine power. From the time of his first vision of the Virgin, as Sono makes abundantly clear, Kolbe's life was on a trajectory of such extreme devotion that martyrdom of one sort or another seemed inevitable. The locus classicus of such faith is found in the paradoxical teachings of Jesus, for example, in Matthew 10:39, which states, "whoever loses his life for my sake will find it." Belief in this paradoxical teaching ("for *my* sake"), Sono implies, is the real miracle.

In fact, what is most interesting about *Miracles*—what it adds to the already well-documented story of Father Kolbe—is the very personal spiritual discovery by Sono, through her journeys in Poland and Italy to investigate the intercessory medical miracles, of how very grounded faith is among European Catholics. Kolbe, she learns, is but an extreme example of a deeply rooted faith in which the expectation of miracles is an integral part. The unspoken contrast between this and the attitude of her largely non-religious Japanese audience is stark, and one is struck by the disparity between the Japan she depicts, where her Christian faith can be a source of embarrassment, something to downplay or even hide, and these European countries, where for many faith, prayer, and the possibility of miracles are the very air they breathe.

Throughout the book, which could be easily categorized as a travelogue, Sono reminds us of her unease with the saintly and her hope that she will encounter flesh-and-blood people of faith. Visiting Kolbe's hometown, she learns that his mother, while devout, had a reputation as a voluble woman: "I was relieved to hear she was 'talkative' [*oshaberi*]. I was afraid that during my investigations the only people I'd encounter would be the completely admirable" (55). And of Kolbe himself she is happy to discover a human side —his deep concern over politics, for instance: "If through God Kolbe was a person far above other people, I don't think I would have been interested in him. Because people like that who are so outstanding have nothing to do with me" (67–68). A "warped person" like herself (*hinekure mono*, 67) then, is predisposed to search for the ordinary, for faith and saints at eye level, so to speak. And indeed this is precisely what her journey brings her face-to-face with: a down-to-earth, living, flesh-and-blood faith.

Like many before her, Sono is astounded by the hold that Catholicism still has on the people of Poland, and surprised by the numbers of people who attend services. (Her visit in 1971 was at the height of the Cold War and Poland's Communist regime.) Attending Mass at Kolbe's hometown church, she imagines Kolbe's long-dead mother praying here: "For [Kolbe's mother] coming to pray here was something absolutely *necessary* to live. Praying wasn't a duty, it wasn't a rule. She came to offer up to the Lord the feelings that overflowed from her. And the women who were praying here now weren't any different" (51). And reviewing the sorrows of Polish history, she notes:

> Poland's sufferings are not over even now. Ever since the general election
> of January 1947, when the Communist Party, under the name of the Unity
> Labor Party, took power, the people have continued to battle for their
> faith. The churches survived because in people's hearts belief was not an
> ideology, but an emotion blazing within them. Once more I felt how the
> Poles don't go to church on Sundays to fulfill an "obligation," but rather
> joyfully go through "love" of God. (52)

Interestingly, she uses the term *koi* here, which refers less to spiritual love than to the earthly, and earthy, affections between men and women—again

Sono's attempt to situate what she experiences at the level of the ordinary. This "fight between liberalism and Communism," she writes, was "predicted two thousand years ago by Christ," who was an "astute psychologist" in his insistence that "man does not live by bread alone." Communism's promise of bread alone, inadequate to fulfill the spiritual yearnings of the people, led to "these crowds of people in church earnestly praying . . . one thing I never could have imagined in this socialist state of Poland" (66). In this sense she is impressed later, at the beatification ceremony at the Vatican, where even the Polish ambassador and his wife take Communion (217). As for the sufferings of Poles under Communism, she quotes Kolbe on how the early church thrived on persecution: "During its first three centuries the early church was persecuted. The blood of its martyrs became the seeds of Christianity. Afterwards, when persecution ended, one of the church fathers lamented the mediocrity of the faith. And he rejoiced when persecution started up once more" (66). Sono concludes that, through its opposition to Christianity, it is Communism itself that supports faith in Poland.

The second half of *Miracles* traces in detail the author's visit to Italy to investigate the medical miracles attributed to Kolbe's intervention. Poland, she writes, was just the background to her real interest in taking a cold, hard look at the possibilities of the miraculous in the present day (123). In passing, she notes a number of miraculous cures attributed to prayers to Father Kolbe, including that of the famous atomic bomb survivor and writer of Nagasaki, Dr. Nagai Takashi, author of *The Bells of Nagasaki*. But she concentrates on the two mentioned prominently in the case for Kolbe's beatification, Francis Ranier and Angelina Testoni.

Through access to relatives, documents, and in the case of Testoni to the woman herself, Sono delves deeply into the record of these healings. It is unnecessary to rehearse the mass of details she reviews concerning the illnesses. In brief, Ranier (who died of heart disease in 1969, nearly two decades after his miraculous healing) suffered a crippling infection in his leg; a partial amputation did not slow his deterioration, and the village doctor announced he had only a day or two to live. Ranier was given a picture of Father Kolbe, of whom he had never heard before, prayed to him, and by the following day was completely recovered.

As in a good detective story, clues and mitigating circumstances raise questions about the "purity" of this particular miracle. Inconsistencies in his statements raise doubts about the timing of Ranier's receipt of the picture of Kolbe (134); likewise, one wonders if, in his sometimes delirious, sometimes unconscious condition, he could have prayed with any concentration. Unlike some of the other Kolbe miracles, this case relies wholly on family members as witnesses to the healing. Some of them, Sono speculates, may have been simply going along with the testimony of the son-in-law, who happened to be a physician (148). The only thing that encourages Sono is one family member, who says that seeing Ranier's overnight recovery was like "seeing the resurrection of Christ": "Those words alone seemed real to me, but since the first miracle ended up being too insubstantial [*hagotae no nai*], I fell into a dark mood" (148). (This dark mood is somewhat alleviated, for Sono and for the readers, by the occasional flash of humor in the text; one Japanese Sono meets in Rome comments that it would have been a more complete miracle if the man's leg had grown back! [146])

Some fifty pages of this 250-page book are devoted to Sono's investigation of Testoni. Sono interviews Testoni, numerous witnesses, and conducts an extensive review of the medical record and report to the Church. Testoni's case involved years of chronic abdominal pains. In 1948 her condition worsened, and she was pronounced near death by her doctor. She asked for the last rites, but a priest also put a picture of Father Kolbe on her stomach so that she would pray to him. (She later put the picture under her pillow, but continued to pray.) Instead of dying five or six hours later, as the doctor had predicted, she made a complete recovery. One doctor downplayed any miraculous elements in her cure; another concluded that, for a case of abdominal tuberculosis like hers, it was an unusual, though not necessarily miraculous, recovery (172). Eventually, though, as with Ranier, the Church accepted the evidence as sufficient to prove that a miracle had taken place.

As Sono meets and interviews Testoni, a nurse who tended to her, and various friends and family members, there is a gradual shift from her original goal of determining the miraculous nature of these individual cases to the issue of the faith that supports these ordinary Italians' lives. As she talks with an eighty-year-old friend of Testoni, Sono writes, "I came to see her less out of interest in hearing the story of Miss Testoni's miracle than out of interest in this indomitable old woman's life" (193). Talking with nursing nuns, she is once more amazed at how their lifestyle of service and devotion, which puts them in daily contact with the depths of human suffering, also contains elements that "transcend the realities of human life" (180). And about talking with a widow who works at an orphanage, she writes, "As I listened to her I was struck by a kind of deeply religious lifestyle that permeates the lives of ordinary Italians. The term 'religious lifestyle' needs some explanation. According to my common [*tsūzoku-teki na*] interpretation, it means that throughout his life a person has a transcendent goal" (188). When Testoni told this widow of her cure on the day it happened, the woman treated the subject lightly; if it had been her own friend who had been so cured, Sono writes, she would have spread the news far and wide (190). Both of those cured tended to minimize their miraculous cures, and Testoni never once even referred to it as a miracle (209).

At the end of her journey Sono arrives at a strong sense of the transcendent and the ordinary coexisting in the lives of these believers, the "transcendent goal," as she puts it, being ever present in their ordinary existence. At one point, referring to the kindness of the people of Sardinia, she writes of their "ordinary, yet tremendous good will" *(heibon de idai na zen'i),* a throwaway comment that nevertheless reveals the natural juxtaposition of these very elements—the tremendous and extraordinary always coexisting with the commonplace and mundane. For Testoni and all those around her, faith, prayer, and the expectation of miracles are part of everyday life. Saints are not worn-out tapestries of some forgotten age, but living spirits they clasp to their breast for all they're worth.

Returning to Kolbe and the nature of miracles, Sono confesses that she doesn't believe in eternal life, or at least not in the usual Christian notion of it:

> Most of the time I believe that when you die everything vanishes. So where does that leave God? Sometimes I feel like I've seen God in this world. I'm not saying I've had some great experience. My faith isn't that deep. But in the confusion of this terrible world, in the fascinating special qualities of people, in the mysteries of being swallowed up by a fate in which good and evil intentions coexist, I have tasted focused, passionate lives that cannot be explained without God.
>
> If you die and return to nothingness, people might say, then where does that leave eternal life? But I believe in eternal life that takes a different form. Like that of a single thread, for instance, from Father Kolbe to Miss Testoni.
>
> Father Kolbe didn't have his own children. Biologically he didn't pass down life. But he did pull at the hearts of any number of young monks. And in the concentration camp, when his own life was on the point of vanishing, when he had lost all outward human dignity, he had a deep influence even on his enemies. Isn't that eternal life itself—this transmitting of the shining essence of the spirit? Even if one lacks a sense of sharing in the overly grand, supernatural eternal life brought about by Christ, it is possible, in this way, to transmit a definite sense of an eternal life. (208)

Ultimately, though she witnesses the transcendent brought down to earth in Kolbe's life and in the lives of ordinary believers, Sono concludes that much is unknowable, both about Father Kolbe and about miracles. Taking a clue from the work of Viktor Frankl, she writes how people's inner world and motivations, remain an enigma to those around them.[22] In the midst of the horrors of Auschwitz, with people crammed up against one another like "sardines in a can," where privacy and private thoughts might seem a forgotten memory, there is an "inner world unknown even to your 'neighbor'":

> One person will, in his inner world, shine a light on it, thus positioning it in eternity, gaining life in the midst of death and nothingness. Another person lacks the power and dies, hurried on by fear. What Frankl writes about is how, no matter what the situation, there were people who did not cease being human. And Father Kolbe was one of these. (214)

The only ones, she concludes, "able to comprehend the meaning of Father Kolbe's actions are God and the Father himself" (215). Still, in the pages that follow, she makes a strong case for Kolbe's motivation as springing from the intensity of his devotion to the Virgin Mary (she discusses at length the appeal of this veneration in Catholicism), ending with the notion that for the Virgin Kolbe committed *junshi,* the ritual suicide of a feudal retainer after the death of his lord (235). Having lived under the white crown offered in his childhood vision, the purity of a life spent in devotion, in the final days of his life Kolbe grasped the red crown of martyrdom, which he always knew was coming.

Likewise, after all her travels and investigations, the question of miracles is left in the realm of the undecidable, the ultimately unknowable. Back in Tokyo, Sono shows the evidence of Testoni's cure to a doctor, who says he cannot declare it a miracle: "Whether you see it as a miracle or not depends entirely on your way of thinking." Sono writes, "And at that point, I'm back to where I began. Is everything that happens in the human world a result of human power, or not? And if miracles are not simply miracles, but 'coincidence,' then what is coincidence, and where does it come from?" (247). For a believer such as Sono, such inconclusiveness may be troubling; but for a novelist, particularly one of Catholic persuasion, perhaps this abiding sense of questions yet to be answered is only to be expected. To quote Flannery O'Connor again, "The fiction writer presents mystery through manners, grace through nature, but when he finishes there always has to be left over that sense of Mystery which cannot be accounted for by any human formula."[23]

Like *Miracles,* Miura Ayako's *Shiokari tōge* (translated in 1974 as *Shiokari Pass*), was first serialized in a Christian journal, in this case *Shinto no tomo,* from April 1966 to August 1968.[24] As a single-volume novel it was her fifth published work, coming chronologically between *Freezing Point* and its sequel. Of the eighty-some volumes in her published oeuvre, *Shiokari Pass* ranks second in total sales (2.96 million copies) and first in popularity among her readers, beating out *Freezing Point.* Interestingly, it was also Miura's own favorite among her novels.[25]

Nonomiya Noriko classifies Miura's works into five categories: novels dealing with original sin, love, and forgiveness (e.g., *Freezing Point*); historical novels; biographical novels; autobiographical novels; and essays and biblical commentary. *Shiokari Pass* essentially falls into the third category, for it is based on the life of a certain Nagano Masao; unlike the life of Father Kolbe, which is well documented, the life of Nagano, a railway employee in Miura's hometown of Asahikawa (the setting of *Freezing Point*) was known mainly to a small circle of friends and fellow church members, with little documentary evidence for the biographer. After his death, following his request in his will, his letters and diary were burned. The only written evidence remaining to document his life was scant—a short pamphlet on his life put out shortly after his death, two memorial postcards with his photograph and will, and some short items about him in a published church history.[26] Miura first learned about Nagano in July 1964, right when the prize for *Freezing Point* was announced, from an elderly member of her church (the Rokujō Church in Asahikawa) who had himself been brought to faith by Nagano. Subsequent interviews with this church member, as well as the member's own writings about his younger days, added to her meager store of facts about Nagano's life.[27]

Miura learned that Nagano, a devout Christian, was a model of devotion and service. As the translators of the novel sum up her findings:

He was an unpretentious person, choosing to live simply and to dress even shabbily, in order to support his mother and to give his earnings to people in need and to deserving causes. Awarded a princely Imperial Grant for his services to the State during the Russo-Japanese war, he gave it all to found a Young Railwaymen's Christian Association.

Nagano was, in fact, a highly respected public servant, renowned for his integrity and popular with his men. . . . Problem personnel tended to be sent to him because of his ability to handle them and win their confidence. . . .

Masao Nagano was a brave man too. A missionary in Hokkaido came under suspicion of being a wartime spy and suffered a great deal of hostility. Disregarding the repercussions upon himself, Nagano wrote to the newspapers and tackled the security authorities on the foreigner's behalf.[28]

Nagano was also an effective and powerful speaker on Christian causes, and it was on his way back from an evangelical meeting at which he had spoken that the incident that made him live on in the memories of his contemporaries, long after his untimely death, took place.[29] On the evening of February 28, 1909, as the train Nagano was riding back to Asahikawa ascended the steep Shiokari Pass north of the town, the last car in the train came uncoupled and started to race backward down the tracks. In the ensuing panic, Nagano, according to eyewitnesses, attempted to stop the car with the emergency handbrake. When this failed, he threw himself onto the track so that his body would stop the runaway car. He succeeded, but was killed instantly. Various theories of his death—as accidental instead of intentional, as a suicide he had been planning all along, and so on—surfaced during the ensuing years. Miura addresses all of these in an afterword to the novel. From Miura's point of view, Nagano's death was a conscious act of self-sacrifice to save others.

Shiokari Pass is a biography of sorts, but Miura has freely invented episodes and events, while toning down the overall depiction of Nagano. She was unable to locate any living relatives, so the lack of resources forced her to invent many characters and events. Renaming the main character Nagano Nobuo (as well as changing one of the characters in the name "Nagano" to a homonym) to indicate the semi-fictitious nature of her narrative, she comments that what little she could gather about the real-life Nagano indicates that he was a much more admirable man, and of much stronger faith, than her fictional Nobuo.[30] Hearing from his friends that he was an "incarnation of love" who lived a "life of pure gold," Miura says she found it hard to imagine the real life of such an exemplary figure.[31] While a good deal of hagiography is no doubt at work in these public memories, readers of Miura's novel (more properly dubbed biographical fiction), many of whom surely find Nobuo too good to be true, should understand that the author consciously humanized her protagonist by portraying him as a man full of doubts who comes to faith only after an enormous inner struggle.

While undoubtedly moved by his life, and by his sacrificial death, in *Shikokari Pass* Miura was also continuing her exploration of original sin. Wakasa Tadao sees the novel as revealing a much more open awareness of "original sin and blessings" than *Freezing Point. Shiokari Pass,* then, represents a continuing exploration of the nature of sin after the incomplete, inconclusive ending to her first novel.[32] In *Shiokari Pass* Miura also constructs a *bildungsroman* of faith that takes the spiritual journey of the protagonist far beyond anything in either *Freezing Point* novel. Here the main character moves from contempt for anything to do with Christianity to an extreme dedication to his faith and devotion to others, a movement spanning the extreme poles of faith. With their own biographical predilections when it comes to literary interpretation, some Japanese commentators have identified various characters in the text with Miura herself, her husband, and others, in an attempt to unravel the novel as a disguised autobiography (using Miura's early antipathy for Christianity as a point of departure). These interpretations may have some validity, but the novel can stand alone—apart from any connection with either the real-life Nagano or with Miura—as a moving portrayal of the slow and often painful passage from unbelief to belief.

Shiokari Pass begins in Tokyo, where Nagano Nobuo is born in 1876 and raised by his grandmother, Tose, and his father, Masayuki. Nobuo has been told that his mother died soon after he was born. For some reason that eludes him, his grandmother has a great antipathy toward her. One day, though, when Nobuo is walking in town with his father, they are greeted by a young girl who calls Masayuki "Father," confusing Nobuo greatly. Eventually the secret comes out: Nobuo's mother, Kiku, is still alive, living apart with her daughter Machiko, the little sister Nobuo never knew he had. Kiku, a Christian, refused to renounce her faith, and Tose, as was typical in this time of loathing for foreign religions, banished Kiku from their house. After Tose's death, though, Kiku and Machiko move back in with Masayuki and Nobuo. Now it is Nobuo's turn to feel antipathy toward Christianity, which he resists at every step.

Meanwhile, Nobuo forms a strong friendship with a classmate named Yoshikawa. When Yoshikawa reveals his intention of becoming a Buddhist priest when he grows up, Nobuo, partly from hatred for his mother's religion and partly from friendship, declares his intention of doing the same. Yoshikawa, though, along with his family, suddenly flees to escape creditors—a kind of second abandonment for Nobuo—and ends up in Hokkaido. Correspondence with Yoshikawa gives Nobuo a chance to philosophize about all the issues stirring in his adolescent heart: love, death, freedom, and especially sexual yearnings. Nobuo struggles with his sexual desires for women. In one memorable scene he is taken to the Yoshiwara red-light district by his older cousin Takashi to have sex for the first time, but he runs home before they enter the brothel. (Nobuo remains a virgin until his death.)

Masayuki suddenly dies, and in order to help support the family Nobuo gives up his dream of attending college and becomes a secretary at the law courts. There he encounters another childhood friend, Torao, who has been arrested. For Nobuo this meeting opens a series of speculations on sin, righteousness, and pride that is furthered by his reading a novel, written by an acquaintance, in which a minister betrays his wife. Nobuo is also growing fond of Yoshikawa's sister, Fujiko, but she is already engaged.

At the age of twenty-three Nobuo sets off for Hokkaido at Yoshikawa's invitation. Partly he wants a new start in life, and partly he wants to meet Fujiko again. She has fallen ill with tuberculosis, and her engagement has been broken off because of her illness. When Nobuo begins to work for the Hokkaido railway, his boss, Wakura, attempts to marry his daughter Misa to him. Nobuo, though, asks Yoshikawa to let him marry the sickly Fujiko, but Yoshikawa refuses, surprising Nobuo with the information that Fujiko is a Christian. Spurred on by his love for her, Nobuo begins reading the Bible, but comes to faith only after an encounter with a preacher on the streets of Sapporo. The preacher challenges Nobuo, who here declares his intention of becoming a Christian, to try to put one Bible story into action. Nobuo chooses the story of the Good Samaritan and attempts to care lovingly for a miscreant colleague of his, Mihori, who has stolen a pay envelope from another railway worker. When Wakura is transferred to Asahikawa, he orders both Mihori and Nobuo to join him, Nobuo ostensibly to guide Mihori and keep him out of trouble. As Nobuo and Fujiko grow closer, Nobuo declares his love for her and pledges to wait until she is fully recovered to marry her, even if it takes his whole life.

In Asahikawa Nobuo is baptized, begins attending church for the first time, and becomes a popular Sunday school teacher (later principal). He is also busy giving talks on the Bible to railway employees and spends much time traveling around Hokkaido to do so, which keeps him from seeing Fujiko often. In the meantime, Misa, who still has feelings for Nobuo, has become pregnant by Mihori, and they marry. Mihori goes off to the Russo-Japanese War. He returns gloomy and cynical, constantly questioning Nobuo about his faith and abstinent lifestyle, at one point accusing Nobuo of being "abnormal," and serving as a foil to allow Nobuo to expound his beliefs.

Fujiko's condition improves markedly, and she and Nobuo fix a date for their engagement ceremony, February 28, which is seven years since they pledged their love to each other. Nobuo, who is worried about his aging mother, plans to move back to Tokyo in April with Fujiko and begin attending seminary. The evening before the ceremony, Nobuo is in Nayoro, a nearby town, giving yet another talk to the Young Railwaymen's Christian Association. He exhorts them to "be ready at any time to give [their] lives for God" (254). The following morning, in the incident that gives the novel its title, Nobuo is on the train back to Asahikawa when the accident occurs in which he sacrifices his life to save the other passengers.

The novel ends three months after Nobuo's death, as Fujiko and Yoshi-kawa visit the site of Nobuo's martyrdom. Nobuo's death has had a great impact locally, helping dispel prejudice against Christianity and turn people toward faith. Ten young railway workers convert because of his example, including Mihori. Nobuo's will is read aloud at his funeral; copies of it are later distributed to his friends and other associates. Mihori, whose life is "changed . . . completely" by Nobuo's sacrifice, comments, "Nobuo's sacrificial death, which I saw, was a more eloquent message to me than his will or anything else" (268–269). The novel ends with Fujiko at the site of the accident, weeping.

Perhaps one of the most surprising things about *Shiokari Pass* to the Western reader is the depth of the prejudice and antipathy toward Christianity that it portrays and which continued well into the modern age. Christianity was officially banned in Japan in 1614, and the ban was lifted only in 1873. As Yamaji Aizan notes in a 1906 work, the Meiji government at first adopted the Tokugawa attitude toward Christianity, setting up notice boards proclaiming, "The heretical sect of evil Christianity is banned as before." Soon, though, the government reversed itself, advocating a policy of "appeasement" and allowing the establishment of churches. In 1872, four years before the birth of the protagonist of Miura's novel, the first Christian church was established in Japan in Yokohama.[33] As Karatani Kōjin has argued, it was not the powerful former samurai (the Meiji leaders) who took to Christianity so much as the lower level, powerless former samurai: "Since the ethos of the warrior class was in every sense the ethos of Hegel's 'Master,' samurai who could no longer be masters in reality had to search for a new way to maintain this identity. *Bushidō* was Christianized."[34]

Instead of the lukewarm official tolerance for the religion or the embracing of it by those who had fallen from power, *Shiokari Pass* underscores the lingering antagonism of a generalized former samurai class, and of ordinary Japanese, toward this foreign religion. Tose in particular is representative of the old-school attitude toward what she views as an evil religion. Tose's intolerance for the "Yaso" religion (the derogatory name for Jesus) drove Nobuo's mother, Kiku, from the house. In a scene soon after Tose dies and Kiku returns, Masayuki and Nobuo discuss this vehement opposition:

> "Your mother is a Christian. Your grandmother disliked 'Yaso,' as she called him, more than anything else. 'I won't have a Yaso daughter-in-law in this house!' she said, and told your mother to get out."
> "Did you say 'Yaso'?" Nobuo suddenly looked scared.

He did not know who Yaso was, but he remembered Tose having said that he sucked human blood and ate human flesh. He could not forget how she had told him that Yaso was an evil creature who did all sorts of frightening things, such as deceiving people by magical powers in order to destroy Japan.

So, to Nobuo, Yaso was an unforgivably wicked person. . . . Taking a stealthy glance at his mother, he felt that it was better to have no mother at all, than to have a follower of Yaso for a mother. (35–36)

Miura's narrator adds a historical reminder: "In those days there were many instances when sons were even disinherited and disowned by their parents because they became Christians. It could not be said that only Tose was bigoted" (38). For his part, Nobuo's father, Masayuki, is a member of the more enlightened, modern Meiji generation for whom Tose's prejudice is anathema. Having "grown up to have liberal and progressive views, in spite of, or maybe because of, Tose's strict upbringing, he could not understand how Tose should look upon Christian believers with such hatred" (37). Still, the old prejudices are strong, and the threat of being disinherited very real, so he gives in and sends Kiku away, playing the part of a filial son. Masayuki's true position, though, comes to the fore in an early incident involving his son. Nobuo is playing on the roof with his friend Torao, the son of an itinerant peddler, when they quarrel and Torao pushes Nobuo off. To his credit, Nobuo tries to protect Torao from punishment, denying he was pushed off and saying, "Of course [I fell off the roof by myself], do you think I'd let a slum kid push me off the roof?" (20). Masayuki is greatly upset at this epithet and lectures him on Fukuzawa Yukichi's Enlightenment notion reflecting the official end of the class system ideology: "'Heaven makes neither one man above, nor one man below another'" (21). Nobuo refuses to apologize to Torao for his prejudiced words, and it is left to Masayuki, the educated, white-collar worker, to bow abjectly to Torao and his father in a memorable scene that is "unforgettably engraved on Nobuo's mind" (22).

The death of Tose may seem to symbolize the end of diehard opposition to Christianity in Japan, but prejudice against it lingers far into the Meiji Period. Early in the novel, Miura describes how children taunt street-corner preachers:

"Yaso, Yaso, born in a stable! Ya! Ya! Ya!" Nobuo knew how the children sometimes made fun of the open-air preacher with this song, a parody of the respectful greeting to a royal prince.

"Ah, now you've come," the preacher would begin. "Today I want to tell you an interesting story." No sooner had he said these words than the children would start to run away, shouting. (36)

Years later, when Nobuo lives in Hokkaido and runs across another street preacher, Iki Kazuma, whose challenge to him brings him to faith, the preacher is similarly taunted by children, some of whom try to pelt him with snowballs (198). In fact, it was a similar scene of brutality toward evangelists and the sense of "righteous indignation" it aroused in Kiku that brought her to faith. She recalls a scene from her childhood:

> Everyone was shouting "Yaso priest, filthy priest!" and cursing a young man. He was standing there quietly, but a man came up and said, "If you're a filthy priest, eat this," and took a dipper from the cesspit and poured the filthy stuff over him. Although his head, his eyes, and his mouth were all covered with muck, the young man said nothing but went off to the nearby river. The heartless villagers all scattered, but I was just a child and watched him from the bridge. And what do you think happened? When he had finished washing his face and hair, he began to sing at the top of his voice. His face was so radiant that it made an indelible impression upon me. (128)

Even at the end of the novel, after Nobuo's death, people's remarks indicate the extent to which, well into the twentieth century, ordinary people looked harshly on Christianity:

> "I thought the Yaso were an evil sect, but look how splendidly one of them died. You can't say Yaso is a bad religion," people were saying.
>   At a time when a man had to forfeit his inheritance because he became a Christian, Nobuo's death dispelled this ignorance. (267)

After Tose's death, it is Nobuo who takes up the mantle of anti-Christianity. Living in a family of Christians (his mother and sister) and liberal thinkers (his father), Nobuo is adamant in his opposition to the religion, scoffing at mealtime prayers and church attendance and falling back on Tose's injunctions about proper samurai behavior (the precedence of stoicism, the strict sexual division of labor, etc.) as his own guide to right conduct and thought. Nobuo constantly feels like an outsider in his own home and questions whether Kiku is indeed his mother (56–57). He laments the fact that the Buddhist family altar in his home has remained shut, and that, unlike in his friend Yoshikawa's home, no priest has come to chant the requisite sutras

(56), berating Kiku for not burning incense in memory of Tose. And, of course, partly out of loyalty to Yoshikawa and partly to spite Kiku and defend the old values against the new, Nobuo declares his intention of becoming a Buddhist priest when he grows up (59).

In *Freezing Point* and its sequel, Miura showed a much narrower range of spiritual movement, depicting how two Japanese (Keizō and Yōko), one of whom had a youthful interest in Chritianity, while the other was uninterested but not antagonistic, came to Christian faith in a more contemporary setting, where the religion is far less persecuted. In *Shiokari Pass* Miura has set herself a far greater challenge, tracing in this spiritual *bildungsroman* a drastic transformation in an age of persecution. Nobuo grows from being someone who detests the religion to becoming an evangelist whose sacrificial death brings even hard-nosed opponents to conversion. It is as if Miura is asking her non-Christian readers a pointed question: if someone like Nobuo can become a strong Christian, can't *anyone*?

Though he dies early in the novel, Masayuki's role in Nobuo's spiritual journey is crucial. In Miura's spiritual world, Masayuki is a transitional figure. On the one hand he acquiesces in the dictates of an antiquated ethos by sending Kiku away, while on the other he maintains a secret relationship with her and welcomes her back into the house as soon as Tose is gone. By portraying him as a modern, liberal Meiji man who cannot turn his back completely on the past, Miura raises the intriguing question of whether he is a closet Christian as well. Masayuki is openly sympathetic to Kiku's beliefs. In one scene he and Tose quarrel over Kiku:

> "There's nothing specially wrong with being a Christian" [Masayuki says].
> "... Do you know what you are saying? How can you stand there and talk to your mother like that? This proves that you have been bewitched by Yaso, without a shadow of a doubt!" Tose was in a rage.
> "Bewitched? There's no such thing in this civilized, scientific age. I can't bring myself to think that Christians are particularly bad."
> "Japan has always had Shinto and Buddhism. We don't have to worship a foreign god! Don't you understand what a shameful thing it is for a Japanese to do?"
> "Mother, this Buddhism which you believe in came from a foreign country during the Nara Period, you know." (37)

Masayuki is also the one who explains Kiku's stance to the dubious Nobuo. When his son wonders why Kiku cannot simply give up her belief in "Yaso" because of all the problems it causes, Masayuki says, "Human beings are creatures who must have something to cling to, even if it costs them their very lives" (45). But what does Masayuki himself cling to? When he dies suddenly, the issue of his funeral becomes a point of contention within the family, with Tose's relatives vehemently arguing for a Buddhist funeral and Kiku insisting on a Christian one. Kiku, though, silences all opposition when she produces Masayuki's will, which states, among other things, "I wish to have a Christian funeral." Miura never reveals if Masayuki is a professed Christian. He does attend church with Kiku sporadically, and Nobuo calls him a Christian, but there is little evidence to support the claim (87; 134). It seems more likely that he is what is called in Christian circles a "seeker," one who is attracted to Christian teachings, yet remains unconverted. More crucial to Nobuo than the funeral arrangements, though, are the other injunctions in the will: his father wishes for something other than "worldly success" for his son and advises him, "Learn from your mother how men should live" (106). Furthermore, Masayuki sees his whole life—"what I have said to [you] in everyday conversation, and what I have done" as his personal legacy to his family (108). To Nobuo this is a compelling legacy indeed:

> This was the attitude of a man who had come to be prepared for death at any time. During his peaceful day-to-day life, he had nevertheless wrestled with this great problem.
>   "Would I be able to live a model life every day like that, so that it could speak like a will for me?" (108)

One thinks here of another famous literary legacy between father and son, that found in Shimazaki Tōson's *Hakai* (translated as *The Broken Commandment*), published in 1906. There the protagonist, Ushimatsu, has to contend with the prejudice against the *eta,* the untouchable class of the time (known now as *burakumin*). Ushimatsu's father, an upright cowherder, commands his son never to reveal his *eta* origins, so that he may succeed in the world. Throughout the novel Ushimatsu's inner struggle is between this commandment and the dictates of personal freedom, which compel him to break his father's commandment and declare his true identity. The difference between these two literary commandments is marked. Shimazaki's is a negative injunction that *suppresses* a young man's freedom, while Miura's is a positive injunction that, in Miura's telling of it, *leads* to freedom. Masayuki's will foreshadows the trajectory of Nobuo's life. He (1) follows his mother in converting to Christianity, (2) makes his entire life a legacy to others, and (3) comes to terms early on with death.

As all of this unfolds as an outline for the life to come, Nobuo struggles with some typically youthful issues, most notably sexual desire. Undoubtedly one of the key reasons for the enormous popularity of *Shiokari Pass* is the way in which young readers can identify with the protagonist's sexual struggles. Nobuo experiences all the stages of sexual desire save one, sexual consummation. Meeting pretty young girls makes him blush; whenever he reads of a beautiful woman in a book, the face of either his mother or of Yoshikawa's sister Fujiko comes to mind (79–80); and he often dreams longingly of a fantasy beauty. His old cousin Takashi reassures him that despite a lingering, samurai-inspired notion that "it's unmanly to think about women. . . . Thinking about women is neither unmanly nor dirty" (84). Takashi is the one who later leads him off to the Yoshiwara red-light district to lose his virginity, a memorable scene in which Nobuo, enjoined, "Act like a man!" abruptly flees. What is particularly distinctive about this scene is the language in which it is couched. According to the narrator, "In those days [after the Sino-Japanese War], before becoming a soldier it was the accepted custom that a man should have sexual experience of a woman. More than half of Nobuo's school contemporaries had proudly boasted about their own" (98). When Nobuo makes the sudden decision to flee from such experience, the command he gives himself is a clipped military one: "About face!" *(Maware migi!)*. This use of parade-ground language as he flees from what is a soldier's "right" is humorous, but also demonstrates what Wakasa Tadao terms the novel's "heterogeneity" *(ishitsu sei)*, the way in which it heads in the opposite direction from which common sense is heading.[35] One example of this is how Kiku, when she abandons the infant Nobuo, goes against the "common sense of putting her child first" (which Wakasa relates to Abraham's willingness to sacrifice Isaac). A second example of the novel's oppositional character, as *ishitsu sei* might also be translated, is this depiction of Nobuo's reaction to sexual desire. Nobuo is in all ways shown as a man of normal sexual appetites (at one point giving in to these and satisfying himself), but, like Augustine, Wakasa writes, he struggles to direct these desires onto a higher plane. While many readers would see these as nonsense, insisting that one should look for an outlet for sexual desire, Miura clearly positions her Christian values to stand in opposition to the common sense of the times.[36] Miura is not known for providing a strong historical context for her stories, in the sense of situating her figures in the flow of extra-textual history—here war and military service, economic depression, and Hokkaido as a place to which debtors escape are all mentioned only in passing—but in Kiku's reaction against putting family above faith, in Nobuo's about-face from the expected behavior of soldiers-to-be, and in Masayuki's surprising anti-materialist success stance, which flies in the face of the *risshin shusse* (careerist) spirit of the times, she does give evidence of Meiji period Christians opposing the centrality of the family-state, state-directed loyalty, and the materialistic ethos of the time.[37]

Sex continues to be an issue for Nobuo, but it is mainly defused by his love for Fujiko who, as a tuberculosis patient, is off limits sexually. (Miura, herself a longtime tuberculosis sufferer, raises these effects of tuberculosis on sexual behavior in her *Freezing Point* as well; the reason Natsue ends up with the infamous "kiss mark" on her neck is that her lover, Murai, suffers from tuberculosis, so refrains from kissing her on the mouth.) To the end of his life, though, Nobuo continues to be berated by "normal" men, such as Mihori, who cannot comprehend his sexual abstinence.

Interestingly, Miura uses literature—a novel within a novel—to introduce Nobuo to the nature of sin and human conduct. One day Takashi introduces Nobuo to his novelist friend, Nakamura Harusame, who gives him a copy of his novel *The Fig Tree*,[38] a discussion of which occupies one whole pivotal chapter of *Shiokari Pass*. The complex, melodramatic plot of *The Fig Tree* involves a Japanese man named Hatomiya who, following an affair with a woman named Sawa, goes to America, where he becomes a Christian and marries an American girl, Emille. Upon their return to Japan, Hatomiya, though he becomes a minister, resumes his affair with Sawa, who is hiding out from the police after murdering her husband. Emille, meanwhile, starts a home for "three beggar children," not realizing that one of them is her husband's illegitimate child by Sawa. Eventually Sawa and Hatomiya are sent to prison, where Sawa commits suicide. Hatomiya, in remorse, also kills himself. Interestingly, plot elements are recycled here from *Freezing Point*—the foreigner (Emille) is the true Christian, unwittingly raising a "child of sin."

Nobuo and his sister, Machiko, read this morality tale, and both, as far as Kiku is concerned, fail to learn the proper lesson from it. Nobuo feels sympathy and admiration for Emille, who endured abuse from her in-laws and even gave her adulterous rival Sawa a proper burial:

He [Nobuo] felt more sorry for the angelic Emille than for the dead Hatomiya. No matter how much one is oppressed by a sense of guilt and sin, surely it is not necessary to torture oneself to that extent. Thinking about Hatomiya gave him a feeling of self-satisfaction. "If a man who has faith finished up in such a way, then I, who do not believe in anything, am better off." This was the conclusion he felt compelled to draw. (121)

For her part, Machiko criticizes the novel as an unfair portrayal of Christian ministers, saying, "A minister would not betray his wife. Novelists don't know much about ministers" (123). Kiku adds a Christian corrective:

As long as you're a human being, no matter how splendid your faith may be, you can't say that you will not fall to Satan's temptations. . . . Machiko and Nobuo, listen to me. You are thinking that there are two kinds of people, good and bad, but there is only one kind. It's just like Nobuo said before, "There is no one righteous; no, not one." In the sight of God it is quite certain there is no one who is just. . . . No, if anybody thinks they are superior it shows they are not. (123)

Nobuo and Machiko also have a chance to quiz Nakamura about his novel. As a Christian, he seconds Kiku's reading, adding that we "tend to trust in our own strength" rather than in God's, and pointing out to them the quotation from Luke 13:1–8 at the beginning of the novel, which contains both Jesus' call to repent, or "you too will perish," and the parable of the fig tree that will be cut down because it does not bear fruit. Nakamura concludes, "A novel is a complicated thing. The minister who betrayed his wife, even when she was so kind and generous, is a picture of ourselves, Christian believers who, although we experience God's love, still fall into unbelief" (131).

Nobuo continues to defend the Japanese faith, here Buddhism, questioning why Kiku had to become a Christian: "There was no need to believe a foreign religion, was there?" (129). But he is shown wavering in the face of these two mature Christians' arguments. Significantly, it is not theology or doctrine that sways him, but the human character of the Christians he encounters. In Kiku's gentle steadfastness he finds the ultimate example of a loving, caring Christian (as well as the model his father had exhorted him to follow); in her story of the young evangelist mistreated by villagers in her childhood, he is presented with a moving example of faith in the midst of persecution. As Kiku puts it, "It was the faith of the man who suffered silently and then sang with joy which commended itself to my way of thinking, rather than the faith of his persecutors" (129). Though the book is laced with biblical quotations and contains a number of interludes of extended discussion, Miura steers the reader away from a too intellectual reaction to faith to a more visceral, emotional one. This, like the faith of the early followers of Jesus—decades, even centuries before an elaborate theology grew up around him—is the faith that truly draws us in, Miura would argue. It is the faith shown by a single person, one whose very life and actions we admire and wish to emulate. And what *Shiokari Pass* illustrates is the process whereby Nobuo—the man who detests Christianity—becomes such a person.

After this debate about Nakamura's novel, as the next chapter states, "Nobuo's thoughts imperceptibly turned to God" (133). Another person who nudges Nobuo in spiritual directions is his friend Yoshikawa. Yoshikawa's main concern is always his ill, crippled sister, Fujiko: "I wonder if sick and deformed people and suchlike are not in this world for a special purpose," he tells Nobuo, "to soften people's hearts" (140). Impressed, Nobuo begins to feel that "each and every thing on earth had a purpose," and tells his friend, "I used to be fairly self-reliant, but lately I've begun to feel that my existence has no particular value. Now, listening to you, I'm beginning to think that after all I may have some mission or other to fulfill" (141). And speaking of the deaths of both his father and Yoshikawa's father (the premature deaths of their fathers are another thing they share, as well as having sisters who are Christians), Nobuo notes, "Don't you agree that we could say that we who are left behind experience the life of those who are dead living within us?" (142). In these words one sees the three stages Nobuo has gone through; first, the self-confidence that needs no spiritual direction, which leads, in his brushes with Christian faith, to the next stage, one of low self-esteem in the face of man's sinfulness, and then his coming to a sense that life's purpose is the fulfillment of one's mission. Recall here what Sono Ayako wrote about the discovery of this sense: "the mission has absolutely nothing to do with happiness," but its fulfillment leads to a brief, "miserable sort of happiness." Nobuo's words about experiencing the "dead living within us" also echo Sono's interpretation of eternal life. In *Shiokari Pass*, these words about how the dead live on presage Nobuo's ultimate sacrifice.[39]

Despite this movement toward faith, Nobuo is portrayed as continually struggling with issues typical of many Japanese who encounter Christian teachings. Fujiko's words as she contends with illness—"Death is not the end for anybody" (160)—force him to consider the Christian understanding of the eternal nature of the soul. (Kiku makes the same point, saying, "Nobuo, I don't think death is the end of everything" [159].) Gazing at drifting clouds one day (ever since Futabatei Shimei's groundbreaking mid-Meiji novel *Uki-gumo* [The drifting clouds] a strong symbol in modern Japanese literature of rootlessness and transience), Nobuo laments the fleeting nature of life and can "only think of life as purposeless" (161–162). But two years later, when he takes the ferry to move to Hokkaido, he does not seek any purpose in life outside a self-centered one: "He did not think of himself as a weak person who needed to depend on God" (163). Likewise, he cannot accept Fujiko's suffering as in any way justified. In compressed form, then, one sees Nobuo reacting in a very typical negative fashion to the claims of Christianity. He has grave doubts about the eternal nature of the soul, about death as anything other than a complete end to life, and about the question of theodicy (high-lighted by Fujiko's innocent suffering). He sees life as purposeless and tran-sient, yet finds meaning in a self-centered, stoical overcoming of the trials of life (as in his conquering of sexual desire). Like many people, Nobuo sees Christianity as the refuge of the weak, among whose number he does not count himself.

Gradually, however, the influence of others he admires and loves has an effect on him. As his love for Fujiko grows (after the shock of learning she is a Christian wears off), Nobuo discovers in her a living faith that soon turns him in new directions. Despite her desperate physical condition, Fujiko insists that "God is love," the same phrase Nobuo's brother-in-law, also a Christian, wrote inside the Bible he presented to Nobuo when Nobuo departed for Hokkaido.[40] Up to this point Nobuo has not even opened this Bible, but now, in the face of Fujiko's reliance on a loving God to see her through her trials, he is impressed enough to declare, "I don't have a blind dislike for Christianity" (179) and to begin reading Scripture.

Because of his lifelong struggle to overcome sexual desire, Nobuo is first drawn to the Bible through Jesus' teaching on adultery: "Everyone who looks at a woman lustfully has already committed adultery with her in his heart" (180–181). He connects this with the biblical quotation he read in Nakamura's novel: "There is no one righteous; no, not one." These disconnected words suddenly come home to Nobuo:

> When he had read it before, it had not penetrated so deeply. But now, to his surprise, this sentence claimed a place in his heart and he could not get rid of it. He suddenly realized that he understood in his deepest consciousness what the words meant. Nobuo suddenly wanted to read the Bible, every word of it. He had the feeling that it was filled with wonderful teachings that he had not yet discovered. (181)

Like his general reaction to Christian teachings, Nobuo's first reaction to the Bible is also one typical of many Japanese. He starts with Matthew, and in a rare humorous section in this generally earnest novel, finds the opening genealogy a "long boring list!" and the story of the Virgin Birth unbelievable and "stupid" (182). The counterintuitive nature of the New Testament's teachings, especially those about revenge and loving one's enemies, forces him to confront, yet again, the samurai stock from which he sprang and the attendant ethos in which he was raised:

> As he read on Nobuo came immediately to the words, "Love your enemies and pray for them that despitefully use you." This teaching was completely incompatible with Japanese feeling. Japanese liked stories of formal revenge. Nobuko earnestly considered what the forty-seven samurai retainers of

Ako would have done if they had lived by this teaching of the Bible. . . .
For in the world of the samurai, taking revenge on the enemy was an honorable deed. If his father, if his feudal lord had been killed, would this man Jesus have avenged them? Was it possible to love such an enemy? "He must have been a very remarkable man," Nobuo thought.

"'Do not hate.' Is that such an important thing? To hate someone who deserves hate, isn't that what people should do?" Nobuo thought so, but without conviction. He had to admit that it was rather a shallow philosophy. (183–184)

Nobuo's former convictions are clearly wavering. After his meeting with the street preacher Iki, and under the continuing influence of Fujiko, he reaches the stage where he is ready to pledge his life to God. One final barrier remains, however: Nobuo's understanding of the problem of sin. When Iki insists that Nobuo was the one who nailed Christ to the cross, in a somewhat comical retort Nobuo interprets this literally, insisting on the impossibility of his having done such a thing to anyone two thousand years ago, instead of taking Iki's point that all mankind are equally sinners, and that Christ died for the sins of all. "Do you see yourself as a great sinner?" Iki asks, to which Nobuo concludes that, despite the lust in his heart, "I don't think I'm so conscious of sin as to admit that I am a great sinner" (200–201). Unless Nobuo can "realize that the problem of sin is your own problem," Iki cautions him, "you have no relationship to Christ" (201).

The primary barrier to faith, then, and one that Miura emphasizes again and again in her fiction and essays, is this: "The greatest sin is not being able to recognize sin as sin."[41] A related theme, found in her earliest work of fiction, *Freezing Point,* is the sense of pride and superiority that results from egocentrism. In her essays, too, Miura often points out the ethical double standard by which most people live—judging others more harshly than themselves and forgiving their own actions but not those of others. All this stems from an egocentric view of oneself as superior.

At Iki's suggestion, Nobuo selects a Bible passage and attempts to put its teachings into practice. Here it is the parable of the Good Samaritan, and Nobuo, attempting to be a "good neighbor" to the incorrigible Mihori, accepts a transfer to Asahikawa from Sapporo in order to help his colleague, despite the pain it causes him to live apart from Fujiko. Finally, though, Nobuo confesses to Mihori that the exercise has made him reinterpret the parable completely. At first Nobuo had been seeing himself as the Good Samaritan, and Mihori, who rebuffs his efforts, as the wounded traveler. In the testimony he will give at his baptism, Nobuo writes:

I thought that, seeing I had loved him from the heart and been a good friend to him, naturally he would be glad. But he did not accept my efforts, and I built up a great hatred toward him.

I was like the Samaritan, putting all my efforts into helping an injured, half-dead man on a mountain road, and I could not understand why he should shout at me. I was trying to help him, but he roughly pushed off my helping hands. When he did that, I hated and cursed him in my heart. I became more and more filled with hatred toward him, until at last I realized what was happening.

I realized that, right from the beginning, I had looked down on him. Every day I was unhappy and prayed to God. Then I heard God's voice, "You yourself are the wounded traveler, fallen on the mountain road. The fact that you are continually crying out to Me for help proves it." I was the sinner who needed help. (226)

A similar testimony has appeared before in Miura's work, that of the young nursing-home worker in *Freezing Point* who realized her "love" toward her charges was actually motivated by self-interest (see chapter 1). In *Shiokari Pass*, and in Miura's theology, with his own realization, Nobuo is truly saved. Miura returns here—reinterpreting, as with the parable—to two ideas set out at the beginning of the novel: Masayuki's insistence that all men are equal, and the opening line of the novel, in which Tose says to Nobuo, "There's no getting away from it, you're just like your mother—not only in looks but in character as well" (13). Miura takes these two notions out of the materialist realm, rereading them as spiritual insights. The Enlightenment idea of equality becomes, not the end of a discriminatory class system, but rather the notion that all people are equal as sinners in God's sight. Likewise, the inheritance of all humanity is shown as going far beyond any superficial traits to encompass the inherited sinful state of all.

All that remains in Nobuo's spiritual journey is his sacrifice to save others. The incident of the train accident is itself compelling and dramatically portrayed. Though some people react in shock to the news of his death, Miura shows his sacrifice as a natural outgrowth of the love he has developed for man and for God, not as something extraordinary. Those who knew Nobuo best see it, in retrospect, as completely understandable and in keeping with his character. To Yoshikawa, for example, "It was a death worthy of Nobuo, and somehow he [Yoshikawa] had known about it for a long time" (*tō no mukashi ni, konna shi o, Yoshikawa wa shitte ita yō na ki ga shita*) (262). Unlike Sono, who in her study of Kolbe laments the fact that his sacrifice did not bring happiness even to the man whose life he saved, Miura clearly shows the immediate and dramatic effect Nobuo's death had on those around him: "In exchange for his own life many lives had been saved. And not just people's bodies, but many souls also. In Asahikawa and Sapporo now, the beacon of faith was burning brightly and there was an intense spirit of earnestness in the churches. Her [Fujiko's] own faith had been strengthened and made new" (271). The memorial postcard with the real-life Nagano's photograph and will printed on it, in fact became a popular item throughout Asahikawa and Sapporo in the months following his death, and Miura reports that in real life, as in her novel, many people in these towns became Christians as a direct result of Nagano's sacrifice. For the characters in the novel, Nobuo's death to save others brings about a renewed commitment to their faith (Fujiko and Kiku), the nudge that some needed to become Christians (some of Nobuo's young subordinates), and in at least one case a dramatic spiritual turnaround paralleling Nobuo's own, as Mihori proclaims to Yoshikawa, "Nobuo's sacrificial death, which I saw, was a more eloquent message to me than his will or anything else" (269).

Though in the novel version Nobuo's death is unequivocally a selflessly courageous sacrifice, in an updated addendum to the paperback edition of *Shiokari Pass*, Miura confronts conflicting theories about the real-life Nagano's death.[42] After the novel was first published in 1968, one reader wrote to Miura charging her with romanticizing what may very well have been an accidental death. Miura reviews three theories about Nagano's death—accident, suicide, or deliberate self-sacrifice. One of Miura's main informants, a Mr. Fujiwara, claims there was an eyewitness who saw Nagano turn around toward the railway car and give a farewell gesture before throwing himself on the tracks. Fujiwara's own comments, in a volume celebrating the sixty-fifth anniversary of the Rokujō Church, however, indicate Nagano's willingness to die, but imply also that he may have slipped and fallen on the icy platform as he struggled with the hand brake. Miura speculates that Fujiwara's support of the accidental-death theory is motivated by fear that Nagano's death might be considered a suicide, a notion abhorrent to Christians such as Fujiwara. Sugiura Hitoshi, son of the pastor of the church at the time of the incident, supports the sacrificial-death theory, citing accounts by numerous railway employees who claimed that Nagano's death was an intentional sacrifice to save others. But he writes that at the time many people—noting that Nagano had a copy of his will on his person at the time of his death—interpreted the death as a suicide. Interestingly, Sugiura also observes that on the night of the incident (Miura has changed the time of the incident to the morning), church members could not believe that Nagano had died at all. Some of them claimed to have just seen him, in his usual front row pew, praying. In *Shiokari Pass*,

Miura transforms this into Fujiko's illusion of seeing Nobuo arrive at the station at the appointed time.

Terms used to discuss Nagano's death, too, are indicative of subtle interpretive differences. Nonomiya Noriko, for instance, labels it *junshi* (compare Sono's depiction of Father Kolbe's sacrifice), an antiquated term indicating the suicide of a loyal samurai following his lord's death.[43] The use of such a term risks not only lending support to the suicide theory, but also placing Nagano's death back in the pre-modern, samurai context to which Miura very carefully, in the novel, opposes his life. For her part, Miura calls the death *junshoku no shi* "death out of loyalty to one's profession."[44] Neither of these terms indicates the loyalty of the sincere Christian to God that Miura really wishes to depict. The lack of a completely satisfactory term may well indicate the difficulty Japanese in general still have in contextualizing and digesting a death motivated by loyalty to a power beyond the temporal plane of feudal lord, job, family, or nation (or, by implication, emperor).

No one will ever know what was going through the mind and heart of the real-life Nagano at the time of his death. As with the Gospels themselves, the accounts are those of survivors and witnesses, not the direct testimony of the person most involved. Despite this limitation, Miura has crafted a compelling fictional biography that—while melodramatic at times and open to the criticism that she has created, in the figure of Nobuo, an almost impossibly pure and devoted believer—portrays the road from unbelief to belief, as traveled by one young man, in a thorough and convincing way. Western readers will find little in her presentation of Christian beliefs that is new or startling—perhaps only her unconventional interpretation of the parable of the Good Samaritan—but for her intended audience of ordinary Japanese, *Shiokari Pass* reads like a primer of Christian beliefs. Avoiding more difficult and contentious theological issues (free will, predestination, theories of the end times, and the like), Miura concentrates on presenting a step-by-step view of how an ordinary Japanese, filled initially with ignorance of and antipathy toward Christianity, comes to understand the Christian teachings about man's sinful state and how it can be overcome through complete reliance on God. The novel is her fullest treatment of Christian theology in her early literature. By analogy, if the *Freezing Point* novels are comparable to Paul's shorter epistles, *Shiokari Pass* is Miura's Romans, her theological magnum opus. At the same time, the novel presents Japanese readers with the radical nature of Christianity as it confronts the givens of their society. The religion's radical egalitarianism and call to a duty beyond family and state run counter to much of the accepted ideology of modern Japan, and make the novel a challenge to readers even today.

Inevitably Japanese critics have seen the novel as reflecting the author's own experiences and life. Though there is much to justify this view, by the time one unravels all the interpretations it is clear that the situation is not that simple. Wakasa sees Kiku as the spokesperson for Miura's viewpoint and Nobuo representing the ordinary reader, with the mature Christian teaching the non-believer.[45] Nonomiya, however, drawing on the fact that Miura spent years suffering from tuberculosis, views the characters Fujiko and Nobuo as reflecting the real-life Miura and her husband, a patient and loving man who sustained her over her long recuperation.[46] Though one could indeed argue that both Kiku and Fujiko, as the two most devout Christian women in the novel, reflect Miura's mature beliefs, both of these viewpoints fail to acknowledge the fact that it is in *Nobuo*'s spiritual transformation from Christian-hater to devout believer that the novel most closely parallels Miura's own spiritual development. Readers, of course, are free to interpret *Shiokari Pass* in any way they like, as fictionalized biography, as autobiography, or as pure invention. Who resembles whom, and the facts of the real-life Nagano Masao's death, are, in the end, less important than the road map to belief that Miura has drawn.

This notion of a "road map to belief," of course, underscores an important issue raised above, namely, the tension between art and faith, between being a writer of fiction and being a devout individual. To what ultimate end do Christian writers in Japan (and elsewhere) write? If it is primarily to evangelize, then is art always secondary to faith? If art shades over into apologia, then doesn't art suffer, and if it suffers, doesn't it lose its effectiveness as spiritual guide? Taken the other way, if the artist binds her talents by artistic requirements alone, then what distinguishes her work from that of the secular artist?

Endō Shūsaku's fiction has been described as depicting "the individual torn between a series of conflicting identities," an apt description for Japanese Christian writers, who are often caught between the desire to create moving, lasting literature and the desire to remain true to their understanding of their faith.[47] One aspect of this that Endō notes is the tension between the "desire, as author, to scrutinize human beings," complete with sins, and the "Christian yearning for purity."[48] If the Christian author opts for purity, does he "have a responsibility to remove the very essence of his work out of concern for his audience?" Quoting the same biblical passage as Endō (Mark 9:42), Flannery O'Connor writes that in honestly depicting the concrete world, the Christian writer does indeed run the risk of "corrupting those who are not able to understand what he is doing. It is very possible that what is vision and truth to the writer is temptation and sin to the reader. There is every danger that in writing what he sees, the novelist will be corrupting some 'little one,' and better a millstone were tied around his neck."[49] O'Connor concludes, however, that to "force this kind of total responsibility on the novelist is to burden him with the business that belongs only to God" and that "the artist has his hands full and does his duty if he attends to his art. He can safely leave evangelizing to the evangelists."[50] In O'Connor's world, then, and in Endō's, the Christian writer is ultimately an artist who, while focused on artistic integrity, not on proselytizing, still has another, spiritual, responsibility to "penetrate the concrete world in order to find at its depths the image of its source, the image of ultimate reality."[51]

But what happens when a writer attempts to take on the task of being both serious artist and unapologetic evangelist? Is she bound to fail in one or the other? If, as Asai Kiyoshi sees it, the trajectory of Miura's work is toward creating a powerful and unique "evangelizing literature," a literature that unapologetically comes down on the side of spreading the Christian gospel, must it also abnegate the requirements of art? One might defer the question by arguing that Miura's motivation in writing a work like *Freezing Point* is less to spread the gospel and make converts than it is to present a personal confession: "this novel is a confession of my faith" *(iwaba kono shōsetsu wa watakushi no shinkō no akashi na no de aru).*[52] This novel (and *Shiokari Pass* as well) can then be read as fictionalized autobiography, confessional novels rewritten in the guise of domestic melodrama or historical biography. But while arguably containing these elements, the ambitions of Miura's literature reach beyond this. They contain purposely didactic elements designed to bring the non-Christian reader to an understanding of certain elements of Christian theology, most notably, in *Freezing Point,* of sin. "If only even one person would read this novel," she wrote, "If only he would then comprehend the meaning of the 'sin' that every human has."[53] What I argue is that, until Miura built up a loyal following of readers and established herself as a novelist, she subordinated the demands of theology to those of art. Only later did she shift to fiction of a more openly apologetic type.

It seems clear that Miura's readers had difficulty comprehending her theology even at its simplest and most watered down. Typical of reactions to the theology in *Freezing Point* is the comment of one critic who states, "It is difficult . . . in a popular format like this, to convey to readers what original sin means," and another who writes, "In a country such as Japan where Christianity is not commonly followed, presenting original sin in one fell swoop is impossible."[54] Miura's limited treatment of the concept indicates that she probably agreed with the second assessment. Still, when she wrote more evangelistically and from a deeper theological stance, she retained her enormous readership. If there was any "artifice or distortion" in the depiction of her characters, to borrow Endō's phrase, because of her attempts to spread her religion, it certainly did not lead to a diminution of her popularity.[55]

In the balance that Miura attempted to strike between art and faith one needs to shift the focus to her readers; successful as a popular writer of fiction, was Miura equally successful as an *evangelical* writer? It is relatively easy to gauge popularity, but measuring the impact of an openly evangelical message is much harder, perhaps impossible. Ordinary readers of her works may just read *around* the message that she so fervently wished to convey, finding a simpler pleasure in the unexpected twists and turns of plot, in the narrative of the downtrodden but plucky stepdaughter, and in the *bildungsroman* of the pure-minded young man struggling with, among other things, sexual desire. If so, the arguments made by both Endō and O'Connor, namely, that the novel is from the first the wrong vessel for the kind of openly religious aims Miura aspired to, gain in validity.

If Miura lies at one extreme of the tension between art and evangelism in fiction, and a writer such as Endō somewhere in the middle, at the other pole is Shimao Toshio (1917–1986).[56] In looking at Shimao's work, one can legitimately ask what, if anything, makes it the work of a Christian writer. Far from openly espousing his faith or desiring to make literature a vehicle for evangelism, Shimao was reticent about the relationship between his faith and his art. Unlike Endō, for instance, he almost never offered his thoughts on the subject in essays, nor did his works openly grapple with religious themes, as Endō does in *Silence* and elsewhere. Shimao's works are regularly included in anthologies of Japanese Christian literature, and he is generally described as a leading Catholic writer. Yet his concerns as a writer are usually expressed more in terms of developing craft than in delineating faith. As one critic notes of him, despite his devoutness,

> he was very reticent about his faith and, confronted by the recent trend amongst contemporary Japanese literary figures to proclaim their faith out loud, his whole being manifested a sense of unease, even hatred, as though overcome by an acute sense of shame. It was as though he were trying to say his own religious convictions were a completely personal affair.[57]

Even before he became a Catholic in 1956, some of Shimao's work reveals an awareness of Christianity and of Christian symbolism. Shimao's first published work, "Shima no hate" (translated as "The Farthest Edge of the Islands" [1946]), depicts the island girl Toe both as a kind of local shaman and from a Christian background:

> From the time of her earliest memories she had had in her possession a leatherbound book. She was sure this book must have belonged to her mother. When she prayed to her God, she pressed her cheek to the book. The two narrow intersecting strips of cool gold embossed on the cover stole the warmth from her cheek. That she did this, Toe never revealed to a soul. She was certain that she would be told that these were the teachings of an evil Western religion, the enemy's religion.[58]

The story is full of clearly Christian symbolism: the dagger that Toe, planning to die when her *tokkōtai* (kamikaze) lover departs on his mission, holds "reverently to her breast like a cross";[59] the fish she serves her lover; and the fact that her lover, a naval lieutenant, is the leader of a band of twelve men (his own *tokkōtai* squad within the larger squadron) and will soon sacrifice himself so that others (the islanders) may live. In addition, Kathryn Sparling notes a "conspicuous motif . . . of death and rebirth" with Christian overtones in the story.[60] All of this surely reflects that Shimao was aware not just of the religious affiliation of the islanders (a large number of whom were Catholic) but also, specifically, of the faith of the woman who became his wife (and, in his most sustained and famous series of stories—the *byōsaimono,* or "sickwife stories"—the focus of the bulk of his later literature).

The scene quoted from this early story and the story as a whole serve as a template for Shimao's own attitude toward the tension between being a devout Christian and being a Japanese novelist. Above all there is the awareness of faith as something not to be brought out into the open; as Shimao puts it, there is a "sense of attachment . . . which we Japanese experience and which is totally unrelated to Christianity. That something is very deep-rooted within us, so that, when one enters the Catholic church, one cannot escape a sense of having somehow betrayed something, however illogical that sentiment may be."[61] The underlying tension in the character Toe, between her "hidden faith" and the island's spiritual tradition of the *yuta,* or female shaman, is, retrospectively, a picture of Shimao's own stance in his literature. Though by all accounts he was a devout Catholic, unlike Miura and Endō, he kept his faith well concealed. As Mark Williams notes of Shimao's essays, "The reader searches in vain for specific references in the literature of Shimao to his spiritual struggles." Unlike Miura, Shimao does not consistently invite a reading of his fiction in light of a clearly defined position on Christianity.[62]

Still, like the scattered Christian imagery in "The Farthest Edge of the Islands," Shimao's literature contains enough openly biblical references, especially in titles such as *The Sting of Death* (1 Corinthians); "Out of the Depths" (Psalms); "The Passover," chapter 9 of *The Sting of Death,* and the earlier story "Shutsu kotōki" (Departure from a lonely isle; both titles are borrowed from Exodus) that observant readers may pick up on the fact that they are dealing with a writer of faith.[63]

Shimao's characters do not "talk religion" as the characters in Miura and Endō's works do, but for the reader willing to dig well below the surface, his fiction provides some profoundly spiritual insights. Some have equated the character Miho in the sick-wife stories, with her unending interrogation of her husband's misdeeds, to the God of the Old Testament—she is, in this sense, an all-knowing, omnipotent, wrathful, judgmental figure who severely punishes the hapless husband for his breaking of a covenant (here, of marriage).[64] A key essay of Shimao's lends credence to such a view: "To me, my wife was God's way of testing me. I could not see God: I could only see my wife."[65] It may be best to shift the focus from the wife to the husband, and argue (as I have elsewhere) that these stories are equally sick-*husband* stories.[66] Such a shift shows Shimao's fiction presenting one of the most harrowing tales of the consequences of sin in the Christian tradition: the husband is consigned to a living hell where, because of his sin, he is seemingly permanently alienated from God. In this reading, God's very absence, and the absence of any expressed awareness of God in the characters, may add up to the most telling spiritual message of all. It is in this sense that it is necessary to re-examine, too, the physical blind spots that characterize the Shimao narrator of this period, especially the physical contraction of the field of vision that assails him in such stories as "Shima e" (To the island), and the studied sense of blurring and indistinctness that characterize such stories as "With Maya."[67] Instead of merely classifying these as intrusions of Shimao's noted "dream story" technique into his "realistic stories," one should understand that in Shimao's fictional world the protagonist is less in a dream than in a nightmarish existence, a fallen spiritual state in which his ability to touch the world around him, let alone touch God, is severely circumscribed. For a writer who so prized the ability to depict the real, the depths of alienation from the world that he depicts must be a vision of hell indeed.[68]

Shimao's stance, then, on the relationship between faith and literature contrasts sharply with the stance of a writer such as Miura Ayako. He not only rejects the notion of literature as a vehicle for open evangelizing (a rejection that encompasses his nonfiction writing as well); he also rejects the suggestion that his sick-wife stories, in particular, serve as vehicles for, say, personal atonement, noting that there is a "strong sense of sin" behind his writing, but that, "If there are clearly parts in my stories that are gestures of atonement for sin, then that's because the stories are no good." [69] Though the average Japanese reader may struggle to follow Miura's doctrine as set out in her fiction, one can imagine an even greater struggle to construct a coherent theology from Shimao's fiction. Tracing the contrast between these very different writers, though, is instructive, for it reveals the broad spectrum of Japanese Christian writers' responses to the needs of both art and faith—and the tension between the two.

CHAPTER THREE

Aum, Underground, and Murakami Haruki's *Other Side*

Just as September 11, 2001, is a date seared in the collective memory of Americans, so the Japanese will not soon forget the events of March 20, 1995. In his 1997 book *Underground,* the novelist Murakami Haruki describes the day this way:

> The date is Monday, March 20, 1995. It is a beautiful clear spring morning. There is still a brisk breeze and people are bundled up in coats. Yesterday was Sunday, tomorrow is the Spring Equinox, a national holiday. Sandwiched right in the middle of what should have been a long weekend, you're probably thinking, "I wish I didn't have to go to work today." No such luck. You get up at the normal time, wash, dress, breakfast, and head for the subway station. You board the train, crowded as usual. Nothing out of the ordinary. It promises to be a perfectly run-of-the-mill day. Until a man in disguise pokes at the floor of the car with the sharpened tip of his umbrella, puncturing some plastic bags filled with a strange liquid . . .[1]

The liquid turned out to be sarin gas, a nerve gas used in the Nazi concentration camps, twenty-six times deadlier than cyanide gas. The man in disguise was one of a team of five members of the Japanese religious cult Aum Shinrikyō sent to release the poison where it would do the most harm—on Tokyo subways at the height of the morning rush hour.

Sarin produces a variety of symptoms, from dizziness and difficulties with vision and breathing to heart failure. In the Aum subway attack, twelve people died, and more than five thousand suffered injuries of various kinds, in some cases including permanent speech and neurological disorders, as well as post–traumatic stress disorder symptoms that plagued many victims for months following the attack. Tokyo, and indeed all Japan, was thrown into a panic as doctors struggled to save lives, security personnel rushed to locate those responsible, and the nation reeled from its first major terrorist attack.

The story of Aum's rise from obscure yoga group to deadly cult has been well documented elsewhere; here I briefly sketch its background.[2] Aum Shinrikyō ("Aum Supreme Truth" in one rendering of the name)[3] was founded in 1984 by Matsumoto Chizuko (also known as Asahara Shōko), a charismatic, half-blind individual recently sentenced to death for murder. At first a small, seemingly harmless group centered on yoga and other ascetic practices, Aum attracted a closed, paranoid circle of leaders who increasingly saw the outside world as their enemy and stockpiled a cult arsenal, including large amounts of sarin, in order both to stave off what they saw as the inevitable attack on their group from Japanese authorities and to bring to fruition the violent apocalyptic visions of their founder.

The 1995 subway attack was far from being Aum's first violent act. As far back as 1989, a Japanese lawyer who had been investigating the group, his wife, and their infant child were murdered in their home by members of Aum. And on June 27, 1994, Aum released sarin gas in the city of Matsumoto, killing seven and injuring hundreds more. Of this second attack Ian Reader writes, "This attack—the first use of chemical weapons on a population by a non-state organization—marked a radical shift from individual and directed acts of violence and terror, to more indiscriminate ones in which Aum was prepared to use the weapons at its disposal against the general public."[4] From fairly early in its history Aum had used violence to deal with its enemies, including dissidents within the cult. Everything seemed to be coming to a head in March 1995; the March 20 attack was apparently the direct result of reports Aum had received that the cult would be raided by the police on or about that date.

Murakami Haruki, one of Japan's leading novelists, began interviewing victims of the attack not long afterward, publishing an oral history of the attack in the form of interviews with sixty survivors (*Underground* [1997]). He followed this a year later with *Yakusoku sareta basho de* (translated as *The Place That Was Promised;* hereafter *Place*), extended interviews with eight members and former members of Aum. Why was Murakami so drawn to this event as to spend two years on the project? At first he seems an unlikely candidate to have written so extensively on Aum and the terrorist attack. One of the best-selling writers in Japan, he is still most widely known for his 1987 blockbuster novel *Noruwei no mori* (translated in 1989 and 2000 as *Norwegian Wood*), a nostalgic love story that catapulted him to national fame by selling several million copies, while at the same time bringing down on him the condemnation of literary critics and older writers of "serious" fiction. These included Ōe Kenzaburō, who has been highly critical of Murakami and other popular writers of the younger generation. In his Nobel Prize acceptance speech in 1994, Ōe distinguished between his own "serious works of literature" and "those novels which are mere reflections of the vast consumer culture of Tokyo and the subcultures of the world at large."[5] In other essays appearing at the time, Ōe makes it clear that he includes Murakami, speaking of him as writing only of "politically uninvolved or disaffected" young people. After the Aum attack, though, both Ōe and Murakami focused on the same disaffected youth subculture, namely, the young people who joined Aum. (See chapter 4 for a discussion of Ōe's literary reaction to Aum.)

Even if one accepts Ōe's criticism of Murakami's earlier fiction, Murakami's more recent works show the beginnings of a serious critique of contemporary Japan, and he here comes off as far more than just a chronicler of modern consumerism. The novel *South of the Border, West of the Sun,* published three years before the Aum attack, is certainly a love story in the mode of *Norwegian Wood,* but it also contains stinging criticism of the late-1980s bubble economy and of the widespread empty, materialistic lifestyle characteristic of the period. And in the novel *The Wind-Up Bird Chronicle,* on which he was working at the time of the subway attack, Murakami for the first time delves into the dark side of Japan's World War Two experience and some of the atrocities that took place on the Asian continent. In the 1990s, then, Murakami clearly began to tackle the darker side of modern Japan.

What first drew him to the *Underground* project was a recognition of the potential for violence lying just below the surface of Japan. In a travel essay that took him back to survey the damage done to his hometown of Kobe after the January 1995 earthquake, he writes:

> While I was living away from Japan, in America, first the Kansai earthquake took place, and then, two months later, the sarin attack on the subway. For me this chain of events had a particularly symbolic meaning. That summer I returned to Japan, and after a short break began interviewing victims of the subway attack, and brought these together a year later in the book *Underground.* What I was trying to investigate in this book . . . what I really wanted to know for myself, was the violence that must lie hidden in our society, just below our feet.[6]

The fact that both these events came up from underground, Murakami notes elsewhere, made them all the more compelling for him, for "subterranean worlds" had long fascinated him and are an important motif in his novels, ranging from the underground catacombs of *Hardboiled Wonderland and the End of the World* to memorable scenes in *The Wind-Up Bird Chronicle* in which the protagonist explores a deep well.[7]

Underground, the interviews with victims of the attack, is compelling in and of itself, particularly as it explores multiple perspectives on single events and the question of eyewitness reliability, but one thing that many reviewers have noted is the way many of the victims, barely able to function after being gassed, insisted on going to work, where some of them finally collapsed. In the afterword Murakami writes of the Aum members that they "deposited all their precious holdings of selfhood—lock and key—in that 'spritual bank' called Asahara Shoko." In his interviews with victims it seems that Murakami has discovered a similar deposit made by many ordinary Japanese in the "bank" called the Company.[8] There is at work in Japanese society a kind of blind obedience to the collective—on the part of both victims and victimizers—that Murakami clearly finds disturbing. Talking with one of the Aum members in *Place,* he comments, "When I did my interviews with victims of the gas attack, several of them told me that, based on their experience working for companies, if they had been in Aum and been ordered to release the sarin they might well have done it."[9] Murakami finds conformism, blind obedience, and subordination of the will to be the norm both inside and outside the cult.

After interviewing sixty survivors of the subway attack for *Underground,* Murakami began to feel the need to examine the other side, the story of Aum and its members. He writes:

> After *Underground* was published, and various repercussions from the events had settled down, the question "What was Aum Shinrikyo?" welled up inside me. After all, *Underground* was an attempt to restore a sense of balance to what I saw as biased reporting. Once that job was over, I had to wonder whether we were receiving true and accurate accounts of the Aum side of the story.
>
> In *Underground,* Aum Shinrikyo was like some unidentified threat—a "black box" if you will—which suddenly, from out of nowhere, made an assault on the everyday. Now, in my own way, I wanted to try to pry open that black box and catch a glimpse of what it contained. By comparing and contrasting those contents with the viewpoints gathered in *Underground* I hoped to gain an even deeper understanding.[10]

The result was interviews with eight members and former members of Aum, first published in *Bungei shunjū* magazine under the title "Post Underground," then collected in a single volume, *Yakusoku sareta basho de* (with the subtitle *Underground 2*). This volume of interviews, slightly abridged—and minus an extended interview with the psychiatrist Kawai Hayao—became part 2 of the English translation *Underground.*

Compared to the interviews in *Underground,* in *Place* Murakami more openly foregrounds his own role, debating the Aum interviewees at times, pushing them to clarify their points, often openly disagreeing with them. As he explains in the preface to *Place,* he tried to keep the interviews from "swerv[ing] in the direction of religious dogma," mainly because he knew that as a "rank amateur" when it came to knowledge of religion, "there was little chance I'd be able to hold my own if I got into the ring to debate doctrine with some devout religious believer" (249).[11] Indeed, his stated goals for the project are modest:

> Analyzing the interviewees' mental state in detail, evaluating the ethical and logical justifications for their positions, etc., were not goals I laid out for this project. I leave deeper study of the religious issues raised, and their social meaning, to the experts. What I've tried to present is the way these Aum followers appear in an ordinary, face-to-face conversation. (249–250)

Despite this disclaimer, Murakami does draw out a great deal that is of interest in the average Aum follower's understanding of the cult's teachings, with fascinating discussions of the apocalypse, salvation, the self and individual will, and the role of a religious "guru." *Place* offers one of the more absorbing glimpses into the spiritual search of certain types of young people in Japan.

What first emerges from Murakami's interviews is an encapsulated view of alienated youth in the affluent Japan of the late 1980s and early 1990s. All his interviewees shared a sense of estrangement from ordinary Japanese life; all, in the words of one follower, were seeking a sense of "purity" and, through one means or another, a way to "rais[e] their spiritual level" (259). Motivations for joining are varied: one member had the lofty goal to "theoretize" Buddhist beliefs as a "natural science" and create a rationally convincing, systematic religious doctrine (255–256); another member sought a "purer kind of doctrine" than found in ordinary Buddhism or in new religions such as Sōka Gakkai, with its emphasis on worldly attainment (267); one simply felt a vague sense of lack in his life (a "hole within") and sought refuge from "human relationships and responsibilities" in Aum (282). One member wanted to do away with the "uncleanliness and attachments" of the outside world, and "do away with the Self" as well (297), while a young woman who had little interest in religious doctrine was originally attracted by the health benefits of Aum's yogic practices and ended up joining because of the peaceful, family-like atmosphere of Aum, so different from the superficial nature of relationships in society (335–344). And one member views Aum as attractive to his entire generation, the so-called Moratorium People, that is, the products of Japan's affluence who never want to truly grow up (347–348). Aum is also seen as a way of attaining power and of participating in and surviving the coming end times (271, 276).

Many of the interviewees share a sense of disgust for ordinary secular Japan. One woman, an OL ("office lady," or white-collar clerical worker), after a typical pleasure-seeking, consumerist lifestyle, rejects this as "increasingly pointless," and yearns to make life easier by doing away with the attachments inherent in such a life—"emotional attachments to your parents, a desire to be fashionable, hatred of others" (337). One young girl, only sixteen when she joins Aum, is turned off by her classmates' talk of "boys, love, fashion, where the best karaoke boxes were," feels left out, and seeks refuge in the "liberation" from such worldly interests promised by Aum publications. One young man goes so far as to declare the world evil, and is attracted to Aum because it "clearly stated that the world is evil. . . . I'd always thought that the world was unfair and might as well be destroyed, and here it was all laid out in black and white" (320).

Followers typically developed a hatred, even a phobia, about the outside world once they were in Aum. As one puts it:

> The *samana* [followers], too, had a fundamental loathing of the outside
> world. "The unenlightened"—that was their term for people who lived
> normal lives. Since these people were heading straight for hell, the *samana*
> had some choice words for them. For example, they didn't worry about it
> if they banged into a car belonging to someone from the outside. It was like
> they were the ones practicing the truth, looking down on everyone else.
> They were too busy striving for liberation, so even if they put a dent in
> someone else's car, so what? (325)

The antipathy toward the outside world that drove many to join Aum was further cultivated within the cult to the point where there was a general sense of superiority vis-à-vis non-Aum society. Murakami notes that the cult leaders, while denouncing Asahara at their trial, "still believe they are at a higher spiritual level than 'ordinary people' and have a sense of being specially chosen" (360). This sense lingers among the lower-level followers Murakami interviewed as well, many of whom still believe in the basic aims of Aum despite the subway attack, and keep their distance from family and society in general. In a section introducing an interview with one former follower, Murakami writes, "As we said goodbye I asked her if talking with someone from 'this world' for so long would cause some uncleanliness to rub off on her. Perplexed for a moment, she replied, 'Logically, that's true.'" (304).

What, then, were these ordinary followers seeking spiritually that could not be satisfied elsewhere, and how did Aum satisfy them? How did they view Aum's religious doctrines? And how did their relationship with their "guru" play into this? Murakami's interviewees vary in their reactions to these questions, revealing a less than monolithic view of the cult from the inside. One member, Kano Hiroyuki, who wanted to position the religion in a systematic, scientific, even mathematical framework, is deeply concerned with the afterlife, arguing that "as long as [something] was beneficial to [a] person after death," it is justified (257). Kano rejects the portrayal of Aum as an "eschatological philosophy" as a creation of the media, and states, "I didn't know anybody who cared about Nostradamus' *Prophecies*. Nobody's going to be convinced by something like that" (256). In contrast, another member, Namimura Akio, states, "Nostradamus had a great influence on my generation. I'm planning my life's schedule around his prophecies." Namimura insisted that 1999 was the key year of the end times and wanted to "see with [his] own eyes what will happen at the end." When Murakami asks if "the end" means that the present system will be wiped out, Namimura replies, "I prefer to think of it as being reset. It's the desire to push the reset button on life. I imagine it as a catharsis, very peaceful" (276). One other former member, Takahashi Hidetoshi, seconds Namimura's idea of Aum as an apocalyptic cult, saying, "Robert Jay Lifton [in his book *Destroying the World to Save It*] has said that there were many cults that have an apocalyptic creed, but Aum is the only one that marched straight toward it as part of their program. That makes sense to me" (349). More than any other interviewee, Takahashi delves deeply into the idea of Aum and the apocalypse, agreeing with Namimura on the profound influence of Nostradamus, saying, "I don't want this to deteriorate into some simplistic theory about 'my generation,' but I feel very strongly that all Japanese at that time had the idea drilled into them of 1999 being the end of the world" (348–349). He adds, "Aum renunciates have already accepted, inside themselves, the end of the world, because when they become a renunciate, they discard themselves totally, thereby abandoning the world. In other words, Aum is a collection of people who have accepted the end" (349).[12]

Takahashi and Murakami pursue the idea of an apocalypse further, with Takahashi, rejecting Kano's notion of Aum as a purely Buddhist sect, arguing that the Aum notion of the apocalypse can more accurately be viewed as a subset of larger Western ideas of the millennium. Aum's ideas cannot "compete with the Christian idea," he says. "It's absorbed into the Christian idea. . . . You can't really explain these Aum-related incidents by looking only at the core of what makes up Aum—namely, Buddhism and Tibetan esoteric religion" (356). Takahashi and Murakami agree that Japan is already saturated with a "suppressed, viruslike apocalyptic vision that's invading society." In this sense, the gas attack was (and here Takahashi uses the same term as Namimura) "a kind of catharsis, a psychological release of everything that had built up in Japan—the malice, the distorted consciousness we have. Not that the Aum incident got rid of everything" (357). Rather than presenting Asahara as the one who introduced a new apocalyptic vision to a Japan devoid of any such eschatological ideas, Takahashi portrays him as a man overwhelmed by a pervasive, *already existing* consciousness of the end:

> Even if you could get rid of it at an individual level, the virus would remain on a social level.
>
> MURAKAMI: *You talk about society as a whole, but in the so-called secular world, ordinary people—by which I mean people who maintain a relative balance in their lives—deconstruct that kind of viruslike, apocalyptic vision, as you put it, in their own way, and naturally substitute something else for it. Don't you think so?*
>
> Yes, it does come down to a process of deconstruction. Something like that has absolutely got to take place. Shoko Asahara couldn't deconstruct it, and lost out to apocalyptic ideas. And that's why he had to create a crisis on his own. The apocalyptic vision of Shoko Asahara—as a religious figure—was defeated by an even greater vision. (357)

There is, then, some disagreement within the cult as to the view of Aum as an apocalyptic, eschatological religion, though more voices than not, at least in this account, see it as one.

Likewise, while Kano subscribes to the whole Buddhist system of karma, rebirth, and so on, and sees Aum as the only correct synthesis of traditional Buddhist teachings, Namimura rejects this:

One thing I found strange was that a lot of Aum followers died in car accidents. I asked a woman I knew well—Ms. Takahashi—about it. "Don't you think it's unusual that this many believers have died?" I asked her. "No, it's all right," she replied, "because four billion years in the future the Master will return as the Maitreya Buddha and will raise up the souls of those who died. "What rubbish!" I thought. (272)

This notion of unexplained and possibly sinister deaths also raises the controversial subject of the cult's understanding of *pōa*, the idea that taking another's life can be condoned as an aid to the person's spiritual liberation by allowing him to be reborn on a higher plane—what Lifton terms a "doctrine of altruistic murder."[13] Like most of the other interviewees, Kano places the teachings of Vajrayana (a "fast path" to salvation) associated with the Aum leadership and *pōa* on a plane far above the level of attainment of ordinary Aum believers:

> MURAKAMI: *But the teachings of Aum Shinrikyo went in a certain direction, resulting in these crimes where many people were killed or injured. How do you feel about this?*
> You have to understand that that part—Vajrayana Tantra—is clearly differentiated from the rest.
> Only those people who have reached an extremely high stage practice Vajrayana. . . . We were many levels below that. . . . There were tens of thousands of years' worth of things you had to accomplish before you reached that level.
> MURAKAMI: *. . . For the sake of argument, though, let's say that your level shot way up to the level of Vajrayana, and you were ordered to kill someone as part of your path to reach Nirvana. Would you do it?*
> Logically, it's a simple question. If by killing another person you raised him up, that person would be happier than he would have been living his life. So I do understand that path. . . . Let's make one thing very clear. A person who cannot discern the transmigration of another does not have the right to take their life.
> MURAKAMI: *Was Shoko Asahara qualified to do that?*
> At the time I think he was. (263–264)

Kano's position is extreme among those of the followers interviewed, though it does reveal the power that Asahara and the Aum elite had over ordinary followers—and the fact that Aum operated on two different levels: an inner circle of those who had attained a spiritual level approaching his, and a larger group who had not. Spiritual attainment and ranks themselves existed on two different planes, with elite members of Aum praised for their obvious accomplishments (Kano calls their spiritual power "astounding"). Yet Asahara's system came under attack from the interviewees as elevating those who had contributed the most money to Aum, those who had graduated from elite universities, women who were particularly attractive, and so forth. Just as in the world outside, money, education, and personal appeal were powerful instruments to advancement in the organization.

This kind of favoritism and spiritual ranking system in Aum reveals how, in interesting ways, the cult reproduced aspects of the society from which its members had fled. Iwakura Harumi, for instance, found Aum rife with the sort of "backstabbing" and politicking endemic to corporate Japan. Anticipating a place devoid of attachments, she found Aum "no different from ordinary society" (337). Inaba Mitsuharu likens the way lower-level workers in Aum had to accept orders from the top, no matter how inane, to the way companies in Japan work: "Businesses in Japan are more or less the same, aren't they?" he asks (285). Further, he adds that the situation for new adherents, who must just follow orders from above, is "like when you're a new employee at a company" (282). Overall, though, the followers interviewed in *Place* find more contrasts than similarities between Aum and ordinary society, particularly in terms of how Aum—unlike Japanese society, consensus-driven and lacking in charismatic leaders–was defined by the vision of one man, Asahara.

Again and again the interviewees turn to Asahara's character and influence to define what Aum was all about. Asahara is called by one member a "man of considerable power" (283), the one who would "provide the final answer to Buddhist teachings" (284). Another considered him a person to be trusted absolutely, who "could answer any question I had" (294), a gentle and yet a terribly frightening person (321). Murakami discusses the extremely close "one-to-one relationship between guru and disciple" and how, like a virus infecting a computer, this runs the risk of throwing the system "out of kilter" with "no third party to halt this process." He sees an inherent danger in this absolute devotion, which in turn leads to him to speculate on the position given to the Self in Aum Shinrikyo doctrine (287). Inaba argues that Buddhist meditation of the kind practiced in Aum is a "method to reach the deepest part of your self. From a Buddhist perspective, deep within the subconscious lies each person's essential sort of distortion. And that's what it cures" (288). Another follower, Masutani Hajime, however, sees the Buddhist interpretation of the self as precisely what Aum *perverted*. Responding to Murakami's idea that it is "extremely dangerous to allow another, a guru, to take control of your own ego," Masutani states,

> I don't think many have thought about it properly. Gautama Buddha said, "The Self is the true master of the Self" and "Keep the Self an island, approaching nothing." In other words, Buddhist disciples practice asceticism in order to find the true Self. They find impurities and attachments, and attempt to extinguish these. But what Mr. Matsumoto [Asahara] did was equate "self" and "attachments." He said that in order to get rid of the ego, the Self must be disposed of as well. Humans love the "Self," so they suffer, and if the "Self" can be discarded then a true shining Self will emerge. But this is a complete reversal of Buddhist teachings. The self is what should be *discovered*, not discarded. Terrorist crimes like the gas attack result from this process of easily giving up on the Self. If the Self is lost, then people will become completely insensitive to murder and terrorism.
>
> In the final analysis, Aum created people who had discarded their Selves and just followed orders. (301–302)

Indeed, in many of the interviews Murakami discovers that one of the appeals of Aum for members is this notion of "giving up on the Self" in the sense of possessing a volitional ego. In this way one allows others to control one's life, destiny, and every act, and is relieved to have escaped from freedom. Kano, again, is the minority voice here, portraying Asahara as someone who would "adjust things so you'd be satisfied. So at least for me, he didn't seem to be forcing people to do things" (283). Most members, though, saw things in a different light, depicting Aum as a group in which individual freedom and will were entirely subordinated to the will of Asahara and the Aum elite. Masutani describes how "at first everyone who joined had very strong wills, but after living in Aum you'd lose that." This was "the path to follow in order to do away with the Self" (297).

Murakami confronts this question of individual will, self, and freedom by pressing the Aum members as to what they would have done if ordered to participate in the subway gas attack. Kanda Miyuki questions Murakami's assumption that those who carried out the attack were somehow under Asahara's spell. According to her, "Even the people who carried out the gas attack—and I've seen this with my own eyes—are people with a strong sense of Self. They are people who have their own opinions and are not slow to speak up in front of others" (315). (At this point, it should be noted, she still

has doubts about whether those accused carried out the attacks at all.) Takahashi, in contrast, analyzes the attack as an example of extreme devotion cultivated by Aum and sees even the elite as operating in a milieu of coercion
emanating from Asahara:

> MURAKAMI: *If Murai [Takahashi's boss and a top leader] had told
> you to release the sarin, would you have disobeyed?*
> I think so, but there's a trick to doing it. The people who carried
> out the crime were put in a position where they were caught off guard
> by the orders and couldn't escape. They'd gather in Murai's room and
> suddenly the leaders would broach the topic, telling them: "This is an
> order from the top." *An order from the top*—that was like a mantra in
> Aum. The people who carried out the crime were chosen from among
> the strongest believers. "You've been specially chosen," they were told.
> The leaders appealed to their sense of duty. Faith in Aum meant total
> devotion.

Takahashi goes on to say that if a close friend like Inoue Yoshihiro had handed
him a bag of sarin and said, "This is part of salvation," he might very well
have gone along. "In the final analyis," he argues, "logic doesn't play a strong
role in people's motivations. . . . No one who had the strength to think logically about it would have carried it out. In extreme cases of guru-ism individuals' value systems are completely wiped out":

> No matter how much you resist and try to put a stop to things, the fact is
> that in a group like Aum your sense of Self is steadily deteriorating. Things
> are forced on you from above and you're continually attacked for not
> accepting the status quo, not being devoted enough, and inevitably your
> spirit is broken. (354–355)

What is Murakami's take on all this? It goes without saying that a clear anger
emerges at the gas attack and the senseless killing and maiming of innocents.
As he says in the preface to *Place* (referring to his work in *Underground*), "I
have met some of the victims, many of whom continue to suffer, and I have
personally seen those whose loved ones were stolen from them forever. I'll
remember that for as long as I live, and no matter what the motives or circumstances behind it, a crime like this can never be condoned" (250). But
beyond this anger is his genuine fascination with many followers' and former

followers' continued search for something beyond the empty, materialistic society that prompted them to join the cult in the first place. In the afterword he writes,

> To all of them I posed the same question, that is, whether they regretted having joined Aum. Almost everyone answered: "No, I have no regrets. I don't think those years were wasted." Why is that? The answer is simple—because in Aum they found a purity of purpose they could not find in ordinary society. Even if in the end it became something monstrous, the radiant, warm memory of the peace they originally found remains inside them, and nothing else can easily replace it. . . . They are aware now that it is a very flawed and dangerous system, and agree that the years they passed in Aum were filled with contradictions and defects. At the same time I got the impression that, to a greater or lesser degree, there is still within them an Aum ideal—a utopian vision, a memory of light, imprinted deep inside them. If one day something that contains a similar light passes before their eyes (it needn't be a religion) what is inside them now will be pulled in that direction. In this sense what is most dangerous for our society at the moment is not Aum Shinrikyo itself, but other "Aum-like" entities. (360–361)

The double nature of what Murakami discovered in Aum is summed up in these closing words: the "purity of purpose" and "utopian vision" tending to wind up as something "monstrous" and threatening. At one point in the interviews, Murakami likens the Aum system to wartime emperor worship and the notion of rebirth to the idea that the souls of the war dead "find peace" in the Yasukuni Shrine (256–257). Here, in the afterword, he compares Aum to the pre–World War Two Japanese colony of Manchuria.

Related to this is the compelling and frightening story of Hayashi Ikuo, a well-respected medical doctor who released sarin on one of the subway lines, killing two railroad employees. How is it, Murakami wonders, that someone like Hayashi, a surgeon who had received a first-class education—someone pledged to save lives—would end up caught in Aum's deadly terrorist schemes? He argues that what the elite members of Aum who carried out the attack had in common was a vision of putting to use the "technical skill and knowledge they'd acquired in the service of a more meaningful goal. They couldn't help having grave doubts about the inhumane, utilitarian gristmill of capitalism and the social system in which their own essence and efforts —even their very reasons for being—would be fruitlessly ground down"

(362). In Hayashi's case, this involved a utopian dream of a medical community based on Asahara's teachings, in his words, "a dream of a green, natural spot . . . where truly caring medical care and education were carried out." In looking at the Aum leadership (none of whom he was able to interview), Murakami reiterates a troubling question Japanese have been asking ever since the Aum attack: "How could such elite, highly educated people believe in such a ridiculous, dangerous new religion?" (361). He writes that as he interviewed Aum members over a year's time, "I felt strongly that it wasn't *in spite of* being part of the elite that they went in that direction, but precisely *because* they were part of the elite" (361). Murakami looks back at the history of the Japanese colony of Manchuria in the 1930s and 1940s. Manchuria became a place where many of the most ambitious members of the educated elite went to live out their dreams. "And that's exactly why they sought out this more accommodating, experimental land, even if it meant jumping off the normal track." Their motives were pure and idealistic, but "something vital was lacking . . . an identity between language and actions" (361). These bureaucrats got caught up in the language of their own insipid slogans, mistaking the idealism of their visions for the messy realities of life.

This in turn leads to the idea that young people entered Aum because they were drawn by Asahara's "narrative," which in many ways was far more powerful and magnetic than any narrative the outside world could provide. This idea of Aum and narrative is one that appeals to Murakami the novelist, and he dwells on it at length. In an interview with the *New York Times* a month after the September 11 attacks, Murakami draws the distinction between open and closed circuits: "The open circuit is this society, and the closed circuit is the world of religious fanatics. . . . Their worlds are perfect, because they are closed off. . . . If you have questions, there is always someone to provide the answers."[14] In *Place* he contrasts the confusing, contradictory, and chaotic nature of reality with the simplistic narrative constructed by Asahara Shōko— what he calls a "hermetic logic." Imagining himself trying to convince a Dr. Hayashi how simplistic and alienated from reality his ideas are, Murakami writes, "The sad fact is that language and logic cut off from reality has a far greater power than the language and logic of reality—in the end, unable to comprehend each other's words, we'd part, each going our separate ways" (363). And it is the power of this hermetic logic—in the case of Aum, for example, the idea that murder is acceptable in order to send a person to a higher state of being—that Murakami finds most frightening and most difficult to oppose.

It is important to note that Murakami, though deploring the gas attack, does not reject the type of spiritual search or the motives that propelled people to join Aum. It is only natural, he says, that people search for meaning in their lives, particularly in contemporary Japan, where meaning can often seem elusive. These cult members are not as aberrant as the media would have people believe. He concludes *Place* with this caution:

> We need to realize that most of the people who join cults are not abnormal; they're not disadvantaged; they're not eccentrics. They are the people who live average lives (and maybe from the outside, more than average lives), who live in my neighborhood. And in yours.
>
> Maybe they think about things a little too seriously. Perhaps there's some pain they're carrying around inside. They're not good at making their feelings known to others and are somewhat troubled. They can't find a suitable means to express themselves, and bounce back and forth between feelings of pride and inadequacy. That might very well be me. It might be you. (364)

How has Aum affected Murakami as a novelist? At one point in *Place* he compares the Aum members' religious quest and his own role: "Talking to them so intimately made me realize how their religious quest and the process of novel writing, though not identical, are similar. This aroused my own personal interest as I interviewed them, and it is also why I felt something akin to irritation at times as well" (250). He adds that the interviews and the whole Aum experience are not something he can now easily catalogue and put to rest: "As a novelist, I will be sifting through what remains within me, bit by bit, investigating, putting things in order as I pass through the time-consuming process of shaping this into narrative form. It's not the sort of thing that takes shape easily" (250). Murakami's fiction can be viewed both as a response to Aum and as an extended narrative project focused from the start on many of the concerns that motivated these spiritual seekers. Of his own literature he states, "What I write are stories in which the hero is looking for the right way in this world of chaos. That is my theme. At the same time I think there is another world that is underground. You can access this inner world in your mind. Most protagonists in my books live in both worlds—this realistic world and the world underground."[15] Indeed, as Jay Rubin puts it, there is an unexpected affinity between Murakami as novelist and these Aum members:

> The Aum members fascinate him because they have tried to do what his characters usually give up any hope of doing. Through religion, they have

sought out regions "south of the border" or "west of the sun" where they
hope to find that missing something, that absolute certainty of "liberation"
or "enlightenment" that will give their lives meaning. Unlike the more
passive victims of the attack, the cult members have dared to probe into
the black box at the core of themselves. In the process, some have temporarily been unable to distinguish between dream and reality, another
familiar Murakami motif.[16]

The irritation Murakami felt in interviewing Aum members results from the
conundrum he discovers in the Aum spiritual quest, and in his own writing:
how the strong pull toward this "inner world," the "world underground"—
the probing into the black box, as Rubin puts it—is opposed by the realization of the danger inherent in going too far. In the post–September 11 interview, he goes on to say, "If you are trained you can find a passage and come
and go between the two worlds. It is easy to find an entrance into this closed
circuit, but it is not easy to find an exit. Many gurus offer an entry into the
circuit for free. But they don't offer a way out, because they want to keep followers trapped."[17] Is it possible, though, to create a narrative to counter that
of Aum, that is, a way both to explore this "inner world" and yet be able to
return? In *Place* Murakami stresses only the difficulties. In his fiction Murakami has long been struggling with this issue, and in his post-Aum fiction in
particular, he comes closer than ever to providing an answer in the form of a
counternarrative to Aum.

The most obvious parallel between Murakami's fiction and the Aum followers is that from his first stories and novel (*Hear the Wind Sing* [1979])
onward, Murakami's fictional characters have largely been the kind of sensitive, introspective loners and dropouts found in Aum. Like the young people
who found their way into the cult, Murakami's characters are often people
"outside the main system of Japanese society" for whom there is "no effective
alternative or safety net."

In his comprehensive study *Dances with Sheep,* Matthew Strecher per-
suasively makes the argument that Murakami's fiction depicts the ennui of a
politically impotent generation following the failure of the late-1960s student
movement.[18] Characters include the first person narrator of Murakami's early
trilogy, a directionless college student turned marginal translator; the narrator of "A Slow Boat to China," whose imaginary China is more real for him
than the Tokyo in which he lives; the protagonist of "New York Mining Dis-
aster," trapped in the darkened "mine" of a meaningless urban existence; and
even the narrator of his later novel *The Wind-Up Bird Chronicle,* who loses,

one after another, his job, his cat, and his wife. Those few who, years later, have seemingly become integrated into "the main system" still look back nostalgically on a lost authenticity and regard their present existence as insubstantial. Because of his father-in-law's insider trading schemes, Hajime, the narrator of *South of the Border, West of the Sun,* thinks,

> I felt I was taking a dishonest shortcut, using unfair means to get to where I was. After all, I was part of the late-sixties-early-seventies generation that spawned the radical student movement. Our generation was the first to yell out a resounding "No!" to the logic of late capitalism, which had devoured any remaining postwar ideals. . . . And here I was, myself swallowed up by the very same capitalist logic, savoring Schubert's *Winterreise* as I lounged in my BMW, waiting for the signal to change at an intersection in ritzy Aoyama. I was living someone else's life, not my own. How much of this person I called myself was really me? And how much was not? These hands clutching the steering wheel—what percentage of them could I really call my own? The scenery outside—how much of it was real? The more I thought about it, the less I seemed to understand. (72)

Sputnik Sweetheart, Murakami's first novel following *Underground* and *The Place That Was Promised,* is his first attempt at "shaping [the Aum experience] into narrative form." [19] *Sputnik* is the story of a young man, K, an elementary school teacher, who is in love with Sumire. Sumire is an eccentric, aspiring young writer who struggles with her sexuality and gradually realizes she prefers women to men, in particular an older Korean-Japanese woman named Miu. Miu hires Sumire to work in her import business, and the two of them travel together on business to Europe. They stay on a Greek island for a short vacation after their business, and Sumire makes her feelings known to Miu. Miu, who had experienced a bizarre out-of-body experience years before, is frigid, and rebuffs Sumire. Soon afterward, Sumire disappears, and Miu begs K to fly to Greece to help in the search. Sumire, who is obsessed with dreams and writing, leaves behind some writings that suggest she either wrote or dreamed her way into another world. Sumire is never found ("'As Miu put it,' K says, 'she vanished like smoke'"). K, back in Tokyo, helps out a severely withdrawn pupil of his who has been caught shoplifting. Concluding, "I can't be part of the solution if I'm part of the problem," K breaks up with his lover, the pupil's attractive mother. In the final scene, K gets a "phone call" from Sumire (the ontological status is left ambiguous), who declares she's back. She asks him to come pick her up. The novel ends,

I get out of bed. I pull back the old, faded curtain and open the window. I stick my head out and look up at the sky. Sure enough, a mold-colored moon hangs in the sky [the same one Sumire describes over the phone]. *Good.* We're both looking at the same moon, in the same world. We're connected to reality by the same line. All I have to do is quietly draw it toward me.

I spread my fingers apart and stare at the palms of both hands, looking for bloodstains. There aren't any. No scent of blood, no stiffness. The blood must have already, in its own silent way, seeped inside. (210)

I will return to these lines, for they are crucial in any interpretation of the novel, but will first examine the more obvious influences of the Aum experience on this work.

Reading *Sputnik* after *Place,* one is first struck by the similarities in narrative structure between the two. Though until recently Murakami has favored the first person narrator (the "Boku" of so many early works), giving many of his stories and novels a semi-confessional flavor (*South of the Border, West of the Sun* in particular), several times in *Sputnik* Murakami appropriates the kind of philosophically oriented, oral history–like confessional, especially of early childhood and youth, found in the interviews with Aum members. Sumire's brief written memories of her childhood, for example, the deliberate way she thought as a child and the consequent alienation this produced (131–132) read very much like many of the childhood reminiscences of the Aum members. More striking are the first few pages of chapter 5, in which K, the narrator, echoes the sort of philosophical, inward-looking, painfully logical mode of many in Aum:

I find it hard to talk about myself. I'm always tripped up by the eternal *who am I?* paradox. Sure, no one knows as much pure data about me as *me.* But when I talk about myself, all sorts of other factors—values, standards, my own limitations as an observer—make me, the *narrator,* select and eliminate things about me, the *narratee.* I've always been disturbed by the thought that I'm not painting a very objective picture of myself. . . .

These are the kinds of ideas I had running through my head when I was a teenager. Like a master builder stretches taut his string and lays one brick after another, I constructed this viewpoint—or philosophy of life, to put a bigger spin on it. Logic and speculation played a part in formulating this viewpoint, but for the most part it was based on my own experiences. . . .

The upshot of all this was that when I was young I began to draw an invisible boundary between myself and other people. (54–55)

Readers of *Place* will also notice the resemblance between certain characters in *Sputnik* and the Aum interviewees.[20] In his portrait of confused, yet yearning, young Japanese in the novel, Murakami borrows details and motifs from the lives of the Aum members for his fictional characters. Sumire, for instance, is an amalgam of features of several of them, particularly Namimura Akio, Kanda Miyuki, and Inaba Mitsuharu. From Namimura, Murakami borrows the burning desire to become a writer. Namimura comes to Tokyo to become a novelist, devours surrealist fiction, but ultimately finds the road to being a writer frustrating ("'You want to be a novelist?' one relative asks him. 'Stop dreaming!'"). And the opening page of *Sputnik* reads, "At the time, Sumire—Violet in Japanese—was struggling to become a writer. No matter how many choices life might bring her way, it was novelist or nothing. Her resolve was a regular Rock of Gibraltar. Nothing could come between her and her faith in literature" (3). As the novel progresses, it outlines various trials and tribulations as Sumire struggles to become a writer. Many writers make their protagonists fellow writers, so this should not be noteworthy—except for the fact that Murakami seldom has. A few of his early characters hover on the edges of being writers—they are translators, copywriters, and the like— but no major characters are novelists.

Much more important is Sumire's obsession with dreams, which clearly is a reworking of statements made in *Place* by the young female Aum member Kanda Miyuki. Kanda states,

Ever since I was little I've had mystical experiences. For instance, when I dreamed it was no different from reality. I'd call them stories rather than dreams—they were long and distinct, and after I woke up I could remember every detail. In my dreams I visited all sorts of worlds, had astral projection–type experiences. . . .

It was different from what you usually call dreams. Everything was extremely realistic. It would have been easier if you could make a clear-cut distinction, and say, "Okay, this is a dream and isn't the same as reality," but things very much like those in reality appeared in my dreams and confused me. "Is this reality? Or isn't it?" Gradually I couldn't distinguish between the two, or maybe I should say that my dreams became more real than reality.[21]

In one of the two essays Sumire leaves behind after she disappears she writes,

> So what are people supposed to do if they want to avoid a collision *(thud!)* [between what they know and don't know] but still lie in the field, enjoying the clouds drifting by, listening to the grass grow—not thinking, in other words? Sound hard? Not at all. Logically, it's easy. *C'est simple.* The answer is *dreams.* Dreaming on and on. Entering the world of dreams, and never coming out. Living in dreams for the rest of time.
>
> In dreams you don't need to make any distinctions between things. Not at all. Boundaries don't exist. So in dreams there are hardly ever collisions. Even if there are, they don't hurt. Reality is different. Reality bites. (135–136)

Much of the rest of the story deals with Sumire's attempts to enter the world of dreams and never come out. She first relates a detailed dream involving her dead mother, who calls out to her from a kind of ventilation shaft in a wall. Her mother is "pulled deeper into that hole, as if sucked by some giant vacuum on the other side," finally being drawn back into a "black hole" and "lost forever in that vacant void" (140). This bizarre dream introduces the reader to the idea of the "other side" as the world of death (Sumire's mother died when she was an infant), but in a second document she leaves behind, entitled "The Tale of Miu and the Ferris Wheel," Sumire reveals a different notion of this "other side." Here, one's body remains on this side and one's spirit on the other, an echo of the chilling experience of the Aum member Inaba, who described how his ascetic training made his "subconscious be[gin] to emerge, and [his] sense of reality gr[ow] faint":

> My sense of reality had vanished. My memory became hazy and I couldn't tell whether I'd actually done something or only dreamed it.
>
> My consciousness had gone over to the other side and I couldn't get back.[22]

In many ways, both superficial and more substantial, Murakami's first post-Aum novel reflects his own experience of Aum. But what is most intriguing is the continued focus in his fiction on the this world/other world (outer world/inner world; open circuit/closed circuit) dichotomy. Examining this aspect of his work in four of his novels—*Hardboiled Wonderland and the End of the World* (1985); *South of the Border, West of the Sun* (1992); *Sputnik Sweetheart* (1999); and *Kafka on the Shore* (2002) points up what might best be termed a growing spiritual dimension in his fiction. In discussing these four novels, two pre-Aum and two post-Aum, I focus on how Murakami portrays the two worlds in his fiction. In the pre-Aum fiction the "other world" is mostly menacing, with characters, as Rubin says, who are stymied in any search for spiritual meaning. But in his post-Aum novels—*Sputnik Sweetheart* and *Kafka on the Shore*—Murakami begins to reveal something different: an "other side" that is both accessible and from which one can return. Most important, this other side, while still frightening in some ways, is spiritually restorative.

As Susan Napier notes, in its two parallel narratives *Hardboiled Wonderland and the End of the World* (hereafter *Wonderland*) references a number of genres—cyberpunk and "classic dystopian science fiction" in the "Hardboiled Wonderland" chapters, and fantasy in the parallel "End of the World" chapters.[23] The cyberpunk and science fiction aspects of the novel no doubt reflect the influence of William Gibson, in whose work Fredric Jameson sees a world of "labyrinthine conspiracies of autonomous but deadly interlocking and competing information agencies in a complexity often beyond the capacity of the normal reading mind."[24] Despite their lack of the gritty futuristic feeling of Gibson's work, the "Hardboiled Wonderland" chapters of the novel fit this description in many ways. In contrast, the parallel "End of the World" chapters depict a gentle fantasy, replete with a walled Town inhabited by a gatekeeper, gentle talking shadows, and unicorns, a world where time, memory, and selfhood have faded.[25] In the cyberpunk world of the "Hardboiled Wonderland" chapters, the narrator, a skilled Calcutec, or information processor, finds himself in the middle of a high-tech information war pitting his side against an opposing side known as the Simuteks (and their allies, the mysterious subterranean Inklings). Eventually the narrator learns to his horror that he has been the subject of an experiment gone awry, an attempt to implant circuits in the brain that allow him to switch between "two cognitive systems," one his conscious mind, the other the fantasy "End of the World," which is a version of his "core consciousness," edited and implanted in him by an eccentric scientist. This "third circuit," however, has no override function, so inevitably the narrator's conscious mind will fade away, replaced by the "End of the World." As the scientist explains to the horrified narrator,

> "The vision displayed in your consciousness is the End of the World. Why you have the likes of that tucked away in there, I can't say. But for whatever reason, it's there. Meanwhile, this world in your mind here is coming to an end. Or t'put it another way, your mind will be living here, in the place called the End of the World.

"Everythin' that's in this world here and now is missin' from that world. There's no time, no life, no death. No values in any strict sense. No self."[26]

While the narrator will continue to live in some sense, he will go over to the other side, be dead to the conscious world, and will have lost his "self." The self, and the connection to the normal world, are represented by his shadow (a recurring motif in Murakami's work). As the inevitable end approaches, the shadow and the narrator in the "End of the World" chapters plot together to make their escape from the cozy, yet ultimately frightening, world of the Town. As the shadow argues, those who run the Town "have surrounded the place with fear." If the narrator is to keep his mind and his identity, he must escape back to the conscious world: "It's not the best of all worlds, but it is the world where we belong."[27]

Ultimately, though, as the narrator and his shadow prepare to make their escape through a pool of water—the only unguarded spot in the Town —the narrator backs away from their plan, announcing that that he will remain behind. The Town, he realizes, is his own creation: "I have responsibilities . . . I cannot forsake the people and places I have created." His shadow counters,

> "I cannot stop you," admits my shadow. "Maybe you can't die here, but you will not be living. You will merely exist. There is no 'why' in a world that would be perfect in itself. Nor is surviving in the Woods anything like you imagine. You'll be trapped for all eternity."
>
> "I am not so sure," I say. "Nor can you be. A little by little, I will recall things. People and places from our former world, different qualities of light, different songs. And as I remember, I may find the key to my own creation, and to its undoing."
>
> "No, I doubt it. Not as long as you are sealed inside yourself."[28]

The Woods mentioned here are significant. As the narrator remarks to the Town's librarian, with whom he's fallen in love, "Only those whose shadows have not been completely exterminated, who still bear traces of mind in them, can live in the Woods. I still have a mind."[29] The Woods, then, is a third element, a place where one exists, partly conscious of one's self, yet trapped and unable to be reconnected to the real world or to an intergrated sense of one's being. The narrator, then, through the survival of his shadow (it escapes alone through the pool), and through his love for the librarian and his desire to restore her mind, is condemned to survive, in Napier's words, in an "apocalypse [that] is ultimately solipsistic."[30]

Though it precedes the Aum attack by a decade, there are haunting parallels between the novel and the darker side of cult experience. Like Aum believers, the narrator of *Wonderland* finds himself at the mercy of an ambitious man's designs. Though the "narrative" that is literally embedded in the narrator's brain (an ultimate form of brainwashing?) begins with his own deepest desires, it has been reconfigured ("edited") in such a way that the narrator eventually becomes a prisoner of this narrative, lost in a seemingly "perfect" world where the most precious thing of all—one's self and volition—are lost.[31] Interestingly, elements introduced in *Wonderland,* in particular the shadow and the Woods, are developed in Murakami's later fiction, especially in *Kafka on the Shore.* While in *Wonderland* the shadow is the element of the self that escapes back to the "real world," leaving behind the narrator as but half a person (the question of whether the escape is successful, or even possible, is left hanging), in *Kafka on the Shore* (hereafter *Kafka*), the world on this side is populated by many who have lost their shadow, or a part of it, in some "other world." The Woods that the protagonist explores in the final chapters of *Kafka* is an extension of what is only hinted at in *Wonderland*—the Woods as an intermediate, middle ground, or, as one character puts it in the novel, a spiritual limbo for those who are dead but whose souls have not yet completely gone over to the other side.

South of the Border, West of the Sun (hereafter *South of the Border*) is, as Rubin notes, a spin-off from the more monumental *Wind-Up Bird Chronicle,* a story that "through a mysterious process of cell division" wound up as its own self-contained story. Rubin writes, "This slim novel might intially appear to be a return to the world of *Norwegian Wood,* the sexual experiences of a teenage protagonist occupying much of the book. But whereas *Norwegian Wood* only hints at the life of its 38-year-old narrator, *South of the Border, West of the Sun* concentrates on the later Boku around the same age."[32] Rubin sees the novel as "the ultimate novel of yuppie mid-life crisis,"[33] and elsewhere I have argued for a reading of it as an expression of a "nostalgia for a formerly infantile Japan." As I sum up the plot,

> Here the protagonist [Hajiime] in his late thirties, a successful owner of two nightclubs in the tony Aoyama district of Tokyo, finds his life progressively pointless and empty. Though ostensibly a depiction of a typical midlife crisis coupled with a rekindled desire for his first love who suddenly reenters

his life, the novel deals principally with two dynamics: the protagonist's disillusionment with late-1980s-style Japanese affluence (brought to a head by a confrontation with his wealthy father-in-law's insider stock trading) and his aching nostalgia for when he was twelve, the year 1963. Though the novel is clothed in a love story (and so marketed), the reader soon realizes that the ghostly nature of the protagonist's lover [Shimamoto] is closely linked to his desire for the ghost of Japan's not-too-distant past: the period predating the emergence of Japan's affluence.[34]

Shimamoto's appearance, though, and the other world to which she beckons Hajime, are more than just a bidding to rejoin some idyllic past; they are linked to the world hereafter, specifically, to death.

In terms of presenting a "hero looking for the right way in this world of chaos," *South of the Border* does indeed, as did *Wonderland,* present a dichotomy between the chaos of "this world" and the seeming placidity of the "other world," with the other world represented by Shimamoto. The contrast is set out below.

	Open circuit/This world	Closed circuit/Other world
Wonderland	*Watashi*	*Boku*
	Chaotic techno-wars	Idyllic, pre-modern, pastoral
	Technology gone wild	
South of the Border	*Hajime*	*Shimamoto*
	Bubble economy	Youthful innocence, first love
	Rampant materialism	

Hajime is at first satisfied with his newfound affluence and happy to be the father of two girls, husband to a caring wife, and well-to-do owner of two successful jazz bars. With all the accoutrements of an upscale, affluent Tokyo lifestyle well documented here, the Luciano Soprani suits, the four-bedroom condos, and the BMW 320s, in *South of the Border,* more than in any other Murakami novel, the author opens himself up again to the charge leveled by Ōe that his work merely depicts the "vast consumer culture of Tokyo." And certainly Hajime is happy to have escaped the dead-end low-level white-collar editing job he did before his marriage, the "third stage of [his] life." According to him, he experienced "Years of disappointment and loneliness. And silence. Frozen years, when my feelings were shut up inside me" (51).

But soon Hajime rebels against the very affluence he shares. Hints that he may already be finding the need somehow to tame or hold at bay the chaos of late-1980s Tokyo (where land prices were doubling by the month and gold-flecked sushi was all the rage) are found in the kinds of bars he creates and in the sometimes obsessive personality he displays. While both partaking in and nurturing the chaotic affluence of Tokyo, Hajime's bar is at the same time an "other world," a kind of idyllic space he creates as a personal refuge, where he "construct[s] an imaginary place in [his] head and little by little add[s] details to it" (104). As he tells Shimamoto,

> You know, sometimes my bars feel like imaginary places I created in my mind. Castles in the air. I plant some flowers here, construct a fountain there, crafting everything with great care. People stop by, have drinks, listen to music, talk, and go home. People are willing to spend a lot of money to come all this way to have some drinks—and do you know why? Because everyone's seeking an imaginary place, their own castle in the air, and their very own special corner it it. (105)

The bar becomes the one place where Hajime can exercise control down to the last detail, and he takes exceptional care to ensure that the cocktails and service are perfect, going so far, when he was designing the place, as to spend days scouring Tokyo for the perfect fixtures for the bar's restrooms. Hajime is the latest manifestation of the often fussy, meticulous Murakami male character who endlessly irons shirts just right and is obsessed with making sure the spaghetti is perfectly *al dente.*[35] One might dismiss this as mere quirkiness, but in light of the Aum experience it is more accurately read as attempts, on even the smallest of scales, to gain some measure of control in a chaotic world. For ordinary Aum followers, this meant turning from the "uncleanliness" of the outside world and striving for the personal spiritual "power" that only Asahara could bestow, while letting the ego be dissolved into his powerful "narrative." Here, in the secular space of a downtown bar, Hajime, like many Murakami protagonists before him, attempts to hold back the chaotic by constructing an imaginary world.

It makes sense, then, both that Shimamoto reappears, and that she reappears first *here,* in Hajime's closed-off, imaginary "castle in the air." Shimamoto's ghostly status has been hotly debated. Rubin concludes, "Shimamoto-san is no more nor less a hallucination than anyone else: she 'really' exists in the world of the novel"; Strecher, recognizing that paranormal phenomena play roles in many of Murakami's works, sees her as one of many ghosts, who are actually "nostalgic images originating as part of the unconscious Other, drawn out from within *the protagonist*'s mind, in a concentrated attempt to recover *his* past and thereby reconnect with the constitutive parts of *his* personal identity."[36] Shimamoto is indeed a nostalgic image from Hajime's past, and in their interaction they reproduce the long-lost childhood they once shared—using childhood ways of addressing each other and initially substituting an adolescent masturbatory experience for adult sex.[37]

But Shimamoto is much more than just an "unconscious Other" that points toward, and helps recover, the past. She is from the world of death, the afterlife, and points not merely toward the past, but toward the *future*—and personal, physical extinction:

---

the nostalgic past <<<< **Shimamoto** >>>>> the future: death

---

Like the closed circuit of Aum, Shimamoto beckons Hajime toward a simpler explanatory narrative of the world—in this case a return to an adolescent fantasy of innocence, purity, and isolation from the chaotic world of late-1980s Japan. Hajime is thrilled by the possibility of a return to the world of *tegotae* (lit., a response to one's hand, i.e., the tangible) that he found at age twelve when he first held Shimamoto's hand ("The two of us alone, beneath a faintly flickering light, *our hands tightly clasped together* for a fleeting ten seconds of time" [18; emphasis added]). This sense of the tangible is what is lost in the bubble economy, which is itself a kind of ghostly enterprise where money is reduced to electronic transactions. As Hajime puts it to his wife Yukiko, after telling her to sell all the stock she bought on an insider trading tip: "Listen, Yukiko . . . I'm getting sick of all this. I don't want to earn money in the stock market. I want to earn money by working *with my own hands*" (159; emphasis added).

While Shimamoto is a nostalgic, comforting figure who beckons to Hajime to re-engage with childhood innocence, she is at the same time menacing. Putting aside the question of her ghostly status—that she is connected with death through being herself already dead—throughout her interaction with Hajime there is a constant undertone of death. In one of the more memorable scenes in *South of the Border,* Hajime and Shimamoto fly to Ishikawa for the day, at Shimamoto's request, to take care of a mysterious task that she reveals only once they have arrived beside a snowy river: the disposal of the ashes of Shimamoto's dead baby. After scattering the ashes, Shimamoto explains,

> "My baby died the day after it was born," she said. "It lived just one day. I held it only a couple of times. It was a beautiful baby. So very soft. . . .

> They didn't know the cause, but it couldn't breathe very well. When it
> died it was already a different color."
>> I couldn't say a thing. I reached out my hand and placed it on hers.
>> "It was a baby girl. Without a name."
>> "When was that?"
>> "This time last year. In February."
>> "Poor thing," I said.
>> "I didn't want to bury it anywhere. I couldn't stand the thought of it
> in some dark place. I wanted to keep it beside me for a while, then let it
> flow into the sea and turn into rain." (118)

Just before this scene, as Shimamoto pours the baby's ashes into the river,
there is a glimpse of a possible afterlife as reincarnation, or at least vague hopes
for such:

> "Do you think it will turn to rain?" Shimamoto asked, tapping the tip of
> her boot on the ground.
>> I looked at the sky. "I think it will hold out for a while," I said.
>> "No, that's not what I mean. What I mean is, will the child's ashes
> flow to the sea, mix with the seawater, evaporate, form into clouds, and
> fall as rain?"
>> I looked up at the sky one more time. And then at the river flowing.
>> "You never know," I said. (117)

The connection between Shimamoto and death is again reinforced in this
chapter as they drive back to the airport, when Shimamoto suddenly has
some kind of quiet seizure and is "white as a sheet and strangely stiff," her
breathing a "mechanical rasping":

> "Shimamoto-san," I turned to her. "Are you all right?"
>> She didn't answer. She just sat back against the seat, making that
> unearthly sound. I put my hand to her cheek. It was as cold as the scenery
> that surrounded us. Not a trace of warmth. I touched her forehead, but it
> showed no signs of fever. I felt like I was choking. Was she dying, right
> here and now? Her eyes were listless as I looked deep into them. I could
> see nothing: they were as *cold and dark as death.* (119; emphasis added)

Medicine revives her, and the nature of her illness is never made clear, but
once again, in the final scenes between Hajime and Shimamoto—their long-

anticipated night of passion in Hajime's cabin retreat—death and Shimamoto
are again inextricably linked. As they drive to the cabin on the highway:

> Again she turned to gaze at me. "Hajime," she said after a while. "When
> I look at you driving, sometimes I want to grab the steering wheel and
> give it a yank. It'd kill us, wouldn't it?"
>   "We'd die, all right. We're going eighty miles an hour."
>   "You'd rather not die with me?"
>   "I can think of more pleasant ways to go." (174)

Even when they finally give themselves up to their passion (as Shimamoto
masturbates while fellating Hajime), Hajime cannot help but think of her as
connected to death. He recalls the seizure she had earlier:

> I recalled clearly what I'd seen deep within her eyes. A dark space, frozen
> hard like a subterranean glacier. A silence so profound it sucked up every
> sound, never allowing it to resurface. Absolute, total silence.
>   It was the first time I'd been face-to-face with death. So I'd had no
> distinct image of what death really was. But there it was then, right before
> my eyes, spread out just inches from my face. So this is the face of death,
> I'd thought. And death spoke to me, saying that my time, too, would one
> day come. Eventually everyone would fall into those endlessly lonely
> depths, the source of all darkness, a silence bereft of any resonance. I felt
> a choking, stifling fear as I stared into this bottomless dark pit. . . . Her
> regular breaths told me she was still on this side of the world. But her eyes
> told me she was already given up to death.
>   As I looked deep into her eyes and called out her name, my own body
> was dragged down into those depths. As if a vacuum had sucked out all the
> air around me, that other world was steadily pulling me closer. Even now
> I could feel its power. It wanted *me*. (183–184)

At the very moment that Hajime finally lives out his adolescent fantasy
of possessing Shimamoto, then, he cannot shake the feeling that his innocent
dreams are being subsumed by the "bottomless dark pit" of death. Shimamoto makes this connection even more explicit in a scene just preceding
their lovemaking, as they discuss the old record of Nat King Cole singing
"South of the Border" that gives the novel its title. Shimamoto contrasts the
image she'd had of "something beautiful, big, and soft" lying "south of the
border" with what lies "west of the sun." She tells of an illness called "hyste-

ria siberiana," in which farmers in Siberia, in an endless, featureless tract of land and after the mind-numbing routine of one day after another, find that eventually,

> "Something breaks inside you and dies. You toss your plow aside and, your head completely empty of thought, begin walking toward the west. Heading toward a land that lies west of the sun. Like someone possessed, you walk on, day after day, not eating or drinking, until you collapse on the ground and die. That's hysteria siberiana."
> I tried to conjure up the picture of a Siberian farmer lying dead on the ground.
> "But what is there, west of the sun?" I asked.
> She again shook her head. "I don't know. Maybe nothing. Or maybe something. At any rate, it's different from south of the border." (177)

Readers of *The Place That Was Promised* will be chilled by these words, written three years before the Aum subway attack. As Murakami argues there —using the poem of the same title by Mark Strand—"the place you were promised, you suddenly realize, has changed into something different from what you've been looking for."[38] In the context of *South of the Border,* Shimamoto starkly shows that the "promise" of a return to a narrative of innocence and purity—south of the border—the world to which she seemingly beckons Hajime—is inextricably transformed into a menacing narrative of death, west of the sun. As she puts it, challenging Hajime to join her forever on her side, the other world, "This is very important, so listen carefully. As I told you before, there is no middle ground with me. You take either all of me or nothing. That's the way it works" (178). After their lovemaking, Hajime pledges to cross over to her side, but Shimamoto delays his final decision until the next day when, she promises, she will tell him everything about herself and her life: "Stay the way you are today. If I did tell you now, you'd never be able to go back to the way you were" (186).[39]

The following morning, Shimamoto, and all traces of her, have inexplicably vanished, and Hajime is left forlorn and bewildered on *this* side. Does the book, as Rubin concludes, merely end "in middle-aged defeat"?[40] Though certainly a dream has been shattered, and, as Hajime puts it, the "thrill is gone" from much of what he previously enjoyed, is this really all Murakami wants to show—the crushing of middle-aged fantasies? Reading retrospectively in light of Aum, one finds Murakami, as in *Wonderland,* demonstrating the allure of a simple narrative of escape from the chaotic world, an escape that, in the end, leads to various kinds of death—in *Wonderland* to the death of the conscious self, in *South of the Border* to actual death. In *Place* Murakami imagined trying to change an Aum member's mind about the nature of reality, countering the hermetic, simplified logic of the Aum narrative with the fact that "reality is created out of confusion and contradiction." [41] Hajime is left in the confusion and contradiction of the real world. He is impressed—perhaps even weighed down—by a newly realized sense of responsibility toward his wife and children, creating a somewhat depressing ending. But he has escaped, though only barely, something far worse: he is lucky to have gotten out alive.

Is life always an either-or choice? Must one stay on this side, the chaotic, confused, and contradictory real world, or else give in to an inviting yet ultimately menacing other world from which one can never return? Is there, as Shimamoto tells Hajime, no middle ground? And does entering the other world always have to be fatal in one form or another? One might imagine that a year spent interviewing Aum members would convince Murakami more than ever of the impossibility of a middle ground. In some of the statements in the afterword to *Place,* and certainly in the post–September 11 interview cited above, he sets up an "open circuit/closed circuit" dichotomy that offers little hope of common ground. In the imaginative world of his post-Aum fiction, however, specifically in the novels *Sputnik Sweetheart* and *Kafka on the Shore,* one sees something else: Murakami beginning to construct a kind of counternarrative to the narrative of Aum—and to his own earlier fiction. In terms of a response to Aum, in *Underground* Murakami lays out a challenge to himself: "But were we able to offer 'them' [Aum members] a more viable narrative? . . . That was the big task. I am a novelist, and as we all know a novelist is someone who works with 'narratives,' who spins 'stories' professionally. Which meant to me that the task at hand was like a gigantic sword dangling above my head. It's something I'm going to have to deal with much more seriously from here on." [42] In his post-Aum fiction, I argue, Murakami extends the this world/other world thematic of his earlier work in an attempt to find a different relationship between the two: not a yawning abyss of separation, but rather an overlap in which the two worlds can touch in ways that are not explosive and deadly, but productive. These new narratives, and the characters' interaction with them, evince the other world as hopeful and even restorative to those who, in the final analysis, must live in the chaos that is reality.

In *Sputnik Sweetheart,* making Sumire a struggling writer is much more significant than just having her reflect some of the real-life situations of the Aum interviewees. For perhaps the first time in his fiction Murakami—as the challenge he sets himself above indicates—is seriously contemplating the role of one who professionally "spins 'stories.'" Sumire's writer's block makes for an interesting side plot in *Sputnik,* but it also conveniently allows Murakami to articulate the road ahead for himself and to offer those who feel alienated from contemporary Japan a new and viable narrative. As K explains to the frustrated Sumire, "A story is not something of this world. A real story requires a kind of magical baptism to link the world on this side with the world on the *other* side" (16). Murakami's task as a writer, as he now sees it, is exactly this: to provide, through his fiction, this very link.

The three main characters, K, Sumire, and Miu, share two things in common: they are all, in their own ways, alienated from life, and they all experience, to varying degrees, the other world while traveling abroad. K is perhaps the least obviously alienated of the three. A college graduate, he is like many Aum members in abhorring the typical post-graduation corporate route to "success," saying that, while he gave up on graduate school, this "didn't mean I was about to find a job in a normal company, claw my way through the cutthroat competition, and advance step-by-step up the slippery slope of the capitalist pyramid" (57). Instead he becomes (like one of the Aum interviewees) an elementary school teacher who finds a certain satisfaction in teaching, yet who continues to "draw an invisible boundary between myself and other people" (55); the only person he truly wants to reach out to, Sumire, has no romantic interest in him. Sumire, besides being frustrated in her attempts to become a writer, is confused about her sexuality, something that she connects with her writing: "I'm not proud of it," she tells K, "but I don't have any sexual desire. And what sort of experience can a writer have if she doesn't feel passion? I'd be like a chef without an appetite" (17). Slowly she awakens to the fact that she is a lesbian, but she in turn, much like K with her, finds the object of her desire, Miu, unresponsive. For her part, Miu is a former concert pianist who suddenly, after an uncanny and traumatic experience in Switzerland in her youth that robs her of sexual desire, "shuts the lid" on her piano forever and enters into marriage, and life, frigid. Miu's alienation from life is compounded by her status as a woman without a country: a Japanese of Korean heritage, she finds her parents' hometown "a town in a foreign country I'd never set eyes on before" (36). Though the most outwardly successful of the three (she owns a small but thriving import business and lives a Hajime-like upscale lifestyle in Tokyo), like K she has constructed barriers that prevent any meaningful contact with others.

All three characters' contact with the other world comes abroad and is filtered through the medium of dreams or mysterious visions. Murakami links the notion of temporal travel (in all three cases here to Europe) with travel of a spiritual kind. Abroad, apart from their everyday existence in Japan, these three characters begin to experience a breakdown or dissolution of the self. Sumire makes this point in her first letter to K from Rome:

> I'm writing this letter at an outdoor cafe on a side street in Rome, sipping espresso as thick as the devil's sweat, and I have this strange feeling that I'm not myself anymore. It's hard to put into words, but I guess it's like I was fast asleep, and somebody came, disassembled me, and hurriedly put me back together again. . . . My eyes tell me I'm the same old me, but something's different from usual. Not that I can clearly recall what "usual" was. Ever since I stepped off the plane I can't shake this very real, deconstructive illusion. (71)

For K, this breakdown begins even before he steps foot in Europe, in a dream as he waits in the departure lounge at Narita. As he dozes in an "unsettled sleep," "the world had lost all sense of reality":

> Colors were all unnatural, details crude. The background was papiermâché, the stars made out of aluminum foil. You could see the glue and the heads of the nails all holding it together. . . . In the midst of this illogical dream—or uncertain wakefulness—I thought of Sumire. . . . In the bustle of the airport, passengers dashing here and there, the world I shared with Sumire seemed shabby, helpless, uncertain. . . . There was nothing solid we could depend on. We were nearly boundless zeros, just pitiful little beings swept from one kind of oblivion to another. (84)

Miu's experience comes first, years before, when she is twenty-five and a piano student in Paris. She travels to a small town in Switzerland at her father's request to take care of some business for him. While there, she meets a Spaniard, Ferdinando, whose unexpected presence wherever she goes triggers a kind of paranoia in her mind: "Like a dissonant symbol at the beginning of a musical score, an ominous shadow began to cloud her pleasant summer."[43] A full-scale persecution complex begins to take over her psyche, and she sees the small town and its people arrayed against her. One evening she goes to the amusement park on the outskirts of the town and rides the Ferris wheel there just as the park is shutting down for the evening. The operator inadvertently turns off the ride while Miu is still inside, leaving her trapped high above the park all night. Miu reads, naps, drops notes for help to the ground, and otherwise tries to pass the chilly night. Finally she takes out a small pair of binoculars she has with her (earlier she had used them to spot her apartment building from the Ferris wheel). This time, though, she is in for the shock of her life. She sees *herself* in her apartment, making passionate love to Ferdinando. In Sumire's retelling of the incident she'd written down on her laptop computer,

> Miu couldn't drag her gaze away from this strange sight. She felt sick. Her throat was so parched she couldn't swallow. She felt like she was going to vomit. Everything was grotesquely exaggerated, menacing, like some medieval allegorical painting. This is what Miu thought: that they were deliberately showing her this scene. They know I'm watching. But still she couldn't pull her eyes away. (155)

Miu loses consciousness at this point, and is rescued the next morning by the police. Here again she is in for a shock, for when she looks in the mirror she finds her hair has turned entirely white. Along with this, she has lost any sexual desire:

> And Miu vanished.
> "I was still on *this* side, here [she explains to Sumire]. But *another me,* maybe half of me, had gone over to the *other side.* Taking with it my black hair, my sexual desire, my periods, my ovulation, perhaps even the will to live. And the half that was left is the person you see here. I've felt this way for the longest time—that in a Ferris wheel in a small Swiss town, for a reason I can't explain, I was split in two forever. For all I know, this may have been some kind of transaction. It's not like something was stolen away from me, because it all still exists, on the *other side.* Just a single mirror separates us from the other side. But I can never cross the boundary of that single pane of glass. Never. . . . I guess never is too strong a word. Maybe someday, somewhere, we'll meet again, and merge back into one." (157)

Sumire's journey to the other side is less well documented, for she disappears utterly, leaving behind only the words that preface this journey, most significantly her writing. Yet, as but the latest of many characters who disappear inexplicably in Murakami's fiction, she holds the key to the this world/other world dichotomy, for she—for the first time in his work—is a character who seemingly straddles both worlds. Because of Sumire's obsession with dreams and her view that dreams are the portal to the other side, K's explanation for her sudden disappearance is simply that she somehow dreamed herself there.[44] Comparing Miu's experience with Sumire's writing, K concludes,

This side—the other side. That was the common thread. The movement
from one side to the other. Sumire must have been drawn by this motif. . . .
 I decided to venture a theory.
 Sumire went over to the *other side.*
 That would explain a lot. Sumire broke through the mirror and jour-
neyed to the other side. To meet the other Miu who was there. If the Miu
on this side rejected her, wouldn't that be the logical thing to do?
 I dredged up from memory that she'd written: "So what should we do
to avoid a collision? Logically, it's easy. The answer is dreams. Dreaming
on and on. Entering the world of dreams, and never coming out. Living
there for the rest of time." (164–166)

"Sumire somehow found an exit," he muses further. "Just an ordinary door,
part of an ordinary wall. Sumire happened to find this door, turned the knob,
and slipped outside—from this side to the other. Clad only in thin silk pj's
and a pair of floppy sandals" (167).

In *Sputnik,* though, the journey to the other side is abbreviated, and what
Sumire may have found there can only be speculated about. The closest the
reader gets to the journey is the section in chapter 13, where K has his own
mysterious encounter with what may or may not be this other world. Here,
in a section expanded from the earlier short story "Hito kui neko" (translated
as "Man-Eating Cats"), K awakens one night on the Greek island to the sound
of music from the top of a nearby hill.[45] As he ventures up the hill in search
of the source of the music, he gradually feels a part of himself slipping away:

My hand was no longer my hand, my legs no longer my legs.
 Bathed in the pallid moonlight, my body, like some plaster puppet,
had lost all living warmth. . . .
 An awful chill swept through me and I felt choked. Someone had
rearranged my cells, untied the threads that held my mind together. I
couldn't think straight. All I was able to do was retreat as fast as I could to
my usual place of refuge. I took a huge breath, sinking in the sea of consciousness to the very bottom. (170)

After overcoming this encounter with a mysterious other world—perhaps
the very same journey Sumire took to completion—K speculates on the
nature of this other world that he has, perhaps, just brushed by:

What is it like—on *the other side?* Sumire was over there, and so was the
lost part of Miu. Miu with black hair and a healthy sexual appetite. Perhaps

they've run across each other there, loving each other, fulfilling each other. "We do things you can't put into words," Sumire would probably tell me, putting it into words all the same.

Is there a place for me over there? Could I be with them? (178)

Taken together with the final scene of the novel, where Sumire ostensibly phones K to tell him she has returned (quoted above), *Sputnik* winds up with a vision of the "other side" that differs considerably from that found in either of the pre-Aum novels *Wonderland* or *South of the Border*. In these two novels, the other side, while greatly appealing as a refuge from the chaos of real life, is in the end a negative place, where one loses both the physical self and the conscious mind. Further, it is a world in which there is, in Shimamoto's words, "no middle ground." As in the spiritual world delineated by someone such as Asahara, it is a place with no exit, no escape. One either is taken all the way over, with little hope of real escape (the narrator in *Wonderland*), or remains behind in the world on *this* side (Hajime in *South of the Border*), staring at the yawning abyss separating one side from the other. *Sputnik*, however, through the challenge thrown up by Aum, attempts to create a newly imagined relationship between the two worlds. Instead of ending up a world of loss, the other side is now a world of reconciliation, restoration, and above all, hope. Further, for the first time, with the character of Sumire, Murakami suggests that a positive linkage exists between the two worlds: in the final lines, Sumire is "looking at the same moon" as K, *"in the same world"* (210, emphasis added). Sumire on the other side and K here in the real are "connected to reality by the same line." K imagines, "All I have to do is quietly draw it toward me" (210). In pulling in the line that connects them both to "reality," does K draw Sumire closer to this side, is he dragged closer to the other, or, more likely, do he and Sumire meet in some now possible "middle ground"? As Rubin notes, readers are divided over how to understand this final scene. Is it, as one reader insists, an hallucination, or is it a happy ending showing that Sumire would return? In a world where dreams are as real as anything else, an hallucination may have its own valid reality. Is this all merely K's speculation and wishful thinking?[46] Perhaps, but I opt for something closer to the second reading: if not a "happy" ending, then at least a hopeful one, a tentative step toward a narrative showing that one may not only dream of, but even experience, a place where the promises—unlike in Aum—are actually kept.

In a lengthy interview conducted several months after the publication of his 2002 novel *Umibe no Kafuka* (translated as *Kafka on the Shore;* hereafter

Kafka), Murakami notes that he first intended the work to be a sequel to *Hardboiled Wonderland and the End of the World*. Though soon abandoning the idea of a chronological sequel, however, Murakami retained the basic structure of parallel stories, though not of parallel worlds. Whereas *Wonderland* depicts events in the parallel worlds of the unconscious and the conscious of one protagonist, events that increasingly overlap as the story progresses, Murakami sees *Kafka* as showing a more complex structure in which two parallel stories (again told in alternating chapters) each reveal equal amounts of the "real" and the "unreal" *(genjitsu, higenjitsu),* with these four "factors" overlapping.[47] Thus a two-part structure is now a four-part one.

There are numerous obvious elements in *Kafka* that link it with *Wonderland*. Libraries play a crucial role in both novels, as do woods and shadows.[48] In *Kafka* the main character, Tamura Kafka, ends up living and working in a small library, where (shades of *Wonderland*) he falls in love with the much older head librarian. *Wonderland* ended with the protagonist's bidding farewell to his shadow as he set out to explore the spiritual limbo of the Woods; *Kafka,* with a protagonist who makes extended journeys through the dense forests of Shikoku, offers a glimpse of what this exploration might be like. Likewise, in *Kafka* shadows haunt the landscape, either through their absence —the idea that certain characters have lost half their shadow—or through dialogues between the eponymous Kafka and his own "shadow," an alter ego named Crow.[49] But the contrasts between the books are more striking than their similarities. In *Sputnik,* his first post-Aum work, Murakami had hinted at the restorative nature of contact with the other world; in *Kakfa,* however, for the first time, he details the spiritual journey to the other side—*and back* —and reveals the process by which such a journey leads to healing. In doing this Murakami explores a number of related topics: ghosts, spirits, and the idea, found as far back as *The Tale of Genji,* of *ikiryō* (living spirits), souls or spirits that separate from their bodies while a person is still alive.

Half of *Kafka* (the odd-numbered chapters) is the first person story of a fifteen-year-old boy, Tamura Kafka (his real given name is never disclosed), who runs away from his home in Tokyo to the island of Shikoku. Kafka, the son of a famous sculptor, Tamura Koichi, was abandoned by his mother when he was four (though she took along his older adopted sister when she left). Growing up in a house already "dead," in his words, and totally alienated from his aloof father and everyone else, Kafka spends a lonely adolescence preparing for the day when he can escape both his father and the Oedipal curse laid upon him, that he will one day murder his father and sleep with his mother. As the novel opens, Kafka is packing for his journey, which he decides will take him to Shikoku, while talking with his alter ego, "a boy called Crow."

Crow becomes a kind of one-man chorus (the notion of the chorus in Greek tragedies is explored briefly along the way) or sounding board who appears in particularly stressful times to advise and/or chide Kafka. Kafka winds up at the Komura Library, a small private library specializing in Japanese poetry, where he is befriended by a cross-dressing young woman named Oshima. At the library he meets the mysterious older head librarian, Miss Saeki.

One night Kafka awakens in the woods behind a shrine to find himself covered with blood. He has no memory of what has happened, though he soon learns that back in Tokyo his father was brutally murdered the same night. Is it possible, Kafka asks, that his anger toward his father sent his vengeful spirit out to kill him? He goes to live in a room in the library, where he can hide from the police, who naturally want to question him, and also assist Oshima. At the library Kafka encounters a ghost, that of Miss Saeki at age fifteen. Miss Saeki, it turns out, was in love with the eldest son of the Komura family who opened the library. A talented pianist, at nineteen she composed a haunting song to her lover entitled "Kafka on the Shore," which became an unexpected hit. Her lover, though, was brutally and mistakenly murdered by student radicals during the uprisings in Tokyo in the late 1960s, and Miss Saeki disappeared from Shikoku. Now, some three decades later, Miss Saeki has returned to the library to become head librarian. At night, though, her living spirit awakens as herself at age fifteen and appears in the room where Kafka is staying, the same room where Miss Saeki's lover lived, and where a painting of him, done when he was twelve and also entitled "Kafka on the Shore," hangs on the wall. Kafka falls in love with this ghostly girl and with the echoes of her he sees in the real-life Miss Saeki (who he is convinced is his missing mother).

Eventually he and the real-life Miss Saeki, who shows up in his room in a somnambulistic state, sleep together. She presumably is trying to recreate her adolescent love, while Kafka suffers from a complex mix of desire for the fifteen-year-old ghost and desire to fulfill the curse on him, thereby overcoming it. Meanwhile, Oshima has introduced Kafka to a remote cabin deep in the forested mountains of Shikoku, where he goes for a few days to lie low while the police search for him. Here, on his second visit to the deep forests surrounding this mountain retreat, Kafka undergoes the transformative journey to the other world that is the core of the novel.

The parallel story, told in the even-numbered chapters of *Kafka*, centers on the second main character, an old man named Nakata Satoru. Before meeting Nakata, the reader is given the backstory to his present life in a series of U.S. Army documents, interviews, and a letter. As a young boy he was evacuated to a small town in Yamanashi prefecture during World War Two, and was one of a class of sixteen children who, while on an outing in the hills to gather mushrooms, all simultaneously fell into a brief catatonic state. While the other children regained consciousness in a few hours with no memory of the event, Nakata remained unconscious for three weeks, only to awaken with his mind wiped clean. He was unable to speak and had no knowledge of the world around him. The story rejoins Nakata in Tokyo in the present, where he is a mildly retarded old man living alone on welfare. He picks up extra cash by finding lost cats. Though unable to read and function normally in society, Nakata has special abilities that set him apart, particularly his ability to speak with cats.

In his search for one particular cat, Nakata one day encounters a mysterious "cat catcher" named Johnnie Walker. (Like the later character Colonel Sanders, we are to understand him as, in Sanders' words, disembodied "concepts" beyond our normal world.) Johnnie Walker has found the cat Nakata is searching for, as well as many others. In a gruesome chapter, he demonstrates how, as part of his project to collect souls, he rips out the hearts of his still-living cat victims. Gentle, mild-mannered Nakata can no longer stand watching these vivisections and, at Johnnie Walker's urging, stabs him to put a stop to them. After killing Johnnie Walker, Nakata attempts to turn himself in, but the police rebuff him, thinking his story crazy, and he sets off west, driven to fulfill a mission that becomes clear only later. Along the way he is befriended by a young truck driver, Hoshino, and the two of them end up in Takamatsu in search of a mysterious "entrance stone."

Once Hoshino and Nakata have, with much effort, located and "opened" the entrance stone by flipping it over, Kafka, in his own journey through the forest, is able to enter the other world. There he discovers, in a setting reminiscent of the Town in *Wonderland,* both Miss Saeki as a fifteen-year-old and the present-day Miss Saeki, who during his absence has peacefully passed away. Just before this, though, Hoshino has helped Nakata discover the end of his search, which is the library where Kafka has been staying. There Nakata meets Miss Saeki, who understands him to be the one she has been waiting for, the one who will take her to the other side, facilitating her death. (The reader also learns that Miss Saeki has in the past opened the entrance stone herself and gone over to the other side.) Miss Saeki entrusts Nakata with a huge manuscript, the story of her life, which she has been writing for years, asking him to burn it. Immediately after this she dies, and soon after Nakata also dies. Hoshino, now on the "edge of the world" and suddenly heir to Nakata's ability to speak with cats, receives a warning from one cat. At all costs he is not to let a mysterious creature that will appear pass through the "entrance," for this would have dire consequences for the world. Unable to fend off the steady advance of the slug-like creature that oozes out of Nakata's mouth and heads toward the stone, Hoshino closes the entrance stone, destroying the creature.

Kafka is most certainly Murakami's most intense exploration of violence and evil to date.[50] In an interview about the novel, he states,

> I've been contemplating evil for a long time. For some reason, for a long while I've been thinking that in order to deepen and broaden my fiction, evil would have to be a necessary element. I was considering how I should write about it. This thought first came to me right after I completed *Hard-boiled Wonderland.* After that, the notion of evil was always on my mind.[51]

Yoked with this has been Murakami's stated concern, since the twin 1995 calamities of Aum and the Kobe earthquake, with the potential for violence that is barely hidden below the surface of everyday life in Japan.

Kafka takes violence far beyond anything found in *Sputnik.* In *Sputnik* it is always the *potential* for violence and bloodshed that is underscored, rather than its realization. There, for instance, K calls killing and bloodshed a "metaphor" for the kind of "magical baptism" linking "the world on this side with the world on the *other* side" (16). And in the concluding words of story, where K looks at his hands after his mysterious conversation with Sumire: "I spread my fingers apart and stare at the palms of both hands, looking for bloodstains. There aren't any. No scent of blood, no stiffness. The blood must have already, in its own silent way, seeped inside" (210). For all its own talk of the uses of metaphor, *Kafka* brings violence and evil right to the surface. Blood is not something that has "seeped inside," but something that gushes out, bathing both Kafka and Nakata in red. In the gruesome vivisections of the cats by Johnnie Walker, in both his death and in the stabbing death of what he stands for (Kafka's father), as well as in numerous other scenes—the mindless violence of punk bikers; the instructions of an Imperial army trooper on the best way to kill with a bayonet; Crow ripping Johnnie Walker to bloody shreds; Hoshino stabbing the slug-like embodiment of evil—Murakami more than ever before confronts the presence of evil in the world and the ways in which violence begets violence.[52]

Readers of *Underground,* of course, will note the obvious question Murakami is raising: is violence a necessary step on the way to the other side, to a religious or spiritual experience of something beyond our world? With Aum and so many other cults answering in the affirmative, Murakami counters with a narrative that both confronts and attempts to defuse this linkage. Much of the trail Kafka treads toward his final encounter with the other world in the woods is certainly paved in death and bloodshed. But in the person of his alter ego, Crow, the final violent attack on Johnnie Walker (in a section right after chapter 46), and Hoshino's parallel attack on the slug-like evil being together reinforce a major point: at all costs evil must be kept from infiltrating and tainting the "other side." If violence is allowed to flourish, in this case to enter the other side through the entrance stone, Kafka's spiritual journey will be incomplete; he will remain, like the narrator in *Wonderland,* stuck on the other side—either literally dead or dead to the world. Likewise, the keepers of the entrance to the other world, the two unnamed spirits of former Imperial troopers who deserted in these woods sixty years before, are people who have, significantly, *rejected violence.* (They carry rifles, but these are, in their words, "useless" because they have no bullets in them.) As Kafka first confronts them as he forges deeper into the forest, they explain:

> "If we hadn't found this spot, they would have shipped us off overseas," the brawny one explains. "Over there it was kill or be killed. That wasn't for us. I'm a farmer, originally, and my buddy here just graduated from college. Neither one of us wants to kill anybody. And being killed's even worse. Kind of obvious, I'd say."
>
>   "How 'bout you? Would you like to kill anybody, or be killed?" the tall one asks me.
>
>   I shake my head. There's no way I want to kill anybody, or get killed.[53]

In fact, *Kafka* shows how it is precisely only those who desire to *escape* violence and evil who are able to make the journey to the other side. The two soldiers, of course, with their rejection of violence as a means of countering violence and evil, are examples, but so are most of the main characters in the novel. Miss Saeki, as becomes clear late in the story, found the entrance to the other side soon after the shock of her lover's violent death in the student revolt. Nakata's teacher reveals, years after the mysterious mass coma of children during the war, that her young charge was clearly the victim of an insidious type of domestic violence—thus he is the one who remains, for as long as possible, on the other side after the incident. And of course there is Kafka himself, who is on a mission to overcome the violence and evil he considers part of his genetic makeup, and the anger and hurt his abandonment by his mother have engendered.[54]

Murakami might open himself up to the charge here of naiveté in regard to violence and evil with his suggestion that they can somehow be totally overcome. But the reality is quite the opposite—at every step of the way evil and violence are there, powerful forces that must be acknowledged and confronted, and these forces are forever threatening to reappear. Johnnie Walker is not a being who can be permanently defeated (he literally laughs in the face of this notion); likewise, there is the suggestion that Kafka's own violent tendencies are hardwired into him, part of his DNA, something that cannot be overcome permanently or totally, but only dealt with when they arise. The powerful and disturbing message "kill or be killed" that Johnnie Walker teaches Nakata, as well as the events of the final chapters, show that evil must be constantly battled, a message quite unlike that of Aum. Violence is not the *means* to the other world, as Asahara's confused apocalyptic "narrative" implies, but the exact opposite—a *barrier* to a true spiritual encounter and restoration.[55]

What this other side entails, though, and what humans' relationship to it can and should be, is certainly not simple. On the one hand, there are characters such as Miss Saeki and Nakata (paralleled in *Sputnik* by, respectively, Miu and Carrot), who both have an element missing on this side that is found only on the other—in Miss Saeki's case, normal warmth and loving feelings; in Nakata's, normal intelligence and ability to function in the world. Unlike the narrator of *Wonderland,* whose mind/consciouness remains on the other side while his shadow returns to this side, with Miss Saeki and Nakata the situation is reversed. They must rejoin the other half of their shadows on the other side to be fulfilled and complete. For them, fulfillment can come only in a permanent transition to the other side; hence the inevitability of their deaths. This idea of completeness, not coincidentally, is first raised by Oshima, who tells Kafka of the notion (in Plato's *Banquet*) of human beings as having been split by God into male and female halves, with the resultant loneliness and alienation humans feel as they search for their other half.[56] Miss Saeki, Oshima explains, is a perfect example of this, for her "second half," her dead boyfriend, is on the other side, and her happiness can come only in rejoining him. Likewise, Nakata longs throughout the novel to become once again a "normal Nakata," to reincorporate his normal intelligence, specifically his ability to read, that was left on the other side after his childhood journey there. (And thus the irony, as Hoshino points out, of Nakata's final act on earth—the illiterate man who seeks to be literate burning a manuscript that no one will ever read.)

For some characters, then, the other side is a permanent destination, a place of hoped-for restoration, but also a one-way street to which only physical death on *this* side can lead. To use the image of the library—a repository of knowledge—that infuses the novel, there is on the other side a repository of all that goes up to make the characters complete and truly human. For Miss

Saeki the library is also the concrete site of her fulfillment, the ultimate place "beyond time" where as a young girl she was supremely happy; for Nakata, who is only now, for the first time in his life, visiting a library, it represents fulfillment of a different sort, namely, access to reading, writing, and his own fully functional mind.

For Kafka himself, however, there is time to wrest fulfillment from contact with the other side and yet return, restored, to live in this world. Unlike the older characters, Kafka has not reached the point of no return in life, and this is what the novel is about. *Kafka* highlights the importance of bridges: both Kafka and Nakata must first cross physical bridges to reach Shikoku, and it is the musical bridge in the song "Kafka on the Shore" (and the mysterious two chords that introduce it) that connects this pop song to the world of the surreal.[57] Kafka, in his journey, must cross the forest, which bridges one world and another. The motivation for his journey, parallels Sumire's in *Sputnik,* the search for the lost mother.[58] In the writings she left behind, Sumire longs for her mother, who died when she was a child. Recall her dream of her mother crammed into a small hole, like a ventilation shaft. Sumire cries out to her, but she is eventually "sucked into that black hole."[59] One might easily see Sumire's love for Miu, seventeen years her senior, less in terms of lesbian desire than in terms of looking for a substitute mother figure.

Kafka pushes this motif of searching for the mother further, creating the wrenching alienation of a young boy whose mother abandoned him, not through death, but by choice. Complex emotions of unforgiveness for the mother who abandoned him are what drive Kafka, and it is only at the climax of the story, when he meets his mother, or what he takes to be his mother— the spirit of the dead Miss Saeki in the forest Town—and accepts her plea for forgiveness, that he is saved.

> "A long time ago I abandoned someone I shouldn't have," she [Miss Saeki] says. "Someone I loved more than anything else. I was afraid someday I'd lose this person. So I had to let go myself. If he was going to be stolen away from me, or I was going to lose him by accident, I decided it was better to discard him myself. Of course I felt anger that didn't fade, that was part of it. But the whole thing was a huge mistake. It was someone I should never have thrown away."
>
> I listen in silence.
>
> "You were discarded by the one person who should never have done that," Miss Saeki says. "Kafka—do you forgive me?"
>
> "Do I have the right to?"

She looks at my shoulder and nods several times. "As long as anger and fear don't prevent you."

"Miss Saeki, if I really do have the right to, then yes—I do forgive you," I tell her.

Mother, you say. I forgive you. And with those words, audibly, the frozen part of your heart crumbles.[60]

Readers will recall the climactic scene of Miura Ayako's *Freezing Point II,* when another young person abandoned at a tender age by her mother, Yōko, finally finds it in her heart to forgive her, as well as the shared vocabulary in which both depict a "frozen" life or heart succumbing to the power of forgiveness. Murakami's *Kafka* lacks the Christian message of Miura's novel, but in both the power of forgiveness—in one way or another—rescues the lost. In *Kafka,* as Crow puts it,

Even though she loved you, she had to abandon you. You need to understand how she felt then, and learn to accept it. Understand the overpowering fear and anger she experienced, and feel it as your own—so you won't inherit it and repeat it. The main thing is this: you have to *forgive* her. That's not going to be easy, I know, but you have to do it. That's the only way you can be saved. There's no other way![61]

Only by finally having a forgiving heart can Kafka return from the other side, not only "saved," but also willing to abandon life as a runaway, take responsibility, and live fully as part of a "brand new world."[62]

A related spiritual dimension of *Kafka* goes back to a decidedly Japanese spiritual tradition: the idea of *ikiryō,* or spirits of the living. After his first midnight encounters with the ghostly figure of the fifteen-year-old Miss Saeki, which appears in Kafka's room at the library, sits transfixed for a time gazing at the painting on the wall, then disappears into thin air, Kafka raises the issue with Oshima, who explains about *ikiryō* and the most famous manifestation of these, the incident in *The Tale of Genji* in which the jealousy of one lover of Prince Genji, Lady Rokujo, makes her spirit, unbeknownst to her, leave her body to possess and torment her rival, Lady Aoi. After discussing these spirits as "the darkness within us" that, unlike peoples of earlier times, modern people do not normally acknowledge or confront, Kafka asks,

"What triggers people to become living spirits? Is it always something negative?" I ask.

"I'm no expert, but as far as I know, yes, those living spirits all spring up out of negative emotions. Most of the extreme feelings people have tend to be very individual, and negative. And these living spirits arise through a kind of spontaneous generation. Sad to say, there aren't any cases of a living spirit emerging to fulfill some logical premise or bring about world peace."

"What about because of love?"

Oshima sits down and thinks it over.

"That's a tough one. All I can tell you is I've never run across an example."[63]

The only spirits in the classical canon who act out of love, Oshima notes (citing *Ugetsu monogatari*) are ghosts of the dead. The combination of living spirits and positive, not negative, motivation is most likely unknown. In creating in Miss Saeki's *ikiryō* a figure that combines the two (and I would argue as well that Crow is Kafka's *ikiryō*)—an outpouring of manifested, living spirit in the service of something *positive*—Murakami once again creates his own counternarrative to the dark dreams of the Aum leader Asahara. In no uncertain terms Murakami makes it clear that there is a spiritual side to human beings, and that this (in the form of an *ikiryō*) may reach out in love and hope for healing. Many Aum members seemed to want just this, only to be betrayed by darker visions.[64]

What is apparent, then, in Murakami's post-Aum fiction, is the very process he referred to at the time of *Place,* "the time-consuming process of shaping [the Aum experience] into narrative form." In *Kafka* in particular the vision is of a way into and out of the other side. The other side is seen as a place of reconciliation and restoration, and the return to this chaotic world occurs only after soul-searching of the very deepest kind.

CHAPTER FOUR

Literature of the Soul

Ōe Kenzaburō's *Somersault*

I n September 1994, after he completed the third and final volume of his massive novel *Moeagaru midori no ki* (The Flaming Green Tree; hereafter *Moeagaru*), Ōe Kenzaburō declared that his long career was over and that he would not be writing any more novels. Since Ōe had been making similar statements since the mid-1980s, many editors and critics did not take him seriously.[1] Clearly, though, Ōe felt he had reached a turning point in his career. He had noted his desire to finish writing novels at the age of sixty (1995),[2] and with the completion of the *Moeagaru* trilogy in his sixtieth year, a work that was, in his words, "the product of all my literary themes and writing techniques," he declared, "I have already written what I need to write."[3] On a more personal note, after his son Hikari's career as a composer began to flourish around the same time, Ōe said, "I thought I would give up writing. I wrote always to be a voice for Hikari, but when he found his own voice in music I did not need to write further."[4]

Ironically, it was only a month after his declaration that his career as novelist was over that he was awarded, in October 1994, the Nobel Prize for Literature. Not long afterward, declaring he "felt empty without writing," Ōe began a private project, a chronicle of world history that allows him to "reflect on the nature of the Japanese and contemplate human nature as a whole."[5] As early as the presentation ceremony for the Nobel Prize, Ōe was already having second thoughts, saying he was thinking of writing in a "new literary form that, in the final analysis . . . might be something you would call a novel."[6] It was not, however, until five years later that Ōe broke his self-imposed silence as a novelist with the lengthy novel *Chūgaeri* (translated in 2002 as *Somersault*). Advertising in Japan for the novel played up the notion that with it Ōe had broken his avowed silence, a point made by the title, with its implication of a renunciation or a reversal of belief. The story is both that of a fictional character who has broken his own vow of silence and that of the author himself.

But what compelled Ōe to return to the novel? Critics in Japan have noted two deaths that may have propelled Ōe to write again: the death of his close friend, the composer Takemitsu Tōru (to whom *Somersault* is dedicated), and the tragic suicide of his brother-in-law, the film director Itami Jūzō (on which the novel following *Somersault*, called *Changeling*, focuses).[7] More significant than either was the subway attack by Aum Shinrikyō. Ōe seemed to have been prescient about Aum. The final volume of *Moeagaru*, which deals with a religious cult, a charismatic leader, and violence, was published in March 1995, the very month of the Aum attack. For quite some time before this, Ōe had expressed a desire to write about religious and spiritual issues. In an August 1993 interview just before the first part of *Moeagaru* was published, for instance, he stated a desire to do "spiritual things" *(tamashii no koto)* and a hope that *Moeagaru* would be his final summation of this desire. As the novelist Kaga Otohiko noted, after reading the first two volumes of the novel:

> The novel is laced with episodes of death and rebirth, martyrdom and resurrection, grace and the Holy Spirit, and prayer. Themes Ōe has developed through expressive imagery in earlier works—the cosmos, the mind of the forest, awakening, mythic metaphors, conversion—are presented in *The Flaming Green Tree* as themes bearing on the soul—grace, the Holy Spirit, prayer. I see this as marking the advent of a new "literature of soul." ... Though I do not presume to regard this as representing his approach to a specific religion, I can sense, through the works of the last 10 years, that he has caught sight of a destination.[8]

As Ozaki Mariko notes, though, the ending of *Moeagaru*, the stoning to death of the wheelchair-bound religious leader as he abandons his flock for missionary work, left many readers unsatisfied, and Ōe himself was dissatisfied with the work.[9] Ozaki also points out an interesting pattern in Ōe's work: he follows up a complex novel by rewriting it in a more accessible idiom. He began with the 1979 novel *Dōjidai geemu* (The game of contemporaneity); this work, a dense look at the myths of Ōe's Ur-village in Shikoku, was soon followed by the 1986 *M/T to mori no fushigi no monogatari*, essentially a more accessible retelling of many of the same stories. Likewise, *Moeagaru* was followed by *Somersault*, a continuation of the Shikoku saga (and of the tale of the Church of the Flaming Green Tree), written, as was *M/T,* in a more reader-friendly style.[10] At any rate, by the time Ōe went to Princeton University in September 1996, to begin a one-year position as visiting scholar, he had already announced he would begin writing a new novel. While in Princeton he wrote some 3,600 manuscript pages (Ōe is one of the last Japanese novelists to write out his novels by hand on manuscript paper), which were, over the next year, pared down to half this length. The result was *Somersault,* published in June 1999.[11]

Like Murakami's *Underground, Somersault* is Ōe's artistic response to the Aum terrorist attacks that shook Japan to its core. Unlike Murakami, however, Ōe starts less with the ordinary members than with the leaders of the cult. Ōe states that he began by imagining two different reactions the Aum leader Asahara might have in court: he could either insist he's completely correct, or announce he's wrong and disband the church. In *Somersault,* Ōe says, he decided to explore the second alternative, how someone rebuilds his life after renouncing his spiritual beliefs.[12] Ōe did not forget the role of less exalted members, though, and much of the novel is his attempt to delineate the forces driving a variety of young people toward joining a cult. As he puts it, "Although I think Aum members are wrong, as a novelist it is necessary for me to enter their spiritual world and imagine how their souls function."[13]

The plot of *Somersault* itself is quite simple, with narrative forward movement often coming to a halt as the reader is drawn into lengthy discourses on Patron's and others' views of God.[14] Critics such as Shimizu Tetsuya speculated (before *Somersault*) about a new style Ōe might invent that "freely goes among poetry, essay, and criticism," and indeed *Somersault* is largely constructed of these three elements: in addition to the main plot with Patron and Guide there are numerous theological discourses on outside texts (e.g., Jonah, Ephesians), as well as lengthy discussions of poetry (in particular the poetry of R. S. Thomas).[15]

The plot revolves around the renewed religious movement led by two cult leaders, nicknamed Patron and Guide. In the 1980s Patron and Guide had been the leaders of an apocalyptic religious cult that reached a crisis when radical members, dissatisfied with Patron's simple call for repentance, devised a plan to bring on the apocalypse by occupying and blowing up Japanese nuclear power plants. To defuse this calamity, Patron and Guide went on national television to denounce their beliefs and the cult, then went into a decade-long seclusion. *Somersault* begins ten years after these events, in a post-Aum world, where Patron and Guide are gradually piecing together a new religious group with new followers—most prominently Kizu, a well-known painter dying of cancer; Ikuo, Kizu's gay lover, who is obsessed with the biblical book of Jonah and the notion of apocalyptic destruction it contains; and Dancer, Patron's assistant. Patron's new group eventually moves to the small village in Shikoku occupied by the earlier Church of the Flaming Green Tree in *Moeagaru* (they take over the earlier church's facilities and chapel and work together with the former leader's widow), and it is here that *Somersault* becomes a kind of sequel to the earlier novel.

After Guide dies as a result of his interrogation by former members of the radical faction, Patron undertakes the task of reconciliation, inviting various remnants of his earlier cult to live together in the village. These include the so-called Technicians, former radical faction members, as well as the Quiet Women, a group of women who stayed true to Patron's beliefs, leading an ascetic communal life in hopes of experiencing—as an act of faith—the same feelings of being in "hell" that Patron himself experienced after his apostasy.

As Patron organizes his new church—the activities all aimed at a summer retreat and mass meeting to launch the movement formally—readers learn more about the backgrounds of Kizu, Ikuo, and various other followers. Kizu, seeking comfort in his newfound gay relationship with Ikuo and hoping that Patron will provide a physical cure for his disease, is commissioned by Patron to paint a large picture symbolizing the history of the new movement that will serve as the centerpiece in the chapel. Ikuo, for his part, seeks in Patron an intermediary who can help him regain the voice of God he heard as a young child, when he murdered an American who had forced him into a homosexual relationship.

The climax of the novel comes at a mass meeting in the summer. Patron, delivering his final sermon to launch the new movement, reiterates the idea (from Ephesians) that the "old men" (such as Patron) must step aside in favor of the "new men" (such as Ikuo), who will lead the movement in the future. A fiery bonfire is lit to mark the end of the meeting, and to the shock of the hundreds of spectators, Patron commits suicide in the flames.

The main focus of *Somersault* is the religious vision of Patron and Guide as leaders of the cult. As Numano Mitsuyoshi notes, the novel often takes time out for lengthy religious discourse.[16] While Numano sees this as drawing the reader deeper into the novel, many others have noted that this explication of spiritual views is excessive and repetitive. Certainly the religious discourse in *Somersault* is by far the most detailed and compelling in any of Ōe's fiction to date. If, as Kaga Otohiko writes, Ōe's literature from the late 1980s onward is "literature of the soul," *Somersault* affords us the most detailed portrait yet of Ōe's views on God, salvation, the afterlife, apostasy, faith, and the spiritual life, and is thus by far Ōe's most "soulful" work. The novel also reveals other aspects of great interest. First is the confrontation between an indigenous, pantheistic, animistic spiritual orientation and, in the words of one character, an "anti-Japanese religious philosophy" (508), namely, the more monotheistic, Christian-influenced views Patron brings into the village. Is Ōe aiming at a syncretism, a melding of pantheism and monotheism, or more a dialectic between the two? Second, *Somersault* is an expression of what might best be called Ōe's essential stance of "existential theism," the notion that, in the words of Patron, "even if God is completely out of the picture, one can still speak of belief" (353). Paralleling the decentering movement seen in this and earlier novels, that is, that this peripheral, backwoods village is now a sort of new Center, and that the marginal has become the center, one sees a recentering of the focus of belief away from the typical spiritual center (God, the transcendent) onto something new and still in the process of being defined and configured.

Patron is a visionary, and in his personal visions, seen in trances, he brings back the unique view of the "other side," the "transcendent," that engages his followers and propels his religious movement. Ōe mentions in passing the seventeenth-century Jewish messianic figure Sabbatai Zevi, and it is clear that Patron is loosely modeled on him. Sabbatai, a prophetic and visionary figure who was seen by many Jews worldwide as the messiah until his forcible conversion to Islam, was clearly a manic-depressive, alternating "states of excessive mental exaltation" with "periods of dejection and melancholia." [17] Likewise, one of our earliest and most memorable views of Patron is when he is in the throes of "a state . . . not one of his deep trances, but something close to it":

> What he [Kizu] saw now on the low chair was Patron, legs resting on a stool the height of two shoe boxes, head stuck deep between his widespread knees, arms hanging straight down on each side, unmoving. . . . Patron seemed totally absorbed. He held his body in a way you would never expect from a living human being. He sat there, utterly still, every semblance of humanity gone. (106)

If this prelude to a "deep trance" is the depressive side, Patron's "deep trance" itself more resembles the manic state: his movements are "so violent that after a deep trance he's completely spent, physically and emotionally." Afterward, according to Guide, "He says all kinds of complex things, as if he's possessed. He says he's standing in front of a kind of three-dimensional mesh, a display screen on which a blur of light is continuously changing, receiving information" (106). And, like Nathan of Gaza, Sabbatai's companion, who interpreted his visions, it is Guide's role to put these "complex things" into intelligible language.

> What does Patron see in these visions of the "other side"? As Guide puts it: "Patron seems to confront some kind of white glowing object. . . . Patron can freely view the entire course of human history and experience every last detail. He traces it all with his own body. He conveys to us what he's learned about the history of mankind and even its future, speaking to us—in the *present*—of the end time." (106)

Interestingly, in light of the cult's later move to the "Hollow," a section of a village in Shikoku, the "blur of light" that Patron sees in his trances is "more like a bottomless hollow":

> The entire hollow is a kind of spinning and weaving net, and the net with its countless layers is a screen that reveals human existence in one fell swoop, from its beginning to its end, and each point on that net is moving forward. It covers everything from the origins of time—nothing other than the first signs of the Big Bang to come—to the time when everything flows back to the one ultimate being. That whole huge spinning hollow, Patron told me, you could call God. In other words, as he sits there with his head between his knees like a weighed-down fetus, he's about to embark on a trance in which he'll come face to face with that God. (108)

In a conversation with Kizu, who after the death of the original Guide becomes Patron's new Guide, Patron reveals that, in a mysterious incident when he was a young boy, a stranger came up to him at a concert and said to him, "You are a unique person, and there's something written about you in . . ." (143). Taking a hint from the elusive book referred to, Kizu suggests that the information net Patron sees in his visions is itself a kind of book: "The other day the idea came to me that perhaps this whitely glowing model itself is that one-of-a-kind book you told us about. So when you're in your trance you're focused entirely on reading that book" (144). Patron agrees, adding that, unlike a book, which can't be changed as you read it, in this vision of "rapidly moving particles" and a "glowing white object" you can "read your own present . . . and you can live it and change your future" (145). Later he expands on this point:

To use a simpler metaphor, it's a book unlike any other, a book within a book, which includes the entire world, the entire universe. I'm on the other side, reading it. This means being conscious of things that transcend the real world, that tie together past and future. Reading this book also means I'm alive in this world, and by living I'm writing new sections of it. . . . What I read in that book is the entire past and future of the world—indeed of the universe—but what happens is that even my own insignificant individual actions, my own passing thoughts, very subtly rewrite the whole. And in this I find evidence that my trifling individual self is one of the saviors of humanity. (154–155)

Patron's vision is of a more active, two-way relationship with God, a dialogue with the transcendent that leaves open the possibility of rewriting the "book." As Guide puts it, "Let us have faith that even the prayers of the weak and the helpless such as ourselves may write one new line in that massive book" (155). Human beings' relationship with God is at one point likened also to a "bundle of fiber-optic lines," with individuals at the termini of each line connected to the "enormous structure that is God" (109). This idea comes up in the ongoing concern of Ikuo about whether he will once again be able to hear the voice of God commanding him, "Do it!" that is, take explosive, violent action. But as *Somersault* progresses the human–God relationship changes from a simpler paradigm (God gives commands to humans) to a more complex relationship in which humans retain the right to speak back, to argue with the Almighty—a switch in emphasis from the monologic to the dialogic. The framework of the novel is, in part, a modern rewriting of the biblical book of Jonah, whose protagonist argues with and disobeys God. The question remains, though, as to the extent God participates in the dialogue.

This question of rewriting God's "book" also raises issues of language and interpretation. As Patron puts it,

Maybe that's the fate involved in using language to speak and listen, especially when you're dealing with transcendental matters. There are no direct connections between the visions I see in my trances and our language on this side. If I wanted to go over to the other side permanently, all I'd have to do would be to immerse myself in experiences that have nothing to do with language on this side. (115–116)

This is where Guide's role becomes critical, for when Patron returns to "this side" speaking in a series of unconnected, almost incoherent ways about his

visions, Guide helps makes his visions understandable. While often throughout the novel Patron explains Guide's task as single-handedly interpreting
his visions for the world, this interpretive enterprise—the heart of the cult's
religious vision—is also revealed as more dialogue than monologue. As
Patron explains:

> I'd turn to him [Guide] and talk about the visions I had but couldn't
> understand. Words just spilled out. He'd put what I said into some sort of
> logical order, and I'd tell him his words weren't like the experience. And
> once again, he and I would try to get closer to what I saw in my trances.
> The visions and the new words would illuminate each other. That's how
> I learned the irreplaceable power that words can have. (147)

Here then, are the power and limits of language, the attempt to employ the
"power" of words to interpret that which has "nothing to do with" ordinary
language, as well as the view that human understanding of God is always an
interpretive enterprise, one that leaves open the possibility that we help write
the message ourselves. The Patron-Guide relationship becomes a possible
model for the human relationship with God.

One other important area Guide introduces into Patron's religious
schema is the notion that humans are made up of particles of light or "resonance." Guide, a science teacher in his early days, chooses Patron to be
mankind's savior because he, among all people, has a clear "resonance." As
Patron puts it,

> What's most important exists in every person, the particles of light or
> resonance that flow out from the Almighty, the one Being that was there
> at the beginning, the Always-already who includes the entire universe. The
> only difference is that in some people those particles of light are clearer
> and give off a much more intense resonance. Yours are extraordinarily
> clear and intense, Guide told me when we met; that's where he found his
> surety that I was the one. (140–141)

These particles of light that make up our being are not static, but must flow
back to the Creator:

> People tend to believe that each of us as individuals is the center of things,
> but we really *are* nothing more than vehicles for these particles of light or
> resonance: just portable containers, until the time when each and every

particle of light returns to the Almighty and *becomes* the Almighty. This flowing out and return takes place in a different way from the events we're used to think[ing] about as happening in historical time. Both happen in an instant yet are also occurring eternally. (141)

It is easy to see these comments on people as particles of light as a parody of the work of Carlos Castaneda, and Patron and Guide as some post–New Age Don Juans, but the influence here is more complex and syncretic. Ōe, in his wide-ranging, syncretic reach, turns immediately to such diverse influences as Christianity and Sufi mysticism. In an extended dialogue with Ikuo, Patron makes the following points: that "Thy will be done"—a "universal element of prayer"—is "the basis of everything we did," and that it is the "poor in spirit," like Ikuo, who will be answered by God. Again Patron emphasizes the active role of the believer:

> Recently Guide ran across some words in a sixteenth-century book by a Sufi mystic that supported this belief. *"The process of all creation, which is from God, being restored to its true state,"* the book said, *"requires more than simply a propulsive force from God; it also requires a propulsive force found in the religious activities of the created."* The book goes on to say that *"this is why the prayerful hold a tremendous power in the inner world, and at the same time a tremendous responsibility to realize their messianic mission."* (142)

This mixture of New Age pantheism (at one point Patron says, "There is a God, a God who is the whole of nature, who encompasses everything, your spirit and body included" [300]), the Christian centrality of prayer and humble receptivity to the Almighty, and the Sufi notion of the importance of the relationship with God as requiring an active stance on the part of the believer, is, as Patron puts it, the "basis of our new movement" (142). What constitutes an active stance, though, and how far believers must go to "realize their messianic mission," relates to the novel's genesis in the Aum attack.

As in almost every aspect of Ōe's writing, in *Somersault* there is a constant tension of opposites at work, here between the ecstasy of the return to the Almighty and the danger of being pulled over into the other side too soon. The ultimate human destiny, in other words, is a return to the "Creator" as particles of light/resonance; at the same time it is important to live in this world and avoid being pulled over to the other side prematurely. In one of the more memorable scenes early in the novel, Kizu draws a sketch of himself and Ikuo, hand in hand, stepping upward into the clouds, an archetypal ascension; before he gets a chance to show it to Patron, Patron correctly describes the sketch in minute detail. The scene is important for the way it affects both Ikuo and Kizu, impressing both of them with Patron's awesome powers of insight, but even more so for what Patron reveals about human nature and the ultimate ascent to the divine:

> As Guide always told me, because this great flow itself is God, you can't let yourself get caught up in the flow of ecstasy on the other side. Getting carried away by that flow means becoming one with God, and the ecstasy is a premonition of this.
>
> Of course you could argue that getting caught up in it is actually the most natural thing to do. . . . For an individual, coming to faith means we take these particles of light or resonance so that they're not some vague concept but are resituated in a more favorable environment in our own body and spirit. Those particles of light or resonance are *inside* us, but they don't *belong* to us. Even less are they *created* by us. They're put in our care by the Almighty. Finally—and by this I don't mean just the inevitable result of the passage of time but also through training—we have to return these particles of light or resonance to the Almighty, where they originated. This is why we must keep them alive, unsullied. . . . If we get drunk on the ecstasy of the trance and are swallowed up by this deep drunkenness, we won't be able to return from that huge flow back to this side. But one of the conditions of being a living human being is that you do not stay forever over there. In other words, if you are mechanically returned to this side, you'll never again be able to discover the particles of light or resonance within your body and spirit. (139)

Patron goes on to discuss how European mystics used sacred phrases actually tied around their waists as a kind of "handrail" or "lifeline" to keep them from "falling into the abyss of ecstasy," and how in Kizu's case his lifeline is Ikuo, holding his hand in the sketch and in life.

The message Patron gives here is not a questioning of humans' ultimate destiny of returning to the Almighty—this is always a given in his teachings—but rather instruction on how to live until that time, and on the timing of such a return. In his own fiery death, accompanied by the supremely earnest Ms. Tachibana and her mentally handicapped brother Morio (whose own composition, "Ascending to Heaven," enraptured Patron)—and in the simultaneous thwarting of the Quiet Women's bid to die and ascend to heaven en masse—Patron reveals that for some, presumably those who have kept these inner particles "alive and unsullied," the time to return has come. For the vast majority of believers, however, it is not yet time.

The duality of returning ultimately to the divine, yet resisting the return until the proper moment, also underscores the tension of opposites in Ōe's writing, specifically, the juxtaposition of the intellectual and the profane, the mind and the body. In *Somersault,* this is shown in how the most intellectual discussions about the divine alternate with grotesque representations of sexuality, a pattern that goes back to one of Ōe's earliest novels, *A Personal Matter.* To say that human beings in Ōe's work are constantly pulled in two directions—the sacred and the profane—oversimplifies the case, but the repetition of this jarring contrast in *Somersault* leads one to conclude that graphic sexuality is more than merely a titillating aside in the novel. Rather, sexuality is itself a kind of lifeline to keep people from being "swallowed up" by the "ecstasy of the trance" that is found on the other side. Yet it is a lifeline that, in many ways, mimics or portends that ecstasy.

Despite its complex mix of different religious and philosophical traditions (or syncretic hodge-podge, depending on one's viewpoint) Patron sees his religious message as quite simple: the world is polluted, spiritually and literally, to the point where the end is near; people must come to this realization and repent. In reviewing the history of his first church, which grew from a handful of followers to a multi-million-dollar religion, Patron recalls a time when he was interviewed by a Belgian newspaper reporter:

> "I have trances, I told him, in order to gain a deeper understanding
> of the approaching end of the world. This helps me be more open to it,
> intellectually and emotionally. My goal is complete repentance. As the
> power of the repentant grows, our connection with God will exceed the
> level of each individual and may even influence society.
>
> Suspicious of why the interpreter was silent, the Belgian reporter
> asked, "Is that all?" just to make sure. "Are your teachings really that
> simple?" . . . To tell the truth, though, that was all there was to it. (149)

If his original religious approach is this simple, Patron sees his new church, ten years later, as pared down and simplified even further:

> As I've thought about my own salvation, or my image of salvation in the
> ten years since the Somersault, my ideas have become simplified—boiled
> down to a single mathematical formula, if you will. When a person thinks

about death or is actually facing death, if he's convinced that his life and death are fine the way they are, isn't he saved?

In my new church, my followers should be able to say, when they think about death or are actually facing death, *Let's go! Hallelujah!* is another way of putting it. The basic orientation of my movement is to lead people gently in that direction. In order to do that, though, one has to truly repent. As long as one has a true awareness that the end of the world is near, this can be accomplished.

The new church's religious movement I've been contemplating is that simple—that naïve, even. (299)

Running throughout Patron's views is an almost visceral sense of the approaching end of the world, an apocalyptic vision that underscores all his words and actions. What exactly, then, is Patron's view of the end times? It is, first and foremost, of a world coming to a standstill. People may be discouraged, he says, at how "very ordinary" his vision of the end is.

It's a picture of a medium-sized provincial city here in Japan. The afternoon sun is shining down on the scene, but it's entirely desolate. No dogs wandering around, no napping cats. The streets are filthy with garbage, but the amount remains the same; no garbage has been freshly discarded. All manufacturing facilities have stopped. The people haven't been completely eliminated yet but are living off the remains of what's been manufactured and not replacing them once they're used up. There's no electricity, no running water, no public transportation. Everyone's waiting for death in inconspicuous corners of this city, lying there, curled up, helpless babies once again, bereft of the skills needed to live. (145)

The first time he brings up this vision, Patron hints that it could be the result of nuclear radiation or some terrible epidemic disease; later, post-Somersault, he expands this vision to make clear that the end of the world is the result of a total environmental destruction. As Nature and God are to some extent synonymous, if Nature is terminally ill, so is God. It is not, as in the first vision of the dying city, merely that the end of the world entails humans' destroying a secular environment, but that in making the world ill they are killing off God:

Nature, which makes up the totality of this planet—the environment we humans live in, in other words—is steadily falling apart. We've gone beyond the point of no return. God as the totality of nature—including human beings—is decaying bit by bit. God is terminally ill.

Moreover, our awareness of God as being destroyed, of God with an incurable illness, is itself a part of God. Our crumbling God, our God who is sick, is the one who makes us aware—just like a mother teaching her baby to speak: a mother who is falling apart, who's dying from an incurable disease and is talking to her baby, who is fading along with her, telling the baby what she knew from the start would happen. (217)

"We have a right to stand up to God and say that this wasn't part of the plan!" Patron explains further.

It is in the mother-child dialogue that we should find mankind's true repentance, because the ones who made this happen, who destroyed God and gave him an incurable disease, are none other than *mankind itself*. Isn't this how the church of the one who will lead them to repentance, the church of the antichrist, should be constructed: through protesting to God? (217)

From such early reportage as *Hiroshima Notes* to his first major novel, *A Personal Matter* (with its anti-nuclear protests hovering in the background and the implied juxtaposition of the nuclear threat and the damaged baby), Ōe has long been known as a novelist concerned with apocalyptic visions, particularly the Cold War nuclear threat. In the post–Cold War world, Ōe's emphasis has focused more on an environment ravaged by nuclear and other types of pollution. Coinciding with the collapse of Communism, Ōe published two science fiction novels, his first ventures in the genre—*Chiryō tō* (Healing Tower [1990]) and *Chiryō tō wakusei* (Planet of the Healing Tower [1991])—that related the story of a million human beings escaping a hopelessly polluted Earth for another planet. These novels reflect a general post–Cold War shift from concern for a nuclear holocaust to a more generalized threat of environmental pollution and destruction (which in *Somersault* includes the plans of the radical faction to induce meltdowns at power plants and subsequent nuclear pollution). *Somersault* takes this new concern for environmental destruction and further shifts it from being primarily a secular to being a spiritual problem.

Ōe does not go into detail about the exact causes of pollution in the novel; this is not in any way an "environmental novel." Instead, insistently throughout the work, he explores the relationship of God and man. This is not the

God-the-Father image of Christian theology, but rather the mother-infant relationship.[18] Further, Ōe's logic here implies that while humans are ultimately created by God (like the baby by the mother), who is the fountainhead of the "particles of light," their actions (pollution of the world) can destroy God. Humanity is responsible for making God "sick"; likewise it has the duty to repent and sustain God's very being. Before it can "realize its messanic mission," however, humanity must be made aware of the problem through repentance.

As Dr. Koga, one of the former radical faction leaders, explains it, this is a two-step process: one must first become an awakened person, and then (and only then) repent. In the case of Dr. Koga, this awakening process involves an understanding of the nature of the "fallen" physical body in a fallen world. Early in his career the doctor suffered from a severe form of physical alienation; not only was he unable to touch his patients, but he also loathed his own body so much he could not touch it without using a cloth or a piece of paper. In a move reminiscent of that of the main character in Ōe's 1972 story "The Day He Himself Shall Wipe My Tears Away," Koga ended up totally isolated from the outside world: "I wrapped my hands in bandages, wore tinted goggles, and stayed shut up in a Japanese-style room" (262). He is cured by Patron, who consoles him by saying, "We live in a fallen world. . . . Everything in the world is fallen—from the earth, to the oceans, to the air itself. The same holds true for human beings, who are perhaps the most fallen of all." Patron goes on to explain that his own reactions when he returns to "this side" from the world of his trances are similar, and that such an acute awareness of the polluted nature of the body expresses a "purifying awareness of the soul":

> What you need to be aware of is that your soul is alive inside this fallen world, inside your fallen body. You're suffering because your soul is oppressed, because your soul is awakening. Your soul is not fallen, but as long as it's in this fallen world, because the temporary container your soul is in, your body, is dirty, and the world that surrounds that body is dirty, your soul will indeed suffer. (270)

When Dr. Koga raises the issue of suicide as a possible solution (his mother, in despair over her son's condition, killed herself and invited him to do likewise), Patron rejects this, calling on him—and all his followers—not to look for an easy out: "As long as you don't find a solution here, in this fallen world, no matter where you run your soul will be in the same predicament. Escaping this world is not a guarantee of salvation" (270). And once again Patron returns to his simple message: "People who hear the voice of the soul must do this: Wake up to the fact that our world is a fallen world, that humans are polluted beings, repent, and await the end of the world" (270). Synthesizing some of the earlier ideas, one can conclude that, if only enough human beings are awakened to this realization of the fall and repent, then the flow of particles of light will extend back to God in such quantity that the sick and dying God (whom we have made sick)—and by extension the whole world, including ourselves—will be restored and made whole.

But is merely being repentant and waiting for the end of this fallen world sufficient? Is this passive stance enough, or, as Dr. Koga puts it, "Shouldn't we go beyond that and actually help bring about the end of the world? Isn't that what's necessary to make the great leap?" (271). This is the main religious tension the novel explores. To reiterate the Sufi mystics: *"The process of all creation, which is from God, being restored to its true state, requires more than simply a propulsive force from God; it also requires a propulsive force found in the religious activities of the created."* But what is this "propulsive force"? What are believers called on to do to "restore creation"? In the actions of individual believers, as well as in such subgroups within the cult as the Quiet Women and the Technicians, *Somersault* explores a number of possible answers to these questions that range from prayer to suicide to violent action.

Before exploring these answers, though, one more layer of Patron's theology, this one filtered through the medium of poetry, must be scrutinized. Chapter 4 of the novel, entitled "Reading R. S. Thomas," brings the painter Kizu (later the new Guide) together with Patron for the first time. The meeting reveals a further subtley to Patron's views about God and salvation. Kizu, on a trip years before, had discovered the poetry of Thomas, a Welsh clergyman and poet. During his first extended visit with Patron, Patron asks him to lecture on the poet for his edification. They meet for several weeks late at night, reading through Kizu's translations of selected verse by Thomas. The meetings are less a lecture on the poetry than a series of line-by-line ruminations by Patron, who sees profound parallels between Thomas' poetry and his own life. The chapter is made up largely of five complete poems by Thomas, including "Correspondence," "Suddenly," "Balance," "Sea-Watching," and "Threshold," as well as excerpts from Thomas' prose, one quotation from Kierkegaard, and another from a scholar of Thomas' work. As Numano Mitsuyoshi notes, this chapter and its heavy reliance on Thomas' poetry stick out from the rest of the novel, and Patron's sometimes melodramatic interpretations are overdone. Yet the chapter is important for the way it asks the reader to interpret the religious message of the poetry in the context of the entire novel.[19] Ōe quotes entirely from Thomas' later poetry, which is more openly religious than are his earlier poems of Wales and the land.[20] As Ono Kosei argues, the point of contact between these poems and Ōe's novel is the "search for God in the absence of God," with the major difference being Ōe's rejection of a personified God.[21] In fact, Thomas is best known as a poet of the *deus absconditus,* "the God who hides Himself," in Elaine Shepherd's phrase, and his poetry is a prime example of the *via negativa,* the knowledge of God gleaned through absences and traces.[22] Though not quoted directly in *Somersault,* the best example of this vision of God by Thomas is his poem of the same name, "Via Negativa":

> Why no! I never thought other than
> That God is that great absence
> In our lives, the empty silence
> Within, the place where we go
> Seeking, not in hope to
> Arrive or find. He keeps the interstices
> In our knowledge, the darkness
> Between the stars. His are the echoes
> We follow, the footprints he has just
> Left. We put our hands in
> His side hoping to find
> It warm. We look at people
> And places as though he had looked
> At them, too; but miss the reflection.

Ōe reveals an awareness of this poem, though, when Kizu first broaches the poet to Patron: "About his themes, though," Kizu says, "maybe because his name is Thomas, he wrote several poems about Doubting Thomas. He wrote from Thomas's viewpoint, discussing the reasons why he had to touch Jesus' bloody wounds before he believed in the resurrection" (66–67). This poem (itself known through its absence from the chapter!) becomes even more relevant to *Somersault* as, three chapters later, Patron is revealed to have his own "sacred wound" in his side. As Ono argues, this poem sums up Thomas' later poetry, namely the idea of a personified God (who leaves footsteps and has a wounded body) who is known primarily through traces left behind, through gaps (darkness between stars, echoes). Thomas' poems quite naturally raise phenomenological issues of the knowability of God. Patron's whole religious enterprise rests on his supposed unique ability to touch the "other side" and come face to face with God, and his mainly positive response to Thomas' work makes one wonder whether Patron has seen God, or only His *absence*. Is, for instance, the glowing white screen or hollow he sees in his visions God, or merely a trace of Him?

Certain lines from the poems that *are* quoted in chapter 4 are ones that Patron sees as relevant to his own life. "Correspondence," for instance, talks of one's own silence and the silence of God:

> Younger I deemed truth
> Was to come at beyond the horizon.
> Older I stay still and am
> As far off as before. These nail-parings
> Bore you? They explain my silence.
> I wish there were as simple
> An explanation for the silence of God.

Patron (at this point still in the "silence" of his ten-year post-Somersault retreat) sees this as a response he should have given to Guide, who was urging him once again to take on the mantle of religious savior. Is God silent, or does He answer our calls? This age-old question is raised throughout the novel, in Patron's torment once he renounces God; in the agonzied quest of Ikuo, who heard God's commanding voice once and wants nothing more than to hear it again—directly, or filtered through Patron as mediator; and elsewhere.

A second poem that Patron finds particularly significant is "Threshold":

> I emerge from the mind's
> cave into the worse darkness
> outside, where things pass and
> the Lord is in none of them.
>
> I have heard the still, small voice
> and it was that of the bacteria
> demolishing my cosmos, I
> have lingered too long on
>
> this threshold, but where can I go?
> To look back is to lose the soul
> I was leading upwards towards
> the light. To look forward? Ah,

> what balance is needed at
> the edges of such an abyss.
> I alone on the surface
> of a turning planet. What
>
> to do but, like Michaelangelo's
> Adam, put my hand
> out into unknown space,
> hoping for the reciprocating touch?

Of the last line Patron says, "These past ten years I've been in the dark, but I haven't relied on a reciprocating touch," and of the first four lines: "I've experienced this more often than I can recall, but I never attempted to find God as I passed through these. Doesn't Thomas at times try to be overly suggestive?" (71–72). These quotations reveal major differences between Patron's and Thomas' viewpoints. At this juncture in the novel, Patron is about to "emerge" ("quietly emerge," as another Thomas poem puts it) from his ten-year "descent into hell," in his words, and the major question facing him now that he has renounced God is whether he will again be able to have his visions, or whether he is permanently cut off from God. The world into which Patron now emerges is, in his view, one in which God is not only absent, but possibly silent forever: "The relevant question," he tells Ikuo, is, "Is it possible for someone who's done a Somersault to confront God again?" (125). In other words, while Thomas' work describes an absent, personified God, known through the traces He leaves behind and the desire of humans to touch Him physically, Patron depicts an even bleaker vision of a world in which humans still act as if God is there, but have grave doubts as to whether they will ever, in any way at all, really know His existence, let alone interact with or touch Him.

It is important to distinguish between the pre- and the post-Somersault theology, and the spiritual implications of Patron's apostasy. Patron's renunciation of his beliefs on national television (to defuse the radical faction's violent plans) lands him and Guide in what they describe as an "abyss," a kind of "private hell" (167) reserved for the two of them as apostates. In this condition Patron no longer has visions and is cut off from contact with the "other side" and with God. The catatonic state described earlier, which his followers interpret hopefully as a prelude to a return to his earlier trances, turns out to be nothing of the kind. In addition, with Guide's death Patron realizes that, even if he were once again to contact God through a trance, there would be no one left to interpret God's message. Even as apostate, while Guide is still with him,

Patron sees a possibility that he can be an "intermediary for God's voice" (125), but Guide's death brings on a resignation that all is irreparably altered:

> After ten years passed [since the Somersault] and we were considering climbing out of the abyss—in other words, when we were starting to grope toward a new beginning—Guide was killed. This was exactly the time when I began to find signs that my trances were about to return.
>
> Once more I felt banished to the wilderness. Even if in the near future my painful deep trances were to return, without Guide's intervention I wouldn't be able to put these visions into words. All my suffering would be in vain. (213)

His appointment of Kizu as new Guide should not be interpreted as Patron's hope to revive his own early position as mystic seer. Although he originally instructs Kizu to be the church's historian, a "backward-looking prophet" who will document, through drawings, the church's history, in the end his charge to the artist is to paint a monumental work depicting the future of the cult, the evolution of a Patron-as-savior-centered church into the "Church of the New Man," with Patron not as savior but as *antichrist*. In doing so, the post-Somersault Patron rejects the visions of one of the major subgroups of the cult (the Technicians), whose members wish to turn back the clock and reverse the Somersault. In all of this Ōe's own vision for the novel as his imaginative reaction to Aum Shinrikyō is apparent. As noted above, one of Ōe's imaginative starting points was to imagine what would happen if the Aum leader, Asahara, had renounced his religion.

In his post-Somersault, post-Guide state, what sort of religious vision does Patron develop? His first public pronouncement of his new vision comes with Guide's tragic death at the hands of former radical faction members. In a public statement issued the same day as the death, he states that he is taking a "bold new step forward" (167). What this new step is is fleshed out at a press conference, where Patron declares:

> After the Somersault, Guide and I fell into the abjectness of hell, where I was forced to ponder the salvation of mankind. Guide was the one pilot we could rely on. Just as we resurfaced, though, he was cruelly murdered. At the same time, this proved to me that the time to take action was near. I want to appeal again to people to repent at the coming end of the world. In order to carry this out, I will fight the final battle against the entire human race on this planet. My church does not possess nuclear weapons, nor does it manufacture chemical weapons. People might wonder how we

can possibly carry out such a battle, and laugh at us for trying, but I believe
we can and must fight. At the cost of his own life, Guide protected mankind's Patron—in other words, me. His death has revealed my legitimacy.
In the end people like us will emerge victorious. (172)

This public declaration alarms some of the reporters present, who compare
the new church to Aum and take Patron's "call to arms" as a literal amassing
of weapons, rather than as the spiritual challenge it is intended to be. As the
Somersault demonstrated, what distinguishes Patron most from a leader
such as Asahara is his bitter opposition to church-induced violence.

In the memorial service that follows, Patron delivers a major sermon that
clarifies both the nature of the "battle" and of how he defines his "legitimacy."
The sermon is also, significantly, the first time in *Somersault* that Ōe quotes
from the Bible, using Ephesians to help Patron define further his Church of
the New Man and his role in it. At the memorial service he quotes first from
Mark, the famous line of Jesus on the cross, "My God, my God, why have you
forsaken me?" using it to lament the loss of his companion, Guide. More to
the point as far as his new theology is concerned, Patron quotes from 1 John
2:18–19:

> Dear children, this is the last hour; as you have heard that the antichrist is
> coming, even now many antichrists have come. This is how we know it is
> the last hour. They went out from us, but they did not really belong to us.
> For if they had belonged to us, they would have remained with us; but their
> going showed that none of them belonged to us. (214)

Patron comments on this, saying,

> This particular passage has caused me great pain. In the last trial, you did
> not leave us, and though you continued to belong to us, neither Guide nor
> I remained with you. And I became the antichrist—both when I fell into
> hell, and even now that I have resurfaced. Is there so much misery and
> pain for mankind that this is the only alternative—that I must be seen
> as the antichrist?
>
> Guide was the only other person who agreed that I must tread this
> path. Together with me he did the Somersault and accompanied me to hell.
> This was his choice, I think, because he insisted to the end on the necessity
> of the Somersault. It was a Somersault where the antichrist appears, which
> signals the end of the world. That is the way I understand it now. (214)

The Somersault, then, is reinterpreted by Patron not as a sad, pointless retreat, but as a necessary step—through the creation of the antichrist—on the way to the end of the world. Patron's "bold new step forward" thus is the revelation of the utter necessity of the Somersault in the broader scheme of things. Rather than being merely a tactic to defuse the radical faction's attempts to bring on the end times by violence, the Somersault is now shown as an essential part of God's plan to "signal the end of the world."

Toward the end of the memorial service Patron raises the image of the earth as sick mother, and ourselves as her sick, helpless babies. Here he discusses how his earlier theology of "God as the totality of nature that created this world" is now replaced by "another theology just starting to sprout, a miserable theology that toys with the first" (217). This new, still inchoate theology is this:

> From our viewpoint, as infants whose fate is to die around the same time as our mother, we have the right to stand up to God and say that this wasn't part of the plan! The dying mother hears the nonsensical words of the feverish baby, puts them in the proper context, and returns them to the baby's mouth. It is in that mother-child dialogue that we should find mankind's true repentance, because the ones who made this happen, who destroyed the natural world, who destroyed God and gave him an incurable disease, are none other than *mankind itself.* Isn't this how the church of the one who will lead them to repentance, the church of the antichrist, should be constructed: through protesting to God? . . . I have decided to restart my movement focusing on leading people to this kind of repentance. . . .
>
> Just as there is no doubt that Christ's humiliating death had meaning, there must be meaning in the desperate struggle of the antichrist who has stepped into hell. Otherwise, in the first consciousness of God as he created the world, why did He structure it so that there would appear so many antichrists at the end? God is the very one who, among all the things of creation, cannot be dismissed as a joke, the one existence that has absolutely no reason ever to turn a Somersault. (217–218)

Near the end of his sermon Patron notes,

> I've lost my connection with God and have nothing to do with visions I might see in trances anymore, but I still find myself burning with a desire to communicate the words from the other side. . . . As a sign that the end time is here, antichrists are popping up all over the world, and I am one

of them. . . . Why would you follow a leader, knowing full well he's an antichrist? With the exception of the children, it's because you, too, are all sinners. You're the ones who destroyed God as the totality of nature and have given him an incurable disease. (221)

Note Patron's rejection of the notion of original sin—the children are sinless—as well as his idea that God is the sole unchanging being, and his pantheistic conflation of God with creation (the earth). But more important is his new vision of a church headed by an antichrist, based on "protesting to God," and bringing people to repentance for their sins.[23]

The notion of the antichrist—and of many antichrists—is one that Ōe explores in detail and that becomes crucial to an understanding of Patron and *Somersault*. The term "antichrist" has been much bandied about recently, particularly in the context of the multimillion-copy Christian bestseller *Left Behind* series, which appeals to evangelistic American millennial thinking. Going back to its origins, the term "antichrist" appears only in the epistles of John, but references to a similar idea occur elsewhere in the New Testament, most particularly in Paul's notion of the "man of lawlessness" in 2 Thessalonians. While the basic Johannine idea is of an evil being who will appear to oppose Christ (though not to claim to be the Christ):

> The concept is introduced in John as already well known ("you have heard that antichrist is coming," 1 Jn. 2:18). But though he does not dispute the fact that at the end of this age there will appear an evil being, called "antichrist," John insists that there is a temper, an attitude, characteristic of antichrist, and that already exists. Indeed, he can speak of "many antichrists" already in the world (1 Jn 2:18). He gives something in the nature of a definition of antichrist when he says, "This is the antichrist, he who denies the Father and the Son" (1 Jn 2:22).[24]

Ōe has long been fascinated with the idea of the antichrist. In his 1989 novel *Jinsei no shinseki* (translated in 1996 as *An Echo of Heaven*), for instance, he has characters debate the meaning of antichrist, whether the "anti" means "against" Christ or simply "before" Christ. Little Father, the cult leader in the novel, is particularly concerned about this distinction. As one character says of him:

> As a scholar, he's only an amateur, but he's done a lot of research on the Antichrist, from a variety of angles, particularly the linguistic aspect. He tells me he's sent his inquiries out to specialists on return postcards, but

has yet to receive a convincing reply. The "Anti-" of "Antichrist" has generally been taken to mean "against" or "in conflict with," but Little Father wants to know if anyone has ever interpreted the Greek Antikhristos as a neutral concept; as simply "one who comes before Christ. . . . " [Later, in one of his sermons Little Father says,] "But isn't it possible to think of ourselves as the Antichrist? Not meaning against Christ, but that we're all pre-Christ?" (110, 111)

In *Somersault,* too, a similar idea surfaces. In one scene Ikuo asks Gii what Patron was interested in most about Gii's father's church, the Church of the Flaming Green Tree:

"*Anti* and *ante,*" Gii answered seriously.
    "Patron's talking about the antichrist," Ikuo explained. "Patron is clearly an *anti*christ, while the leader of the Church of the Flaming Green Tree, whom his followers called *savior,* insisted that he was an *ante*christ. He preached that before the real Christ returns there will be countless *ante*christs, *ante* in the sense of *coming before,* and that he was one of them. . . . "
    "When Patron asked me [Gii] whether it was possible for him to be both an antichrist and an *ante*christ in the sense that my father used the term, I remembered something my mother had said and told him that that didn't jibe with what my father taught. And Patron said, 'I guess that's right,' in such a moving way I was quite surprised." (367)

In the Johannine definition of an antichrist as one who denies the Father and the Son, Patron sees himself reflected, for his ultimate definition of himself throughout the book is as one who has "somersaulted," who has renounced God and turned his back on Him. One could argue that in his syncretic viewpoint Patron may not have been denying the Christian Father and Son per se, but this point becomes moot in a later scene when, for the first time since the memorial service, Patron quotes from Christian Scripture to refine his understanding of antichrist. This takes place in an informal talk that finally (430-plus pages into the novel) launches his new movement, which he christens the "Church of the New Man." Referring first to Kizu's major painting depicting himself (Patron) and Ikuo, he says:

The painting portrays the confrontation between the antichrist sponsoring the church, the Old Man, and Jonah, representing the New Man, and the two of them facing the body of believers. The painting boldly depicts the

basic misconception I had till now about the difficulties I've been facing.
My mistake lay in thinking that *I* should be the one to build the new
church. But now I know that's wrong. (433)

Where did he get these terms, "Old Man" and "New Man"? Patron relates
how, in a feverish state, because of his so-called Sacred Wound, he asks Morio
to mark two passages in the Bible at random; these turn out to be the only two
passages in the New Testament that refer to the "new man" and the "old
man," the "new self " and the "old self." Quoting them, Patron says:

> As this world approaches its end, *a savior must appear who will make one
> the two that stand opposed, destroying in his flesh the dividing wall of hostil-
> ity, abolishing the law with its commandment and regulations.* And I believe
> that such a savior will surely come.
>   *He will create in himself one new man out of the two, making peace, and
> in this one body reconcile both of them to God through the cross, putting to
> death their hostility.* This, too, I believe, will come to pass.
>   That being the case, what role will an antichrist play? Precisely this:
> He is the Old Man who acts as herald for the savior. All sorts of antichrists
> will appear—strange, comical types of heralds who clown around and
> make fun of God. All antichrists, though, are united in the role they play
> as Old Man and all that term implies. They are the ones who pave the way
> for the savior. I am firmly convinced of this, which is precisely why I want
> to construct my new church as an antichrist.
>   I also appeal to you through the second passage Morio marked in
> the scripture: *Put off your old self, which is being corrupted by its deceitful
> desires; be made new in the attitudes of your minds; and put on the new self,
> created to be like God in true righteousness and holiness.* I appeal to you as
> an antichrist, as one who will forever remain an Old Man. Even though I'm
> such an Old Man, one thing I can do is challenge each of you to become
> New Men! (434)

These biblical quotations are all from Ephesians. Of this Pauline epistle John
R. W. Stott writes that the passage reveals the situation of "all human beings
[as] alienated from God because of sin" and "the Gentiles . . . also alienated
from the people of God" along with an active enmity between Jew and Gentile. "The grand theme of Ephesians 2," he continues, "is that Jesus Christ
has destroyed both enmities."[25] Ōe, too, has several characters discuss the
believer-versus-unbeliever (heretic or Gentile) angle ("the Japanese are still

all heretics," says one [481]), but what is most important is Patron's interpretation of his new role as antichrist. Here we see antichrists as necessary heralds fulfilling a role reminiscent of John the Baptist's. Like John, whom some mistakenly considered the savior, Patron's original church appellation was indeed "Savior"; likewise, their messages could both be boiled down to a call to repent. But there the resemblance ends. In keeping with Ōe's penchant for the grotesque, the carnivalesque, the antichrist's role here is not, like John's, grimly to predict the end, but to "clown around and make fun of God," as indeed Patron sees himself having done with the Somersault. This is a necessary role, indeed is part of God's plan for the approaching end times, a signal that the end is near; but what is most noteworthy is the notion of the antichrist, as "Old Man," stepping aside to make way for the "New Man." While the fiery ending of the novel, and Patron's gruesome death, may take readers by surprise, Patron is here indicating that his time to exit the stage is fast approaching.

A final point Patron makes about the antichrist comes a little later. As Kizu is sketching Patron for the Jonah triptych, Patron notes,

> In the building of the Church of the New Man we'll be engaged in from now on, the transcendent is indifferent about whether I'm a faithful follower or whether, as an antichrist, I'm trying to regain the will I had in the Somersault. The transcendent is absolutely self-centered. It doesn't stand on the side of those who are trying to do good. . . .
>
> The Almighty is bereft of imagination. Spinoza's completely right on this point. If you call the transcendent God, then you're saying that God has no imagination. Every time I read the section of the Gospels where Jesus is crucified, I find myself thinking that God's son has no imagination. For Christ, there is only this world God made—that is, God Himself and His designs. 'My God, my God, why have you forsaken me?' Jesus cries out, but he accepts everything that happens to him.
>
> The antichrist, in contrast, *does* have imagination. Imagination, in fact, is *all* he has. (463)

What image of man and God (and antichrist) remains here? Patron ends up with a more cynical, deterministic vision of a world operating according to God's "unimaginative," and thereby unchanging, plan, with little regard for human endeavor. (Though he does note that God has "smiled on" Kizu's work, his painting, and has taken away his cancer.) The antagonism between antichrist and God has been transformed from the traditional biblical view of evil versus good to a contrast between imagination and its lack, between a man who is free to act, even to denounce and make fun of God, and a God who will stolidly carry out His plans nonetheless. Patron believes in the "coming savior." In his earlier sermon, where he quotes from Ephesians, he endorses much of the standard biblical rhetoric. Yet what he ends up with is all his own: a view of man as in many ways aware of, but apart from God, of man left with the freedom of his realm of imagination. But free to imagine—what?

One thing humans are left with is the freedom to argue with and protest to God—whether He responds or not. This notion of protesting to God, of course, leads to a consideration of the main extratextual framework by which *Somersault* hangs, its incorporation of the biblical book of Jonah. By highlighting the story of Jonah and the possibility of humans' protesting to God, the novel also underscores the idea of human freedom (including the idea of, ultimately, being free of God). But if God is the sole unchanging being, the only one who will never "turn a Somersault," then what good is any protest to God? Ōe would answer that, through the tortuous process of wrestling with God (the traditional translation of the word "Israel," of course), man wrests a certain realm of freedom *from* God.

The book of Jonah, one of the "strange books of the Bible" according to Elias Bickerman, is an atypical prophetic book, for it is a "story about a prophet rather than a collection of prophetic sayings." In fact, Jonah is "never named 'prophet' in the book that bears his name,"[26] nor are any of his prophecies recorded other than the single-sentence prediction of Nineveh's doom. (Bruce Vawter goes so far as to call the book a "parody of a prophet.")[27] In this short biblical book, Jonah is commissioned by God, "Go to the great city of Nineveh and preach against it, because its wickedness has come up before me." Instead, "Jonah ran away from the Lord and headed for Tarshish" (Jonah 1:1–3). Then follows the storm at sea; Jonah is thrown overboard by the fearful sailors, and he is swallowed whole by a "great fish" in which he stays for three days and nights before he is delivered. After his deliverance, God tells Jonah again, "Go to the great city of Nineveh and proclaim to it the message I give you." This time he obeys, goes to this city, the capital of Assyria and thus of the enemies of Israel, and proclaims that, unless the city repents, it will be destroyed. The people of the city, including the king, immediately repent in hope that "God may yet relent . . . so that we will not perish" (Jonah 3:4–9). As Martin Luther wrote, "In view of this [mass repentance], I am tempted to say that no apostle or prophet, not even Christ Himself, performed and accomplished with a single sermon the great things Jonah did."[28]

Still, though, Jonah is a reluctant prophet; after God has compassion on the repentant Ninevites and spares their city, "Jonah was greatly displeased and became angry" (Jonah 4:1). He had feared from the beginning that his commission would end in God's sparing the city: "I knew that you are a gracious and compassionate God who relents from sending calamity" (Jonah 4:1–2). Jonah goes out of the city to sulk, and God "provided a vine and made it grow up over Jonah to give shade for his head to ease his discomfort." When this vine withers and dies (by a worm also provided by God) Jonah is "angry enough to die," but God admonishes him, saying, "You have been concerned about this vine, though you did not tend it or make it grow. It sprang up overnight and died overnight. But Nineveh has more than a hundred and twenty thousand people who cannot tell their right hand from their left, and many cattle as well. Should I not be concerned about that great city?" (Jonah 4:10–11). Thus ends Jonah.

Jonah is interesting for many reasons. The story of a miraculous deliverance, of course, is echoed in the New Testament when Jesus (only the second prophet, after Jonah, to hail from Galilee), declares, after being asked for a "miraculous sign,"

> A wicked and adulterous generation asks for a miraculous sign! But none will be given it except the sign of the prophet Jonah. For as Jonah was three days and three nights in the belly of a huge fish, so the Son of Man will be three days and three nights in the heart of the earth. The men of Nineveh will stand up at the judgment with this generation and condemn it; for they repented at the preaching of Jonah. (Matthew 12:38–41)

Jonah, as a missionary to Gentiles, can be also be seen as an Old Testament precursor to Paul. In Jonah both the sailors and the Ninevites are Gentiles, and both are the "only truly pious people" in the story.[29] The book has been interpreted in numerous and often conflicting ways over the centuries, though one widely accepted interpretation is of Jonah as a "protest against a narrow, exclusivistic Judaism."[30] In this reading, Jonah desires God's compassion to rest solely on his chosen people; all others should feel His wrath. The book of Jonah, however, reveals a God whose initial wrath can be transformed to compassion and mercy, a God who can change His mind and spare even the most wicked. As Abraham J. Heschel writes,

> God's change of mind displeased Jonah exceedingly. He has proclaimed the doom of Nineveh with a certainty, to the point of fixing the time, as an inexorable decree without qualification. But what transpired only proved

the word of God was neither firm nor reliable. To a prophet who stakes his life on the reliability and infallibility of the word of God, such realization leads to despair. . . . God's answer to Jonah, stressing the supremacy of compassion, upsets the possibility of looking for a rational coherence of God's ways with the world . . . beyond justice and anger lies the mystery of compassion.[31]

Thomas Bolin notes, too, that, "while on a formal level the debate between Jonah and Yahweh is unresolved," " the author indicates through a renewed emphasis on God's unlimited power over creation that to engage in a debate with God in the hope of victory or resolution is pointless . . . [compared to Job,] in Jonah the argument is more subtle: Argue with God if you will; win if you will, but to what end is your victory? Divine power is larger than any human conceptions of justice or logic." [32]

As far as the influence of Jonah on writers and artists is concerned, James Limburg also notes, "The book of Jonah has never been the exclusive property of theologians or members of religious communities. The incident involving the great fish has captured the imagination of poets and novelists, painters and dramatists, sculptors and songwriters . . . to a degree matched by few stories in or out of the Bible." [33] Ōe's artistic appropriation of Jonah, then, joins a long line of predecessors, but while Ōe does highlight the prayer of Jonah for deliverance while he is in the belly of the whale, and is concerned about the fall into "hell" (of Patron and Guide) and their deliverance from it, the two confrontations between the prophet and God that begin and end Jonah are the core model for much of what goes on in *Somersault*. Ōe is fascinated by the notion of protesting to God, and a dialectic develops in the novel between humble repentance (in the original sense of turning toward God) and a more forceful confrontation with Him. This is depicted mainly through an increasing tension between the impetuous Ikuo, who, like Jonah, has heard the voice of God to "destroy," and Patron, inclined toward compassion and nonviolence. As the novel progresses, the huge triptych commissioned by Patron from Kizu for the chapel—that in some interpretations depicts Ikuo and Patron as Jonah and God, respectively—becomes the focal point for an evolving interpretive debate over Patron's role, the meaning of the Somersault, the future of the Church of the New Man, and the ability of man to understand the will of God, or even to hear Him at all.

Ikuo is depicted from the beginning of the novel as a fiery, combative young man enthralled by the possibilities of the kind of total Old Testament–like destruction of a city. In the prologue, where the ten-year-old Ikuo smashes his Lego creation, the narrator comments:

Did destroying the model city he'd taken a year to create afford him a
precocious, lawless sense of confidence—this boy who often fled from the
center of Tokyo? Did seeing his creation as something whose sole purpose
was to be broken to pieces make him wonder if even this huge metropolis
could be razed if one wanted to? (2)

When Kizu meets Ikuo fifteen years after this incident, Ikuo is obsessed with
the book of Jonah. Discussing Jonah and the illustrations Kizu had done for
a children's version of the story is what brings them together. Ikuo admits to
being disturbed by Jonah: "I can't help wondering if the Jonah we have now
is complete, or whether it might originally have had a different ending" (37).
Kizu invites Ikuo to his apartment, where he reviews for him a study of Jonah
by J. M. Meyers, one that emphasizes God's sadness at the possible destruction of Nineveh because of all the innocent children who would die (Meyers'
interpretation of the line "more than 120,000 people who cannot tell their
right hand for their left"). For his part Ikuo is still fascinated with the vision
of mass destruction: "What a terrible thing it must have been to destroy the
whole city of Nineveh. For us now, mightn't it be equivalent to destroying a
city the size of Tokyo?" (40).

Is Tokyo a modern-day Nineveh? Will God call down destruction on the
city? Can a different ending be written for Jonah, one in which Jonah per-
suades God to go back to His original plan of total destruction? In the context
of *Somersault,* the question becomes Can the Somersault be reversed? *Somersault* pits Ikuo's vision and hope—an apocalyptic goal consonant with that
of the former radical faction that attempted to bring about a nuclear holocaust—against Patron's. On the one hand is Ikuo, drawn to the remnants of
the radical faction (the Technicians), as well as to the militant Young Fireflies—and to the burning desire that through Patron's mediation God will
tell him once more *Do it!* (engage in a purifying act of destruction). On the
other hand, opposing this, is Patron, the former "savior" and present "antichrist," who defused the original apocalyptic plans and who similarly defuses
Ikuo's violent visions in a fiery suicide designed in part to satisfy the young
man's apocalyptic desires.

As Kizu works on his Jonah-inspired triptych throughout Part 2 of the
novel, much of the story revolves around shifting interpretations of the
meaning of the painting, and the roles signified by the characters depicted in
it. Ikuo's role in the painting at first seems unambiguous. He is, as Dr. Koga
states, "a Jonah-like personality," so much so that he is nicknamed "Yonah"
(the Japanese pronunciation of the name) by the Young Fireflies. Looking at
one panel of the triptych, one of the Fireflies comments, "But Ikuo as Jonah

wouldn't obey God's suggestion that the people of Nineveh be spared. Didn't Ikuo tell us it's possible Jonah wasn't convinced by the parable of the vine?" (364). Certainly Ikuo isn't the only Jonah-like person in the cult. At one point, discussing the plans for the triptych with Ikuo, Kizu sees the Technicians as "uncompromising Jonahs" (360). Likewise, Patron later likens both the Technicians and the Quiet Women, both of whom have their own agendas, to Jonah. Like Jonah pressing God, saying, "Now, O Lord. Take away my life," the Quiet Women in particular are bent on self-destruction.

Later, when Ikuo has a premonition that something extraordinary will happen at the Hollow and worries that the Young Fireflies may "fall victim" to it, Kizu begins to see him as less like Jonah and more like God:

> "Every time I talk with you about the book of Jonah, I see you standing on Jonah's side, grumbling about what the Lord wants you to do. But your attitude right now isn't just that of a Jonah."
>
> "What do you mean?" Ikuo asked, caught off guard.
>
> "It's a simple thing, really. Not long ago I put it this way: Jonah stands up to God, insisting that he destroy Nineveh the way he originally planned. But God, lamenting the loss of over 120,000 children plus countless head of cattle, doesn't burn the city. And the people repent. And now *you're* worried about children not becoming victims, right? . . . I'm not making fun of you, merely pointing out this contradiction." (404)

Patron himself is also likened to Jonah through his rejection of God in the Somersault. As Kizu comments on his developing painting:

> "The Sacred Wound fits in nicely with the person who acts as mediator between us and God," Kizu said. "But instead of having this wounded mediator trying to *persuade* Jonah, I'm beginning to see him more on Jonah's side, *protesting* with, refusing to surrender to God."
>
> "I like the ambiguity involved—having Patron model for a figure that can be interpreted in more than one way," Ikuo said. "The followers praying in the chapel can read it any way they want." (395)

A little earlier, though, Ikuo sees Patron not as mediator between Jonah and God, but as God himself: "I was thinking it made sense to have Patron in the painting as God, showing him persuaded by Jonah's protest. God's given up on it once but has now completely consigned Nineveh to the flames and is standing there with Jonah gazing down at the burning city. That was the vision of God I had" (380). The interpretation of the painting becomes even more complex when Patron's self-proclaimed role as antichrist is factored in. How might this fit in with an understanding of the triptych? As Patron poses for the painting, he and Kizu have the following exchange:

> "The foreground of the middle panel shows Ikuo as Jonah. Are you planning to use my image in the open part on the left?" Patron asked.
>
> "That's right."
>
> "In other words, I'll be depicted as the Lord?"
>
> "Since that's who Jonah quarrels with, yes, it would be the Lord, though my conception has changed a little since I first started. It doesn't have to be the Lord, exactly, though it *does* have to be someone who transmits God's will to Jonah."
>
> "And he goes to all this trouble of showing this wound in his side to convince Jonah?"
>
> "Rather than the biblical Jonah, I'm starting to see it more as the Ikuo-as-Jonah image the Young Fireflies have, Ikuo as the young man awaiting God's intermediary to give him the word to act."
>
> "Since I'm less a model for God than for the antichrist," Patron said, "even if I tell him to act it makes it a complicated sort of instruction, doesn't it? If you show the antichrist here with a wound in his side debating with Jonah, it's like you're depicting this young man as seeing beyond the antichrist to God."
>
> " . . . You're very perceptive," Kizu said, his comment heartfelt. (427–428)

With his emphasis on his role as antichrist, this appears to be Patron's final word on how he believes the painting should be read. His role as antichrist is as herald to the savior to come, and here again he downplays his role in the cult: though the antichrist debates with Jonah, Jonah's role is to "see beyond" him to God.

All of this presages Patron's announcement of the "Church of the New Man," and his stepping aside in favor of Ikuo. As we have seen, the concept of the "new man" is from Ephesians and emphasizes how, in Christ, the old "enmities" between Jew and Gentile, between man and God, are destroyed, overcome in the self-sacrifice of Christ. Just as Kizu sees a contradiction in Ikuo's stance (now Jonah-like, now more like God), there is a substantial contradiction between the biblical "old man/new man" and what happens in *Somersault*. As one follower, Ms. Asuka, neatly sums it up, "The New Men [in Paul's time] were the ones who were able to overcome the discord between Gentiles and Jews. Jonah ran counter to this trend" (481). In *Somersault*, while Patron sees himself as the "old man" stepping aside to allow the "new man" to lead the church, in reality what takes place is the exact opposite: Patron, through his self-sacrifice, is the one who reconciles (as far as reconciliation is possible) the contending factions in the church, while he leaves the church in the hands of Ikuo—the Jonah-like figure who wants to set the clock back, who opposes compromise and reconciliation. The "new man," in short, gives way to the "old man," not the other way around.

But why does Patron need to die? Why does handing over the church to a new generation require that he commit suicide? As with many aspects of the novel, there is a great deal of foreshadowing, in this case indicating that Patron's days are numbered. As he waits for Guide's memorial service to begin, for example, he comments on his own physical deterioration because of gout: "At first it doesn't hurt so much, but at the end it spreads quite fast. I don't have much time" (212). A few pages later, at the conclusion of the service, he ends his sermon by saying, "Even if I die a death befitting an antichrist, one more horrid even than Guide's, your march must go on. In order that the harvest gained by Guide's death will not be in vain, each one of us must play his part" (222). Earlier in the sermon, Patron refers not to Guide's death, but to his own, contrasting it with Christ's: "just as there is no doubt that Christ's humiliating death had meaning, there must be meaning in the desperate struggle of the antichrist who has stepped into hell" (217). Later, Kizu has a dream of Ikuo and Patron "gazing down on a city engulfed in flames" (381). In a still later dream this is transformed into a scene of Ikuo and Patron standing in the Hollow with a "huge cypress tree towering darkly" (413), the very site of Patron's fiery demise.

Ōe leads the reader to expect Patron's death, but he does not explain it. One simple answer is that Patron wants to follow his beloved Guide in death. Patron's theology of light particles returning to the creator may not provide the comfort of Christian belief in resurrection and heaven, or of the local beliefs in reincarnation of souls, but it does hold out the possibility of a joint return to a source, and of a reunion of sorts, in a vaguely conceived afterlife. Ikuo later interprets Patron's suicide as "heroic, but miserable and comic," and entirely understandable as an elderly man's "winding up his affairs" (565). Patron may also choose to die in atonement for his sins. Though "sin" is a term used sparely in the novel, it is clear that Patron needs to expiate in some way the sin he feels he committed, not so much toward God (for in laughing at God he was only fulfilling the necessary heraldic role, as he sees it, of antichrist), but toward those who trusted and believe in him—most obviously the two major subgroups of the Quiet Women and the Technicians.

Both groups suffer a piercing sense of abandonment and isolation because of Patron's renunciation. Patron's Somersault forced these two groups to suffer—the Technicians by being hunted down and imprisoned by the authorities for following their interpretation of Patron's visions, the Quiet Women by withdrawing to an ascetic, prayerful life aimed at experiencing the "hell" that Patron and Guide lived through. Patron's death offers both a means to expiate his own sense of sin toward them and a substitutionary death to defuse the mass suicide plot of the Quiet Women—he dies, in other words, so they may live. Likewise, his fiery death vicariously fulfills Ikuo's long-held desire for massive destruction and conflagration (Ikuo, urged on by Dancer to *Do it!* is predictably the one who actually sets the blaze). A year after Patron's death, Ikuo has mellowed and is no longer the young man obsessed with God's wrathful destruction: the Young Fireflies who have joined the church "no longer call Ikuo *Yonah*" (556). Ikuo has outgrown Jonah and now "seems to be free from the voice of God" (555). In his final act on earth, it is as if Patron is saying *Let me die instead of you!* to the Quiet Women, and *Kill me instead of the world!* to Ikuo. And in fact, in this novel, so filled with talk of destruction and apocalypse, only two people end up dead—Patron and Guide. The rest are left to pick up the pieces and construct their own vision of the world and of their spiritual search.

And what sort of spiritual vision of the future do Patron and *Somersault* leave? Despite his view of himself as the "old man," in his sacrificial death Patron fulfills more the Christlike role of the "new man" who "makes one the two that stand opposed," "reconciling both of them to God through the cross, putting to death their hostility." (For those searching for a cross in the story, recall that Christ is often described as nailed to a "tree" in his crucifixion.) In the post-Patron world, to what extent has hostility been ended and people been reconciled to God?

To a great extent the hostility between two contending religious visions in the novel *has* been reconciled. In the final chapter, as Ogi visits the Hollow to gather information for the "History of the Age" (his chronicle of the church) the reader learns that Young Gii, the leader of the Young Fireflies, has been "selected to take over the spiritual side of the church eventually" (555), while Ikuo, now married to Dancer, is in charge of the day-to-day running of the church. The Quiet Women and a less radical core of the Technicians have opted to remain in the Hollow and will share the duty of educating Gii. Ikuo recognizes the potentially violent nature of Gii and his cohorts (Gii questions a visiting American reporter about how secretly to obtain weapons from U.S. bases, as well as talking excitedly of a final Branch-Davidian style stand-off between the Fireflies and the rest of the world and the establishment of a "millennial reign"), yet insists that he will stand by this group of youngsters, who are the real "new men" of the church.

This uneasy truce or reconciliation represents Ōe's attempt to meld two different religious views current throughout *Somersault* and present in part in his earlier works as well. On the one hand are the indigenous, animistic traditions of the Ur-village that is the setting of so many Ōe works, most notably *The Silent Cry* and the *Moeagaru midori no ki* trilogy; on the other hand are the intrusive, monotheistic/pantheistic, New Age/pseudo-Christian religious views of someone like Patron. In *Somersault* the local traditions, which have been in decline, are revived by the activist Young Fireflies. These practices are nothing new in Ōe's work, and they include such things as a candlelight procession to the hills in which dead souls are ritually buried at the foot of a selected tree. Later, these souls come down from the hills and are reborn as infants. As Gii points out, in such a reincarnation scenario, the living are all those who have "come back." At one press conference, Patron had been accused of bringing an "anti-Japanese religious philosophy" to the village. Opposition to it is fierce in many quarters, most notably among the Fireflies, who, with the Church of the New Man coming in and taking over the former Church of the Flaming Green Tree facilities, see parallels between themselves and the occupied Palestinian territories, making it known that they are ready to fight the new church to defend their land with its special "power." In *Moegaru*, which precedes *Somersault*, the motif of an outsider's coming to the village to lead a church also appeared. In that case it was an earlier Brother Gii. In this novel, the outsider is in part subsumed by the local belief system by being designated the latest in a line of Brothers Gii, people with special spiritual or other powers. At the end of *Moegaru*, however, when Brother Gii dissolves his local church and sets out to leave the village on a missionary journey, he is attacked by locals and killed. (One is left wondering whether any reconciliation between "local" beliefs and the outside world is possible.) In *Somersault* there is an even starker clash between two systems, both of them based on Ōe's own experiences and study: the local village practices and beliefs inspired by his rural Shikoku upbringing, and the alien amalgamation of readings in Dante, Dostoyevsky, Blake, Yeats, R. S. Thomas, the Bible, and so on. But here, in the end, there is an uneasy, provisional accommodation between the two. Earlier I spoke of *Somersault* as a more simply told version of *Moeagaru*, but this is not wholly the case, for *Somersault* goes beyond the earlier novel in its attempt to synthesize Ōe's contending spiritual inclinations.

This move toward accommodation and reconciliation finds symbolic expression in the final moments of Patron's life. The Spirit Festival led by the Young Fireflies involves a parade of large-scale papier-mâché figures representing legendary and historical figures from the village's past—He Who Destroys, Oshikome, Shirime ("Butthole Eye"), Meisuke-san (leader of a peasant uprising), Jin (an obese woman in *The Silent Cry*), and Brother Gii. The figures are paraded before the audience, then ritually burned in a massive bonfire. Patron dons a special full-body papier-mâché figure of Guide, who is to be added to the pantheon of local legends. In the creation of the Guide figure and in Patron's wearing it, there is a symbolic playing out of the future accommodation between the two religious systems. Patron's participation in the festival signals support for the local belief system, while the addition of Guide to the pantheon of native figures local acceptance of the new church. As is common with Ōe's work, the novel ends with an unresolved tension and many unanswered questions. Will Gii and his Firefly militia wind up repeating the violent apocalyptic visions of the old radical faction? Have Patron's humanistic, pacifist tendencies been passed down to a mellower Ikuo? Or is confrontation between the two inevitable, mimicking the radical faction/Patron crisis that spawned the Somersault? Ikuo's comments on the subject indicate his attitude, at least for the moment:

> "No matter what frightening things the young people in the church do over the next ten or fifteen years," Ikuo continued, "as long as they're New Men I'm not going to drive them out. I imagine that from now on Gii will, in both what he says and does, be the one who fluctuates the most violently, but right now in our church he's the number-one New Man. I want to educate him to be the one who shouts *Long Live Karamazov!* and succeeds the dead. I want to raise him up in our church—and *outside* it, too." (568)

"Inside" and "outside" the church—the implications are intriguing in their ambiguity: now that the outside church has been integrated *into* the village, will some reinvigorated belief system move into the world *outside*? That is what Patron hoped would happen. Ōe's fictional universe, however, leaves the reader hanging, and one can only speculate until the saga is picked up once again.

One thing is clear, though: much of what has taken place will inevitably pass into the realm of legend. In fact, one of the more unusual aspects of the novel is the realization that it portrays the genesis of a legend. Just as the man Guide has already been transformed into a village spirit, so will, in time, aspects of the new church and the fiery demise of its leader become part of village folklore. With typical scatological humor, Ōe suggests that the only thing that will remain is the name given to the place where the Quiet Women suffered their bout of drug-induced diarrhea ("Mountain Stream Where Twenty-Five Refined Ladies Shat"), and that events of the summer conference will "fade into the past" (555). But the evidence suggests the contrary, that legendary figures will continue to be remembered and memorialized. Remembering and memorializing are depicted as active, creative processes. Just prior to the summer conference, as Gii and his cohorts revive the Spirit Festival and the stories of legendary figures, literally sketching their visions of the spirits, one witnesses how the past is always rewritten. Spirits do not come unmediated, but are the product of reinterpretation. Likewise, as Ogi compiles his massive "History of the Age" to document the history of the church, though he strives to capture every moment and every detail he and others can recall, and to write as objective an account as possible, what is underscored is the subjective nature of any such undertaking.

And where is God in all this? Endō Shūsaku writes that Ōe's fiction is "characterized by the quest for salvation without God,"[34] and *Somersault* can certainly be read as Ōe's most complete expression of this view to date. Patron's final interpretation of Kizu's Jonah triptych is as depicting "this young man as seeing beyond the antichrist to God," but by the end of the novel God is essentially out of the picture as well. Patron's shocking death has changed Ikuo, making him "free from the voice of God" he had sought all his life. In the final pages of the novel Ikuo recalls for Ogi how Kizu died, of cancer, a few months after the summer conference. Kizu's final words to him just before he dies are these: "Ikuo—is it really so bad that you can't hear God's voice? You don't need God's voice, do you? People should be free. . . . You say . . . God's voice . . . told you that . . . but I think . . . even without God, I want to say *rejoice*. To me, and to . . ." (569–570). Kizu's mention of freedom harks back to one of the first conversations he had with Ikuo, in which he had recalled an anecdote about a Renaissance painter who, when asked to contribute a drawing in a competition to paint a fresco, submitted a single, perfect circle. "And that circle fits perfectly with the concept of a circle that resides within God," Kizu remarks (41). "The person who can accomplish this is a *free man*." Ikuo, at this point still obsessed with Jonah, finds freedom not in artistic accomplishment but in a Jonah-like ability to confront God:

> Jonah complained to God that he changed his original plan. Aren't you supposed to finish what you first decided to do? he implored. Isn't the way Jonah acted exactly the way a free person is supposed to act? Of course it's

God who makes this freedom possible—and correct me if I'm wrong—but if God doesn't take into account the freedom to object to what He wants, how can He know what true unlimited freedom is? (42)

By the end of the novel, of course, Patron concludes that God is defined by a *lack* of imagination, the antichrist by imagination alone. Freedom is found in the human imagination, in the ability and drive to find *another way*, to confront God's plan, even rail against it if need be. But is this true dialogue? Will God respond? Patron's answer to Ikuo's earlier questions come in his final sermon, moments before his death. Imagining Ikuo's response to the Somersault, he says:

> By your Somersault, [Ikuo would] say, *you made a fool of God, Patron. But how can you make a fool of something that doesn't exist? The fact that you had no choice but to do the Somersault is inescapable proof that God appeared to you. . . . He did it for the sake of God, a God who is real.*
>
> Yonah's positive questions have made me ponder things, and I now recognize that I made a fool of a God who is real though silent, a God who is definitely keeping a watch on me. . . . By making a fool of God, Guide and I made a *confession of faith*. (545–546)

In Patron's final moments it becomes clear that—following the model of Jonah's talking back to God, trying to convince him to reverse a decision —it is *Ikuo* who has taught *Patron*, who has brought him an awareness of what the Somersault was all about, and about the relationship of God and man. In Ōe's fictional universe here, God exists, and in people's making a fool of God He is sustained. It is not particles of light going back to the creator that sustain him, but rather *words*, words from ordinary human beings struggling to make sense of the relationship between themselves and what lies beyond. God exists, God keeps watch over our affairs, but he is ultimately silent. R. S. Thomas' hope for a "reciprocal touch" is not found in Ōe, but this doesn't negate the position that *spirit matters*.

In the final lines of the novel an American reporter asks Ikuo, "Has this become a church without God, then?" to which Ikuo responds with Somersault's final line: "For us, a church is a place where deeds of the soul are done." Ikuo's words echo Ōe's in an interview three years before the novel's publication: "I don't know if there is a god or not; possibly there is. The most important thing for me is the orientation of the soul or the heart to something beyond our world. . . . With God or without God I don't know. But our concentration on something over and beyond our reality is most important."[35]

In Ōe's case one might add that a novel, too, is a place where deeds of the soul are done. And many are done in this, his most soulful work.

What is one to make of *Somersault* as a response to Aum? In writing in response to Aum, Ōe had set himself two goals: first, to imagine the mind-set of young people who are drawn to cults, and second, to imagine the consequences of the apostasy of a cult leader such as Asahara—for himself, for the cult, and for its members. References to Aum as a counterpoint to Patron's church dot the text. Guide first mentions Aum in discussing the reactions of members to the Somersault. Among other reactions, "Some followers were left on their own and joined groups like Aum Shinrikyō and fundamentalist Christian groups" (102). Interestingly, here Patron's old church is seen as a predecessor to Aum, one which in some cases feeds into it. (Assuming that the present time of *Somersault* is approximately the time of composition, 1999, one can place the Somersault in 1989, at which time Aum was a fledgling organization.)[36] Later, as Patron announces his comeback after his decade of silence, his new church is seen more as a successor to Aum. Patron's announcement that he will "fight the final battle on earth" and "never again compromise" (172) spawns fears among reporters that they are about to witness the rise of another Aum-like religion. At yet another press conference, Ogi states, "Patron believes that if there hadn't been a Somersault . . . the church, with the radical faction leading it, would have ended up just like Aum. And if that happened our church, again like Aum, would have been attacked and destroyed. Patron needed to send out a message of healing for his followers" (227). Here the Somersault is seen as a preventative measure to defuse an Aum-like outcome (though years before the Aum attacks of 1995). The idea of healing is important in this context. In the Somersault, Patron's "healing message" is a preemptive strike to save the lives of his radical followers and possibly of innocent civilians; later on, as he begins his new church, it functions as a healing sanctuary for spiritual seekers, as well as for the remnants of Aum. To borrow Murakami's evaluation, it provides a "safety net" for those whose earlier safety net (Aum) proved a dangerous illusion. Patron comments,

> When there is a great desire on the part of young people for spiritual salvation, nothing will be solved by crisis-management measures taken to crush new religious groups just because one group that absorbed these young people committed a blunder. Our attitude is to be open to any and all young people searching for salvation. With none of the established

religions, Buddhism and Christianity, offering this, I believe there is a place for us to care for these young people. (233)

As Henri Nouwen writes, "Healing means first of all allowing strangers to become sensitive and obedient to their own stories. . . . Healers are hosts who patiently and carefully listen to the story of the suffering strangers."[37] In *Somersault* this is exactly what occurs as Patron listens to, and helps heal, a variety of people. Guide is the first "suffering stranger" whom he heals, and Guide is succeeded by a variety of people who become followers, including Dr. Koga, Dancer, Kizu, and Ogi. Most memorable among these are the minor characters Ms. Tachibana and Ms. Takada (one of the Quiet Women). Ms. Tachibana, whose younger brother Morio is a mentally challenged composer (the idiot savant figure found throughout Ōe's oeuvre and inspired by his own son Hikari), first encounters Patron after giving up in disgust on established religions. At a small gathering with Patron, she takes notes on his sermon, writing down thoughts based on the "words of a seventeenth-century philosopher":

God revealed himself in Christ and in Christ's spirit, not following the words and images the prophets had given.

When the true spirit of things is grasped, apart from words and images, then and only then are they truly understood. . . . Christ actually, and completely, grasped this revelation. (89)

As she listens to the sermon, Ms. Tachibana cannot help but speak up:

"Sir," I asked, "I don't know about this special person named Christ, but could this be applied to someone else—say, an unfortunate person? A person who doesn't know he's unfortunate and has a pure heart? Is it possible that God could reveal himself directly, not through words, but through *music?*"

After I said this, Patron wove his way on unsteady legs through the narrow space between the people sitting in front and came and held my hand and whispered to me, *"That's exactly right!"* I was still a young girl, and those words stayed in my heart. I felt as if my body and heart were filled with light.

Ms. Tachibana and Morio become such devoted followers that they follow Patron in "loyal deaths" as the newspaper puts it.

Ms. Takada is a young woman with a terrible facial deformity. A scar runs "from one ear down to her cheek," and "one of her eyes [is] completely covered over by a smooth layer of skin" (198). One day when she is alone with Patron, he bids her come to his side and look deep into his eyes:

> I was afraid he was going to make a pass at me. But he said it so casually I couldn't resist, and though I was wary, I went ahead and knelt in front of him. He told me to look once inside his eyes, and what I saw was this: my own face, *beautiful, completely unscarred.* The face of a young woman, her eyes wide open in surprise.
>
> Next he told me to smile, since then I'd see my own face smiling. I tried to smile, but I was so happy I burst into tears.
>
> . . . And I became convinced that the beautiful face I saw reflected in the Savior's eyes was my real face, the one my soul possessed before I was born, so I was able to forgive him [for the Somersault] and think of him with fondness. (198–199)

These and many other stories of spiritual healing through contact with Patron and his church echo stories of Aum followers in Murakami's *Underground* and elsewhere. In addition, the entire research-scientist-gone-mad scenario played out in the radical faction's Izu research facility parallels much of what happened in Aum. One critical difference between Aum and Ōe's cult, though, lies in the consequences of bringing on the apocalypse for the followers: Asahara's closest aides expected to survive, in fact saw their survival alone as the whole point of Aum and themselves as "chosen," while Ōe's radical faction from the first envisioned themselves dying horrible deaths so that others might be urged to repent and live. This apparent altruism, though, is tempered by the fact that the radical faction was planning, shortly before the Somersault, to assassinate a hundred high-ranking Japanese leaders, in imitation of early 1930s right-wing plots (497). Still, the element of the random mass murder of innocent civilians that characterized Aum was missing from the radical faction's plans, whose emphasis was always on sacrifice of *self,* not of *other.* Even Ikuo, the erstwhile murderer, recalls with fondness how he was influenced by the Miyazawa Kenji story "Gusukonbudori," in which a young man sacrifices himself to stop a volcano from erupting and destroying the world (365); though his interests turn later toward Jonah and an obsession with mass destruction and cities in flames, he recommends both Jonah and the Miyazawa story to the violence-prone Fireflies. This combination of obsession with mass destruction tempered by a more altruistic, self-sacrificing stance is what grounds much of *Somersault* and distinguishes its cult from Aum.

The principal difference between Aum and Patron's cult, however, lies in the persons of the leaders themselves. For all his complexity (his deep interest in music, poetry, literature) Patron is in some ways a simpler soul than Asahara; unlike the Aum leader, he never sought religious power or planned to found a church. He is a mystic who never intended his vision to go beyond himself, a reluctant savior, in other words, and far from power-hungry. The narrative of apocalypse and repentance in *Somersault* several times threatens to overwhelm Patron, but he resists. He is a cult leader who is willing to throw it all away in a moment, willing to renounce everything he's stood for, willing to suffer disgrace and humiliation, as long as he can defuse the radical faction, saving their lives and those of countless ordinary Japanese. Ian Reader has said of Aum that it polarized the world into good and evil, propounded a notion of a sacred war, and emphasized the existence of enemies who conspired to destroy them. He speaks of "Aum's descent from its early optimistic mission of world salvation to the murky depths of murder."[38] In stark contrast to Asahara and Aum, Patron struggles to maintain the earlier part of the equation—the mission of world salvation—from being overwhelmed by the second—the descent into murder and violence.

Indeed, three times in the novel mass violence is planned by members of the church, and in each case Patron preempts and defuses their plans. The first of these is the plan of the radical faction, a decade before the novel begins, to occupy and blow up nuclear power plants, that prompted Patron to renounce his beliefs and go into seclusion. The second incident occurs when the Fireflies, led by Gii and Ikuo, are apparently about to light up the forest surrounding hundreds of spectators so that they die in a fiery blaze. I say "apparently" because it is not entirely clear whether this conflagration was actually going to take place, or was all a figment of Patron's imagination. Either way, Patron is nearly out of his mind with worry, fearing for the lives of hundreds of people. The third and final incident is the attempted mass suicide of the Quiet Women, which is foiled in a humorous way that has the women squatting desperately in the weeds evacuating their bowels, rather than, as they had planned, crumpling over dead from poison or dangling from ropes.

In *Somersault* Ōe creates a parallel world, where Patron and his church are an alternative to Asahara and Aum. Does the narrative of a cult leader necessarily have to end in violence? Can apocalyptic narrative be contained, to lead away from, not toward, mass violence and death? Ōe, in imagination, rewrites the ending not only of Jonah, but of Aum as well. In his 1994 Nobel

Prize acceptance speech, he notes the profound influence of the humanistic education he received and states, "I wish my task as a novelist to enable both those who express themselves with words and their readers to recover from their own sufferings and the sufferings of their time, and to cure their souls of their wounds. . . . I find the grounds for believing in the exquisite healing power of art."

    Somersault is a flawed work in many ways, repetitious and far too long. As one reviewer put it, with all the seemingly endless theological debate, one is not sure if the end of the novel, let alone the world will ever come.[39] But with this novel Ōe has taken an important step toward curing the souls of his readers, the Japanese in a traumatized post-Aum world. In doing so, he has demonstrated not only that spirit matters, but that art can indeed have the power to heal.

Conclusion

Of Christian writers in Japan Mark Williams speaks of the "generation of postwar writers, epitomized by Endō, who remain determined to address in their fiction the issues raised by their faith," but the ones he lists—Endō Shūsaku, Shimao Toshio, Shiina Rinzō, Miura Shūmon, Miura Ayako, Sono Ayako, Takahashi Takako, Yasuoka Shōtarō, and Ariyoshi Sawako (to which I would add Ogawa Kunio and Kaga Otohiko)—are either now dead or in the twilight of their careers, with no successors in sight.[1] These writers have made enormous contributions; as an important minority voice they have added to the vocabulary of Japanese literature such themes as original sin, martyrdom, and the possibility of the miraculous. They have, as in Miura's best-sellers, presented a dramatic and personalized statement of belief—a road map to readers who might be inclined to follow. They have also, as with Sono, laid bare the shadow of doubt that tinges their faith, delineating in personal terms what it means to be both Japanese and Christian. Their influence, though, is gradually receding. Endō, Miura, and Sono in particular will continue to be read, but few if any seem poised to take up the mantle of the committed believer-writer.

More recently, in the words of Ozaki Mariko, Japanese literature has been concerned with the search for "deeds of the soul" *(tamashii no koto)* in an "age without gods" *(kami naki jidai),* along the lines of the ending of Ōe's *Somersault.* The search for spiritual meaning continues, even in a relentlessly secular, materialist world, where traditional (and even less traditional, such as Christianity) foci of belief are largely absent.[2] To put it another way, today Japanese writers are more likely to explore spiritual matters that are not, in a traditional way at least, issues raised by their faith. Their work thus is not an illustration of a firmly held faith, but rather a raising of questions for which there is no set catechism. The answers to these questions are, at best, inchoate and in the process of being formulated. As Ozaki writes of Ōe and others who continue to pursue spiritual matters, the impulse toward spiritual literary pursuits remains both strong and important: "The inner questions of [these writers] are something that continues to be shared by influential writers in our country. . . . Novelists are beginning all kinds of experiments. They understand that the only path is a regeneration of Japanese literature starting now."[3] As evidence of this continued interest in spiritual fiction and the pursuit of "inner questions" Ozaki sites two recent works: Hino Keizō's *Tenchi* (Heaven and earth), which depicts a "creation of myth through human imagination" that in her opinion agrees with Ōe's "vision of god"; and Ikezawa Natsuki's *Subarashii shin sekai* (A wonderful new world). She quotes one of Ikezawa's characters, a woman in her thirties, who asks: "Why did Asahara appear on the scene? And how many more Asaharas will pop up after this? . . . The war is to blame. The country used apocalyptic slogans of a national crisis to steal people's souls away from religion. And then they threw them away."[4] These authors' themes are echoed in *Somersault,* where the reader witnesses both the creation of myth in the enshrining of Guide (and presumably later Patron) in the pantheon of village deities and the role of the war in robbing the Japanese of their "soul." *Somersault,* in fact, could be read as a story of the postwar Japanese struggling to survive abandonment by their "deity" (the Emperor) as much as it is a story of Patron's apostasy and of Aum. As one character in Ōe's novel puts it, speaking of the Emperor's surrender speech:

> When Patron and Guide turned their Somersault . . . I had the feeling
> that I'd already experienced that before. This happened at the time of our
> defeat in World War Two. . . . We were to assemble with our teachers in the
> auditorium to listen to the radio. What really shocked us students was that
> the Emperor spoke in an entirely human voice, just like ours.[5]

The model for Patron's apostasy, then, can be found closer to home than, say, Sabbatai Zevi. In this passage from *Somersault,* the 1945 surrender speech and the "renunciation of divinity" speech a year later are conflated, with the implication that the second speech was unnecessary: by the act of speaking at all, the Emperor/god had already become, suddenly, absent. A god who speaks to us is, in this sense, no god at all. On the final page of *Somersault,* the dying Kizu says, "Even without God, I want you to *rejoice*"; and in response to the reporter's question, "Has this become a church without God, then?" Ikuo declares, "For us, a church is a place where deeds of the soul are done."

One might read this as the Japanese abandonment of hope for a dialogue with the transcendent (just as Patron, after his apostasy, was cut off from "visions" of the other side), while still struggling to cope with the spiritual impulse, the inner desire to accomplish spiritual deeds.

The Christian literary critic Okuno Masamoto argues for what he calls a "paradoxical reversal" at work in *Somersault,* a rupture between inner experience—the experience of God's being—and the external reality of God's absence. Kizu's final words, he maintains, do not deny God's existence. They are instead a statement that God's will cannot be known to people, and that, through resigning oneself to the unknowability of God's will, one paradoxically makes the nature of God evident. Knowing you cannot know God's will, in other words, is true knowledge of God. Okuno goes on to quote Kierkegaard to the effect that "Faith is precisely the contradiction between the infinite passion of the individual's inwardness and the objective uncertainty."[6] In a similar vein, speaking of his Somersault in his final speech to his followers, Patron concludes,

> Yonah's [Ikuo's] positive questions have made me ponder things, and now I recognize that I made a fool of a God who is real though silent, a God who is definitely keeping watch on me. And because this is so, the descent into hell awaited me after the Somersault. If Guide and I really broke all connections with the *other side* through the Somersault, why in the world would we have to suffer in hell?[7]

To extend the metaphor, through the sufferings of a hellish postwar period, the Japanese have *not* "broke[n] all connections with the other side," and continue to insist that spiritual things matter.

No one story can fully capture present-day Japanese literary attitudes toward the spiritual, but the one that perhaps comes closest is Murakami's "All God's Children Can Dance." First published in 2000 as one of six stories in the collection of the same name (retitled *After the Quake* in the English translation), the story (and the collection) is part of Murakami's reaction to the Kobe earthquake of 1995. As the mother of the protagonist, Yoshiya, heads off on a relief mission to the ravaged city, the fact of the earthquake is never far away; likewise, the impact of cults (and of Aum) is present as well in the cult that Yoshiya has left, but to which his mother still adheres. Beyond this nod to the twin tragedies of 1995, though, the story presents a memorable and emblematic vision of the sort of anguished and at times ambiguous spiritual quest of modern Japan.

Yoshiya, a gangly twenty-five-year-old who works for a small publishing company, is viewed by his mother's religious cult as a kind of divine being, a son of God. After Yoshiya's mother becomes pregnant with him (her third unwanted pregnancy)—despite the insistence of her obstretrician lover that his use of birth control was "beyond reproach"—a senior member of the cult, Mr. Tabata, analyzes the pregnancy as a miraculous occurrence of divine intervention:

> You took the most rigorous contraceptive measures, and yet you became pregnant. Indeed, you became pregnant three times in a row. Do you imagine that such a thing could happen by chance? I for one do not believe it. Three "chance" occurrences are no longer "chance." The number three is none other than that which is used by our Lord for revelations. In other words, Miss Osaki [Yoshiya's mother], it is our Lord's wish for you to give birth to a child. The child you are carrying is not just anyone's child, Miss Osaki: it is the child of our Lord in Heaven; a male child, and I shall give it the name of Yoshiya, "For it is good." (65–66)

This passage at one stroke references both Genesis 1:12, "And God saw that it was good" (in Japanese, *Kami wa mite, sore o* yoshi *to sareta;* emphasis added) and the annunciation and birth of Christ. In the story, though, Yoshiya's youthful relationship to God revolves around secular issues: he prays he can shake off his uncoordinated ways, his unpopular status ("I promise to maintain unwavering faith in You if only You will let me catch outfield flies" [61]). At thirteen he renounces his faith, a move that devastates his mother, and he becomes a hard-drinking young man prone to casual sexual encounters. Our first view of him shows him recovering from a crippling hangover after a night of carousing.

Still, throughout his young life Yoshiya is propelled by a desire to meet his "Father," to have "God my father . . . recognize me as His son" (69). The second half of the story narrates this search. When, on the train, he spies a middle-aged man missing an earlobe (a detail his mother has revealed about her lover), Yoshiya pursues him through the darkened Tokyo suburbs, first by cab and then on foot. After losing sight of him, Yoshiya, ironically enough for an unathletic young man who wanted nothing more than to be good at baseball, winds up on a pitcher's mound in a dark, deserted baseball field. Uncertain what to do, he recalls his love of dancing—the gangly yet spontaeous way he used to move that spawned his college girlfriend's nickname for him, "Super-Frog." When he danced in college,

As he let himself go and moved his body in time to the music, he would come to feel that the natural rhythm inside him was pulsing in perfect unison with the basic rhythm of the world. The ebb and flow of the tide, the dancing of the wind across the plains, the course of the stars through the heavens: he felt certain that these things were by no means occurring in places unrelated to him. (77)

Now, on the baseball mound, he is seized by a desire to recapture that sense of one-ness:

Unable to think of a song to match his mood, he danced in time with the stirring of the grass and the flowing of the clouds. Before long, he began to feel that someone, somewhere, was watching him. His whole body—his skin, his bones—told him with absolute certainty that he was in someone's field of vision. So what? he thought. Let them look if they want to, whoever they are. All God's children can dance. . . . He would eventually have to pass through the forest, but he felt no fear. Of course—the forest was inside him, he knew, and it made him who he was. (78–79)

Readers of *Kafka on the Shore* will recognize in this passage the sort of imagery employed in that later novel—the spiritual journey likened to a journey through a deep, dark forest of one's inner self. Watched over by "someone" *(dare ka)*, possibly God Himself, Yoshiya is poised on the edge of a spiritual and personal discovery, taking the first steps into this "forest." It is not, he is beginning to discover, in the *finding* of God that one reaches a spiritual awakening—he essentially gives up his pursuit—but in the continued *process* of the search. His quest for "God the Father" also reveals how, in the end, such a spiritual search is not the sole property of an anointed few, but the legacy of all. ("All God's children can dance," with the emphasis on "All.")

The final pages of Murakami's story leave one with a haunting image of a young man that, I think, says much about the way the search for the transcendent in Japanese literature has been depicted in recent years—and will no doubt continue to be depicted for some time. The final lines are particularly suggestive. After remembering Mr. Tabata's deathbed confession of lusting after Yoshiya's mother, Yoshiya recalls his own incestuous desires for her, thoughts he never revealed to the dying man:

He took Mr. Tabata's hand and held it for a very long time, hoping that the thoughts in his breast would communicate themselves from his hand to

Mr. Tabata's. Our hearts are not stones. A stone may disintegrate in time and lose its outward form. But hearts never disintegrate. They have no outward form, and whether good or evil, we can always communicate them one to another. All God's children can dance. The next day, Mr. Tabata drew his last breath.

Kneeling on the pitcher's mound, Yoshiya gave himself up to the flow of time. Somewhere in the distance he heard the faint wail of a siren. A gust of wind set the leaves of grass to dancing and celebrated the grass's song before it died. "Oh God," Yoshiya said aloud. (82)

Yoshiya replaces the necessity of forgiveness with a mutual, though unspoken, understanding between human hearts of human fallibility and sinfulness. The heart here is far more than the seat of the emotions; it is, in essence, that which connects mortals with the eternal. Giving up organized religion, giving up any pursuit aimed at somehow directly touching God—a description that would fit the majority of Murakami's readers, and most Japanese—does not mean abandoning the spiritual. In fact, it can mean quite the opposite.

The meaning of Yoshiya's final call to God *(Kamisama, to Yoshiya wa kuchi ni dashite itta)* is, like the endings of many of Murakami's stories, more suggestive than clear-cut. Is Yoshiya's groan one of thankfulness that he has finally begun his journey of spiritual discovery? Is he expressing his relief that the pursuit of his "father" need no longer obsess him? Is it, even, a simple prayer for his life to come? Perhaps it is a bit of all three.

Notes

Introduction

1. Whether Murakami Haruki should be classified as a postmodern writer is a matter of some debate. Obviously, I do not see him as such. For differing views see Matthew Strecher, *Dances with Sheep: The Quest for Identity in the Fiction of Murakami Haruki* (Ann Arbor: Center for Japanese Studies, The University of Michigan, 2002), and Chiyoko Kawakami, "The Unfinished Cartography: Murakami Haruki and the Postmodern Cognitive Map," *Monumenta Nipponica* 57/3 (Autumn 2002): 309–337.

2. This story was originally published in *Kaien* (March 1991), and is found in Ogino Anna, *Watashi no aidokusho* (Tokyo: Fukutake Shoten, 1991), 95–134.

3. From Takahashi Genichirō's novel *Yūga de kanshōteki na Nihon yakyū* (Kawade Shobo Shinsha, 1988); a translation by Minoru Mochizuki of part of this is found in *New Japanese Voices: The Best Contemporary Fiction from Japan,* ed. Helen Mitsios (New York: Atlantic Monthly Press, 1991), 102–122, under the title "The Imitation of Leibniz."

4. A. S. Byatt, *The Biographer's Tale* (New York: Vintage, 2002), 4. See Fredric Jameson, *Postmodernism: Or, the Cultural Logic of Late Capitalism* (Durham: Duke University Press, 1991), especially chapter 1.

5. Philip Gabriel, "Dream Messengers, Rental Children, and the Infantile: Shimada Masahiko and the Possibilities of the Postmodern," in *Ōe and Beyond: Fiction in Contemporary Japan,* eds. Stephen Snyder and Philip Gabriel (Honolulu: University of Hawai'i Press, 1999), 219–244.

6. See Donald Keene, "Japanese Writers and the Greater East Asia War," in Donald Keene, *Appreciations of Japanese Culture* (Tokyo: Kōdansha, 1981), 300–321.

7. For a complete discussion of these see Doris Bargen, *A Woman's Weapon: Spirit Possession in* The Tale of Genji (Honolulu: University of Hawai'i Press, 1997).

8. Paul Varley, *Japanese Culture,* 4th ed. (Honolulu: University of Hawai'i Press, 2000), 195.

9. Karatani Kōjin, *The Origins of Modern Japanese Literature,* translation edited by Brett de Bary (Durham: Duke University Press, 1993); see 81 and all of chapter 3.

10. The exceptions are Roy Starrs' study of Shiga, and the work of Mark Williams and Van C. Gessel. See Mark B. Williams, *Endō Shūsaku: A Literature of Reconciliation* (London: Routledge, 1999), and Van C. Gessel, "Voices in the Wilderness: Japanese Christian Authors," *Monumenta Nipponica* 37/4 (Winter 1982): 437–457. For an interesting discussion of religious symbolism in the work of Kawabata, see Gwenn Boardman Petersen, *The Moon in the Water: Understanding Tanizaki, Kawabata, and Mishima* (Honolulu: University of Hawaiʻi Press, 1979), 127–133.

11. The classic early study of this is H. Neill McFarland, *The Rush Hour of the Gods: A Study of New Religious Movements in Japan* (New York: Harper & Row, 1970). After the Aum affair, of course, a number of new studies of this cult appeared.

12. The only exception to this chronological order is the discussion of Miura's *Shiokari tōge,* which comes in chapter 2, though it was published before *Zoku hyōten,* discussed in chapter 1. *Umibe no Kafuka* is the only post-millennial novel, having been published in 2002.

13. Haruki Murakami, *Underground* (New York: Vintage, 2000), 247–248.

14. Comments on Endō and Jung are found in Williams, *Endō Shūsaku,* 51.

15. Sono Ayako, *Kiseki* (Tokyo: Bunshun Bunko, 1977), 180.

16. Ibid., 215.

Chapter 1. The Frozen Soul

1. Asai Kiyoshi, *"Hyōten"/"Zoku hyōten," Kokubungaku kaishaku to kanshō* 63/11 (November 1998): 46.

2. As Asai (ibid.) notes, this was an enormous amount for the time, roughly equivalent to the prime minister's salary for two years.

3. Miura notes that the title *Hyōten* was actually her husband's suggestion. Miura wrote the final section of the novel, Yōko's written testimony/suicide note, first, and her husband suggested using the term, which first appears in this section, as the title of the novel. See Miura Ayako, *"Hyōten" o tabi suru* (Sapporo: Hokkaidō Shimbunsha, 2004), 36–37.

4. Asai, *"Hyōten"/"Zoku hyōten,"* 47.

5. Harada Yōichi, "Kaisetsu," in *Hyōten,* 2: 365–366. The edition used here is the standard paperback edition by Kadokawa Bunko, first published in 1982, and as of 2001 in its fifty-seventh printing. This edition, in two volumes, totals 732 pages. All page references in the text are to this edition, with the volume number given first, and the page number second. Unless otherwise noted, translations from the novel are my own.

6. Its popularity is reflected in its sales figures. *Hyōten's* initial printing of 50,000 copies sold out in a week, and by a year later sales had topped 700,000.

(Ozaki Hokki, "*Hyōten*,'" *Asahi Jyānaru* 9/9 [February 1967], 36.) A recent Japanese website lists *Hyōten* as Miura's number one best-seller, with 3.38 million copies sold. *Zoku hyōten* is in third place, with 2.84 million copies (www .hamashon.com/miura-ayako/guide/n-ayakoguide03.htm).

7. Harada, "Kaisetsu," in *Hyōten*, 366.

8. *Zoku hyōten (Freezing Point II)* was serialized from May 12, 1970, to May 10, 1971, in 360 installments. On a personal note, I vividly recall being given a copy of *Hyōten* by a student of mine soon after I first arrived in Nagasaki in 1977 to teach English at a women's college. It was the first Japanese novel I ever owned, and I recall how excited the student was, assuring me that the work was one of the best novels she'd ever read. Hiromu Shimizu and John Terry, the translators of *Freezing Point*, note that in a January 1986 poll of ordinary Japanese readers, Miura was chosen as the most popular author in Japan, beating out such competitors as Mishima and Kawabata, and that the book had sold 1.5 million copies. (Miura Ayako, *Freezing Point*, translated by Hiromu Shimizu and John Terry [Wilmington, DE: Dawn Press, 1986], unpaginated afterword.)

9. The information on television, film, and stage versions comes from Asai, "*Hyōten*"/"*Zoku hyōten*," 52.

10. Ibid., 47.

11. Ibid., 50.

12. Miura, *Hyōten*, 1: 71–72.

13. Miura, *Freezing Point*, translated by Shimizu and Terry. This edition is obscure and is generally not found in either U.S. or Japanese bookstores. As far as I know, *Freezing Point II* has not been translated into English.

14. This trilogy includes *Michi ariki* (1969), *Kono tsuchi no utsuwa o mo* (1970), and *Hikari aru uchi ni* (1971). The first volume has been translated into English as *The Wind Is Howling* by Valerie Griffiths (Downers Grove, IL: Inter-Varsity Press, 1977).

15. Quoted in Kubota, *Kindai Nihon bungaku to kirisutosha sakka* (Osaka: Izumi Shoin, 1992), 54.

16. Ibid., 55.

17. Ibid., 57. For details of Miura's life and struggles, see her autobiographical trilogy.

18. Kubota, *Kindai Nihon bungaku*, 57–59.

19. By familiar I mean that much of the novel, as Asai notes, incorporates and recycles familiar elements. The novel follows a long line of classical Japanese stories (e.g., *Utsubo monogatari*, *Sumiyoshi monogatari*) that depict the abused stepchild, and it combines the well-worn notion of retribution for previous actions ("karma" is another way of putting it) with the three main elements of popular newspaper novels: light tempo, interesting plot development, and attractive characters (Asai, "*Hyōten*"/"*Zoku hyōten*," 51–52). Asai also notes how the conventions of overhearing conversations and glancing at diaries are put to good use in the novel as devices through which characters learn certain secrets.

20. The Shimizu and Terry translation makes the obliqueness of Murai's declarations much more openly affectionate. His calling her "Natsue-san" in the original becomes "Darling" in English, while the "feelings" he declares for her are translated as "love," in "You must have understood how much I love you, but . . . " (Shimizu and Terry, *Freezing Point*, 9). Throughout, the Shimizu and Terry translation is more interpretive, adding a certain smoothness to the text. My own translations are deliberately more literal and closer to the original.

21. This is not to imply that Ruriko's murder is a surprise to any reader, for the paperback edition gives away this and other salient plot points in its blurb.

22. This pronouncement comes at the end of the first volume of the two-volume paperback edition and effectively marks an end to one part of the story. As originally bound, however, the novel was in one volume, and there was no indication that the story should be seen as being in two parts.

23. See, for instance, Carol A. B. Warren, *Madwives: Schizophrenic Women in the 1950s* (New Brunswick, NJ: Rutgers University Press, 1987).

24. Miura, *Hikari aru uchi ni* (Tokyo: Shinchō Bunko, 1996), 33.

25. Ibid., 37.

26. Ibid., 26.

27. Harada makes the same point in "Kaisetsu," in *Zoku hyōten,* 2: 369. (The edition used here, as with *Hyōten,* is the two-volume paperback edition from Kadokawa, in its sixty-fifth printing as of 2000. Again, page references are given in the text with volume first, page second.)

28. Quoted in Harada, "Kaisetsu," in *Hyōten,* 2: 370.

29. Cf. the early poetry of Yosano Akiko, for example, especially the collection *Midaregami.*

30. Donald G. Bloesch, *Essentials of Evangelical Theology* (Peabody, MA: Prince Press, 1998), 92.

31. John Irving, *A Son of the Circus* (New York: Ballantine Books, 1994), 324.

32. Bloesch, *Evangelical Theology,* 95.

33. Quoted in ibid., 104.

34. Ibid., 107.

35. Last page of Shimizu and Terry, *Freezing Point* (unpaginated).

36. Ibid., 495.

37. Flannery O'Connor, *Mystery and Manners* (New York: Noonday Press, 1995), 161.

38. Ibid., 154.

39. Kubota, *Kindai Nihon bungaku,* 58–59.

40. Quoted in Ozaki, "*Hyōten,*" 38.

41. As Ozaki (ibid., 36–37) argues, although Asahi mounted an extensive public relations campaign to promote the serialization, the book's boom was nevertheless genuine.

42. Ibid., 36.

43. Ibid., 38.

44. Miura, *"Hyōten" o tabi suru,* 155.

45. Quoted in Harada, "Kaisetsu," in *Zoku hyōten,* 2: 370.

46. Ibid., 2: 369.

47. Miura, *"Hyōten" o tabi suru,* 142.

48. Bloesch, *Evangelical Theology,* 98.

49. By the time Miura wrote these words she had published *Shiokari tōge* (see chapter 2), a study of this very notion of the giving of one's life as the ultimate expression of love.

50. Philip Yancey, *What's So Amazing about Grace?* (Grand Rapids, MI: Zondervan, 2002), 98.

51. Henri J. M. Nouwen, *Reaching Out: The Three Movements of the Spiritual Life* (New York: Doubleday, 1995), 97.

52. Kuroko Kazuo, "Miura Ayako no shizenkan." *Kokubungaku kaishaku to kanshō* 63/11 (November 1998): 30.

53. Asai, *"Hyōten"/"Zoku hyōten,"* 50. Of course publishing exigencies come into account as well when considering the relationship between the timing of publication and the content of the novel.

54. Harada, "Kaisetsu," in *Zoku hyōten,* 2: 374.

55. Yancey, *Grace,* 98.

56. Asai, *"Hyōten"/"Zoku hyōten,"* 49.

57. O'Connor, *Mystery and Manners,* 163.

58. Ibid., 167.

59. Harada, "Kaisetsu," in *Zoku hyōten,* 2: 374–375.

Chapter 2. The Seed Must Fall

1. Recently a second translation of a Sono novel has appeared: *No Reason for Murder* (original title: *Tenjō no ao*), translated by Edward Putzar (New York: ICG Muse, 2003).

2. All page references to *Kiseki* in the text are to the paperback edition of the work, first published in 1977 by Bunshun Bunko. The book was originally published in 1973 by Mainichi Shimbunsha.

3. Robert Royal, *The Catholic Martyrs of the Twentieth Century* (New York: Crossroad, 2000), 210–211.

4. Several English websites list the following information about the two: "the July 1948 cure of intestinal tuberculosis of Angela Testoni, and August 1950 cure of calcification of the arteries/sclerosis of Francis Ranier" (Patron Saints Index, http://www.catholic-forum.com/saints/saintm01.htm). An Italian website agrees with Sono's use of "Angelina" as the woman's first name, and I follow this version of the name. (See www.smbsassari.com/milizia/milizia.htm.)

5. These are listed in her own bibliography. In addition to her own I would add the ones I have consulted in writing this chapter: André Frossard, *"Forget Not Love": The Passion of Maximilian Kolbe* (San Francisco: Ignatius Press, 1987);

Susan Bergman, ed., *Martyrs: Contemporary Writers on Modern Lives of Faith* (San Francisco: HarperSanFrancisco, 1996); and Royal, *Catholic Martyrs.*

6. Frossard, *Maximilian Kolbe,* 23.

7. Paul Mariani, "Maximilian Kolbe Poland, 1941." In Bergman, ed., *Martyrs,* 216–233.

8. Royal, *Catholic Martyrs,* 205–206.

9. Mariani, "Kolbe," 221.

10. Ibid., 219.

11. Sono, *Kiseki,* 101.

12. Mariani, "Kolbe," 223.

13. Ibid., 219.

14. Ibid., 229.

15. Ibid., 230.

16. Sadists like the Nazis, she argues, who find *sustained* pleasure in cruelty, should be distinguished from their wartime allies the Japanese: "Atrocities in the war by the Japanese were impulsive [*hossateki*]. They blew up in anger and then killed" (100). Sono's dismissal of Japanese atrocities is troubling and does not square with information that surfaced after the publication of *Miracles* about sustained atrocities like the Rape of Nanjing. Be that as it may, Sono writes of the intertwining of sadism like the Nazis' with the existence of God.

17. Sono Ayako, "Ochiba no koe." *Gendai Nihon kirisutokyō bungaku zenshū* 7 (Tokyo: Kyōbunkan, 1973): 129.

18. Ibid., 131.

19. Ibid., 131–132.

20. Ibid., 140.

21. The translations from Gardavsky are taken from Vitezslav Gardavsky, *God Is Not Yet Dead,* translated by Vivienne Menkes (Harmondsworth, England: Penguin Books, 1973). Sono's quotations from Gardavsky are taken from the Japanese edition of the book, *Shi ni hatenu kami,* translated from the German by Shigeru by Aoki and Shigeru Kobayashi (Tokyo: YMCA Shuppan, 1971).

22. Viktor Frankl was a psychiatrist who survived the Nazi concentration camps. He is the author of numerous books, including *Man's Search for Meaning.*

23. Flannery O'Connor, *Mystery and Manners* (New York: Noonday Press, 1995), 153. For more about the possibility of miracles from a Christian standpoint, see C. S. Lewis' classic *Miracles* (New York: Touchstone, 1996). For an informed discussion of the historicity of miracles, see John P. Meier, *A Marginal Jew: Rethinking the Historical Jesus,* vol. 2, *Mentor, Message, and Miracles* (New York: Doubleday, 1994).

24. *Shiokari Pass,* translated by Bill and Sheila Fearnehough (Tokyo: Charles E. Tuttle, 1974). In contrast to the more interpretive and problematic translation of Miura's *Freezing Point* discussed in chapter 1, the Fearnehough translation is

generally accurate and fluent. Unless otherwise noted, it is this translation that is quoted in the above discussion, and page references in the text are to this edition. References to the Japanese original are to *Shiokari tōge* (Tokyo: Shinchō Bunko, 1998).

25. Nonomiya Noriko, *"Shiokari tōge," Kokubungaku kaishaku to kanshō* 63/11 (November 1998): 65.

26. Miura Ayako, "Afterword" [*Atogaki*], in *Shiokari tōge,* 375.

27. Ibid., 374.

28. *Shiokari Pass* (Fearnehough translation), 9–10.

29. Miura notes how, thirty years after his death, when most people would be remembered only by close relatives, Nagano's life and deeds remained firmly in the minds of members of his church (Miura, "Afterword," 374).

30. Ibid., 375.

31. Ibid., 378.

32. Wakasa Tadao, "Genzai no bungaku—*Shiokari tōge*," *Seiki,* no. 413 (October 1984): 79.

33. Yamaji Aizan, *Essays on the Modern Japanese Church: Christianity in Meiji Japan,* translated by Graham Squires (Ann Arbor: Center for Japanese Studies, The University of Michigan, 1999), 62–64.

34. Karatani Kōjin, *The Origins of Modern Japanese Literature* (Durham: Duke University Press, 1993), 84–85. (Translation edited by Brett de Bary.)

35. Wakasa, "Genzai no bungaku," 79.

36. Ibid., 79–80.

37. As far as the pursuit of material success is concerned, it is ironically Masayuki's death that forces Nobuo to part ways with the standard path of success, the economic pinch following his father's death making it impossible for him to pursue his dream of attending college.

38. Nakamura Harusame's novel *The Fig Tree* was published in 1901. The author's name is alternately read Nakamura Shun'u.

39. Additional examples are found on pages 253 and 254 of the translation. Here Nobuo, shortly before his death, reads the following passage from the Bible: "By this we know love, that he laid down his life for us. And we ought to lay down our lives for the brethren." And later, at a public talk, Nobuo says, "If it be necessary, let us be ready at any time to give our lives for God."

40. The phrase is from 1 John 4:16.

41. Miura Ayako, *Hikari aru uchi ni* (Tokyo: Shinchō Bunko, 1996), 26.

42. These remarks are in the Japanese paperback edition of *Shiokari tōge* (Tokyo: Shinchō Bunko, 1998), 380–383.

43. Nonomiya, *"Shiokari tōge,"* 69. This is the same term used in Natsume Sōseki's *Kokoro* to describe the death of General Nogi at the end of the Meiji period.

44. Miura, "Afterword," 374.

45. Wakasa, "Genzai no bungaku," 84.

46. Nonomiya, *"Shiokari tōge,"* 67–68.

47. Mark B. Williams, *Endō Shūsaku: A Literature of Reconciliation* (London: Routledge, 1999), 34.

48. Ibid., 34–35.

49. O'Connor, *Mystery and Manners,* 187.

50. Ibid., 187, 171.

51. Ibid., 157. See Williams, *Endō Shūsaku,* 35, for a discussion of how Endō placed himself in the camp of those "for whom artistic integrity remained of paramount importance."

52. Miura Ayako, *"Hyōten" o tabi suru* (Sapporo: Hokkaidō Shimbunsha, 2004), 26.

53. Ibid., 26.

54. Ibid., 159.

55. Quoted in Williams, *Endō Shūsaku,* 36.

56. For a fuller treatment of Shimao's work see my *Mad Wives and Island Dreams: Shimao Toshio and the Margins of Japanese Literature* (Honolulu: University of Hawai'i Press, 1999).

57. Okuno Takeo, quoted in Mark B. Williams, "Shadows of the Former Self: Images of Christianity in Contemporary Japanese Literature" (Ph.D. diss., University of California at Berkeley, 1991), 193.

58. *"The Sting of Death" and Other Stories by Shimao Toshio,* translated by Kathryn Sparling (Ann Arbor: Center for Japanese Studies, The University of Michigan, 1985), 23.

59. Ibid., 29.

60. Ibid., 149.

61. Williams, "Shadows of the Former Self," 147.

62. Ibid.

63. Ibid., 223–224.

64. Ibid., 231.

65. Ibid., 211.

66. See Gabriel, *Mad Wives and Island Dreams,* chapters 3 and 4.

67. Williams notes a similar inability to "see" in depictions in "Shima e." Williams, "Shadows of the Former Self," 212.

68. See Shimao's essay "Dōshite shōsetsu o watakushi wa kaku ka," in *Shimao Toshio zenshū* (Tokyo: Shōbunsha, 1986), 261–266, for a discussion of how Shimao desires purely to "record" reality as it appears to him.

69. Discussed in Gabriel, *Mad Wives and Island Dreams,* 256. One cannot escape the sense that Shimao's work does serve as a vehicle for a fictionalized confessional that is quite in keeping with the practices of a man who, by all accounts, was a devout Catholic.

Chapter 3. Aum, *Underground*, and Murakami Haruki's Other Side

1. Murakami Haruki, *Underground*, translated by Alfred Birnbaum and Philip Gabriel (New York: Vintage, 2000), 8. Unless otherwise noted, all page references in the text are to this edition.

2. Noted studies of Aum include Robert Jay Lifton, *Destroying the World to Save It: Aum Shinrikyo, Apocalyptic Violence, and the New Global Terrorism* (New York: Henry Holt, 1999); Ian Reader, *Religious Violence in Contemporary Japan: The Case of Aum Shinrikyo* (Honolulu: University of Hawai'i Press, 2000); and David E. Kaplan and Andrew Marshall, *The Cult at the End of the World* (New York: Crown, 1996).

3. Reader, *Religious Violence*, discusses the meaning of the name in his book; see especially page 61.

4. Ibid., 209. Lifton, *Destroying the World*, notes, "Between 1990 and 1995 the cult staged at least fourteen chemical and biological attacks of varying dimensions" (6).

5. Quoted in Stephen Snyder and Philip Gabriel, eds., *Ōe and Beyond: Fiction in Contemporary Japan* (Honolulu: University of Hawai'i Press, 1999), 1.

6. Murakami Haruki, *Henkyō, kinkyō* (Tokyo: Shinchōsha, 1998), 239.

7. See Murakami's comments in *Underground*, 239–241.

8. Ibid., 231.

9. Ibid., 354.

10. Ibid., 247–248. Page references are hereafter given in the text.

11. One notes Murakami's worries about whether his interviewees are representative members of Aum (*Underground*, 248).

12. This notion of Aum members' having already lived through "the end" is fascinating, but unfortunately Murakami does not pursue it. See Ōe, *Somersault*, on this idea of salvation—or the end of the world—as both experienced always and as a single historical event. (Note that the published English version of Murakami's text, in English *Underground*, does not use diacritic marks for Japanese words; thus I have omitted them in quotations from this volume. Personal names are also in English order, with the given name first [Shoko Asahara, instead of Asahara Shōko], and I have referred to given names in this fashion when quoting from this volume. Discussion apart from direct qotes uses Japanese order.)

13. Lifton, *Destroying the World*, 8.

14. Murakami, interviewed in Howard French, "Seeing a Clash of Social Networks, a Japanese Writer Analyzes Terrorists and Their Victims," *New York Times*, October 15, 2001, sec. E, p. 1.

15. Ibid.

16. Jay Rubin, *Haruki Murakami and the Music of Words* (London: Harvill Press, 2002), 243.

17. French, "Seeing a Clash of Social Networks."

18. Matthew Carl Strecher, *Dances with Sheep: The Quest for Identity in the Fiction of Murakami Haruki* (Ann Arbor: Center for Japanese Studies, The University of Michigan, 2002).

19. Murakami Haruki, *Sputnik Sweetheart,* translated by Philip Gabriel (New York: Vintage, 2001). Page references to the novel are given in the text.

20. The Aum interviews in the translation of *Underground* have been edited, with some of the cuts coming precisely in these types of reminiscences of early childhood.

21. Murakami, *Underground,* 304-305.

22. Ibid., 281.

23. Susan Napier, "Ōe Kenzaburō and the Search for the Sublime at the End of the Twentieth Century." In Snyder and Gabriel, eds., *Ōe and Beyond,* 21.

24. Fredric Jameson, *Postmodernism: Or, the Cultural Logic of Late Capitalism* (Durham: Duke University Press, 1991), 38.

25. In a recent interview, Murakami said these were the hardest parts to write. See "*Umibe no Kafuka* o kataru," *Bungakukai* (April 2003): 10-42.

26. Murakami Haruki, *Hardboiled Wonderland and the End of the World,* translated by Alfred Birnbaum (Tokyo: Kodansha International, 1991), 270.

27. Ibid., 386.

28. Ibid., 399.

29. Ibid., 350.

30. Napier, "Search for the Sublime," 22.

31. There is a limit of course, to this analogy. The old scientist whose experiments on the narrator have disastrous consequences is portrayed throughout as a genial, well-meaning man, truly concerned about the narrator's well-being, and far from the image of Asahara one gets from *Place.*

32. Rubin, *Music of Words,* 194.

33. Ibid., 195.

34. Philip Gabriel, "Dream Messengers, Rental Children, and the Infantile: Shimada Masahiko and the Possibilities of the Postmodern." In Snyder and Gabriel, eds., *Ōe and Beyond,* 224.

35. See the opening of "Nejimaki dori to kayōbi no onnatachi" (originally published in *Shinchō* in January 1986), translated by Alfred Birnbaum as "The Wind-Up Bird and Tuesday's Women" in Murakami Haruki, *The Elephant Vanishes* (New York: Knopf, 1993), 3-33. This was later incorporated into the opening of the novel *The Wind-Up Bird Chronicle.*

36. Rubin, *Music of Words,* 199; Strecher, *Dances with Sheep,* 97.

37. Rubin, *Music of Words,* points out both of these ideas.

38. Murakami, *Underground,* 364.

39. This passage shows the influence of the Edo period gothic work *Ugetsu monogatari* on Murakami and, by extension, on the notion of Shimamoto as a ghost. He discusses this in the interview "*Umibe no Kafuka* o kataru" and has suggested in a personal conversation that his reading of *Ugetsu monogatari* influenced his portrayal of Shimamoto.

40. Rubin, *Music of Words,* 200.

41. Murakami, *Underground,* 363.

42. Ibid., 233.

43. Murakami, *Sputnik,* 146. One senses, however, that as a member of the Korean minority in Japan, Miu has often felt alienated there as well. The feelings she has in Switzerland are perhaps only the most extreme manifestation of a feeling of disconnectedness she has already experienced in her "native" land.

44. Rubin, who sees this novel as one of Murakami's weakest, is particularly critical of the way Sumire's journey to the "other side" is left unexplained (*Music of Words,* 250–255).

45. Murakami Haruki, "Man-Eating Cats," translated by Philip Gabriel (the *New Yorker,* December 4, 2000): 84–94. It should be noted that the published English translation of the short story, at the request of the *New Yorker* editor, ends with an edited version of the ending of the scene as it appears in *Sputnik Sweetheart* rather than with the original short story ending.

46. Rubin, *Music of Words,* 255.

47. Murakami, "*Umibe no Kafuka* o kataru," 12–13.

48. As of this writing Murakami has just published a children's book, *Fushigina toshokan* (The strange library) that, as the title indicates, is set in a library, continuing the theme.

49. Murakami informs the reader that "Kafka" is Czech for "crow." Likewise, in *Sputnik* one is told that "sputnik" means "traveling companion."

50. *The Wind-Up Bird Chronicle* may approach the same level in terms of violence.

51. Murakami, "*Umibe no Kafuka* o kataru," 24.

52. Despite the comments in *Sputnik* on the necessity of blood's being shed, that novel depicts no such scene directly.

53. Murakami Haruki, *Kafka on the Shore,* translated by Philip Gabriel (New York: Knopf, 2005), 374.

54. Murakami also describes the journey of Hoshino from being a violent youth to, through his encounter with Nakata, becoming an increasingly sensitive, caring individual.

55. The question remains, however, as to whether force used to overcome evil may in itself become a prelude to evil, whether by accepting the axiom "kill or be killed," one becomes what one opposes. *Kafka* indicates various reactions to this challenge: Nakata—unable to resist being "invaded" by other minds—lashes out and kills, while the two unnamed soldiers, more mentally able to resist, take flight rather than accepting this alternative.

56. Murakami, *Kafka,* 37.

57. This idea is found in the Bungakukai interview, "*Umibe no Kafuka* o kataru," 23.

58. In "*Umibe no Kafuka* o kataru," Murakami calls *Sputnik* the "shadow" of *Kafka,* which is the same relationship obtaining between *South of the Border* and *Wind-Up Bird.*

59. Murakami, *Sputnik,* 138–140.

60. Murakami, *Kafka,* 411.

61. Ibid., 372.

62. The theme of reconciliation is far from a passing interest with Murakami. His most recent novel, *After Dark,* depicts the reconciliation of two sisters, while a recent story, "Gūzen no tabibito," leads to the reconciliation of an estranged brother and sister. See Murakami Haruki, *Afutādāku* (Tokyo: Kōdansha, 2004) and "Gūzen no tabibito" (*Shinchō* [March 2005]: 6–22).

63. Murakami, *Kafka,* 208.

64. Note that Crow is Kafka's *ikiryō,* because, as mentioned above, Kafka means "crow" in Czech. A second element that possibly connects *Kafka* with traditional Japanese spritual notions is that of *kami,* noted by John Updike, for instance, in his review of the novel. Updike argues that "*kami* pervades Murakami's world," and that the "novel's two heroes interact only in the realm of *kami*" (*New Yorker* [January 24 and 31, 2005], 91–93). In my opinion, while Murakami does utilize the vocabulary of *kami* in the novel, his imagined spiritual realm is in no way limited to traditional views of the spiritual.

Chapter 4: Literature of the Soul

1. In fact, one of Ōe's novels of the period is entitled *Saigo no shōsetsu* (The last novel [1988]). *Moeagaru* was serialized in three parts in *Shinchō:* the first part appeared in September 1993, the second in June 1994, and the third in March 1995. Ozaki Mariko, "Ōe Kenzaburō no *Chūgaeri*=Tenkō," *Chūō kōron* 114/8 (August 1999): 284.

2. Ozaki, "*Chūgaeri,*" 282.

3. Caroline Moseley, "Start from the Personal," www.princeton.edu/pr/pwb/ 97/0303/0303-oe.html. (Reprinted from the *Princeton Weekly Bulletin,* March 3, 1997.) (Last accessed October 10, 2002.)

4. Ibid., 3.

5. Ibid., 1.

6. Ozaki, "*Chūgaeri,*" 285. Critics in the December 1994 issue of *Bungakukai* speculated about what form this might take.

7. Ozaki, "*Chūgaeri,*" 282. At the memorial service for Takemitsu (February 1996), Ōe declared he had wanted to write a novel for Takemitsu to present to him (ibid., 286).

8. Otohiko Kaga, "Ōe Kenzaburo, Literary Pathfinder," *Japan Echo* 22/1 (Spring 1995). http://www.japanecho.com/

9. Ozaki, "*Chūgaeri,*" 285. According to Ozaki, Ōe was already thinking of writing a continuation of *Moeagaru,* though in a new style. After writing *Somersault,* he said he was trying to grasp what he could not easily grasp in *Moeagaru* (ibid., 287).

10. According to some, then, *Somersault* is nothing new, but a continuation of his saga (setting the stage for yet another Gii to appear), and Ōe himself has

not done a "somersault" with this work. See Fukuda Kazuya, "Nan no tame no keikensa ka," *Bungakukai* (October 1999): 163.

11. Despite the fact that, as Ozaki notes, this novel has been gone over particularly carefully by editors, there is at least one error, a misquotation from a John Donne poem. (Ōe conflated two poems; the error has been rectified in the English translation.) When Ōe learned the novel was to be translated, he contacted the translator and made changes and additions to the text, adding material equivalent to three handwritten manuscript pages.

12. Ozaki, "*Chūgaeri*," 288.

13. Moseley, "Start from the Personal," 1. One could argue, though, that most of *Somersault* focuses on the characters—Patron, Guide, Kizu, Dancer, Ikuo, Ogi—who form the core leadership of the church, not on the rank-and-file members.

14. Numano Mitsuyoshi, "Tamashii no koto o suru basho to shite no shō-setsu," *Bungakukai* 53/10 (October 1999): 141.

15. Ibid., 137.

16. Ibid., 141.

17. Scholem, Gershom, *Sabbatai Sevi: The Mystical Messiah, 1626–1676* (Princeton: Princeton University Press, 1973), 126. For a discussion of how Nathan reinterpreted Sabbatai's messianic mission after his apostasy, see pp. 800–820. It is also interesting to note, in light of the importance Jonah plays in *Somersault*, that as part of his attempt to interpret Sabbatai's message, Nathan touched on an unusual interpretation of this biblical book (ibid., 315–316).

18. The mother-infant image is reminiscent of Endō Shūsaku's ideas about the nature of worship among the so-called Hidden Christians of the Edo period, namely, their development of a "mother-oriented religion." See Endō Shūsaku, "Religious Consciousness of the Japanese," in *Nihon no kokoro* (Tokyo: Kōdan-sha, 1985), 6–21.

19. Numano, "Tamashii no koto," 144.

20. Elaine Shepherd, however, argues that all of Thomas' poetry is religious, including the "non-religious" poems (Elaine Shepherd, *R. S. Thomas: Conceding an Absence: Images of God Explored* [New York: St. Martin's Press, 1996], 186).

21. Ono Kōsei, "Ōe Kenzaburō *Chūgaeri* ni okeru R. S. Tomasu," *Kirisuto bungaku kenkyū* 17 (2000): 57.

22. Shepherd, *R. S. Thomas*, 109.

23. One might, of course, see this as an inversion of Christian belief: humans are so depraved that the best they can hope for is not a savior, but an antichrist.

24. J. D. Douglas, et al., eds., *New Bible Dictionary*, 2nd ed. (Leicester, England: InterVarsity Press, 1996), 50.

25. John R. W. Stott, *The Message of Ephesians: God's New Society* (Leicester, England: InterVarsity Press, 1979), 92.

26. James Limburg, *Jonah: A Commentary* (Louisville, KY: Westminster/John Knox Press, 1993), 19, 39.

27. Bruce C. M. Vawter, *Job and Jonah: Questioning the Hidden God* (New York: Paulist Press, 1983), 98.

28. Quoted in Limburg, *Jonah*, 120.

29. Thomas M. Bolin, *Freedom beyond Forgiveness: The Book of Jonah Re-Examined.* (Sheffield, England: Sheffield Academic Press, 1997), 118.

30. Douglas et al., eds., *New Bible Dictionary*, 614.

31. Abraham J. Heschel, *The Prophets* (Peabody, MA: Prince Press, 1999), 66–67.

32. Bolin, *Freedom beyond Forgiveness*, 177.

33. Limburg, *Jonah*, 9.

34. Quoted in Susan Napier, "Ōe Kenzaburō and the Search for the Sublime at the End of the Twentieth Century," in Stephen Snyder and Philip Gabriel, eds., *Ōe and Beyond: Fiction in Contemporary Japan* (Honolulu: University of Hawai'i Press, 1999), 32.

35. Napier, "Search for the Sublime," 32.

36. In 1989 the Shōwa Emperor died. Though one might imagine Ōe at this point moving beyond his earlier focus on the Emperor, *Somersault* marks a continued fascination with the spiritual consequences of the Emperor's change in status in the postwar period.

37. Henri J. M. Nouwen, *Reaching Out: The Three Movements of the Spiritual Life* (New York: Doubleday, 1995), 96.

38. Ian Reader, *Religious Violence in Contemporary Japan: The Case of Aum Shinrikyo* (Honolulu: University of Hawai'i Press, 2000), 229, 234.

39. See Alan Cheuse's review, "A Powerful Story about Fanaticism and Faith," *Chicago Tribune* (March 2, 2003), 3.

Conclusion

1. Mark B. Williams, *Endō Shūsaku: A Literature of Reconciliation* (London: Routledge, 1999), 33, 246.

2. Ozaki Mariko, "Ōe Kenzaburō no *Chūgaeri*=Tenkō," *Chūō kōron* 114/8 (August 1999): 289.

3. Ibid.

4. Ibid.

5. Ōe Kenzaburō, *Somersault*, translated by Philip Gabriel (New York: Grove Press, 2003), 220.

6. Okuno Masamoto, "*Chūgaeri* o yomu," *Kirisuto bungaku kenkyū* 17 (2000): 50–51.

7. Ōe, *Somersault*, 545–546.

Select Bibliography

Akinari Ueda. *Tales of Moonlight and Rain: Japanese Gothic Tales.* Translated by Kengi Hamada. New York: Columbia University Press, 1972.

Anstey, Sandra., ed. *Critical Writings on R. S. Thomas.* Mid Glamorgan: Poetry Wales Press, 1982.

Asai Kiyoshi, *"Hyōten"/"Zoku hyōten." Kokubungaku kaishaku to kanshō* 63/11 November 1998): 46–53.

Bargen, Doris. *A Woman's Weapon: Spirit Possession in* The Tale of Genji. Honolulu: University of Hawai'i Press, 1997.

Bergman, Susan, ed. *Martyrs: Contemporary Writers on Modern Lives of Faith.* San Francisco: HarperSanFrancisco, 1996.

Bickerman, Elias. *Four Strange Books of the Bible.* New York: Schocken Books, 1967.

Bloesch, Donald G. *Essentials of Evangelical Theology.* Peabody, MA: Prince Press, 1998.

Bolin, Thomas. M. *Freedom beyond Forgiveness: The Book of Jonah Re-Examined.* Sheffield, England: Sheffield Academic Press, 1997.

Breen, John, and Mark Williams, eds. *Japan and Christianity: Impacts and Responses.* New York: St. Martin's Press, 1996.

Cheuse, Alan. "A Powerful Story about Fanaticism and Faith." *Chicago Tribune,* March 2, 2003, p. 3.

Craig, Kenneth M., Jr. *A Poetics of Jonah: Art in the Service of Ideology.* Columbia: University of South Carolina Press, 1993.

Davis, William V., ed. *Miraculous Simplicity: Essays on R. S. Thomas.* Fayetteville: University of Arkansas Press, 1993.

Douglas, J. D., et al., eds. *New Bible Dictionary.* 2nd ed. Leicester, England: Inter-Varsity Press, 1996.

Eagleton, Terry. *After Theory.* New York: Basic Books, 2003.

Endō Shūsaku. "Religious Consciousness of the Japanese." In *Nihon no kokoro,* 6–21. Tokyo: Kōdansha, 1985.

Enomoto Masaki. *Ōe Kenzaburō no hachijū nendai.* Tokyo: Sairyusha, 1995.

French, Howard. "Seeing a Clash of Social Networks, a Japanese Writer Analyzes Terrorists and Their Victims." *New York Times,* October 15, 2001, sec. E, p. 1.

Frossard, André. *"Forget Not Love": The Passion of Maximilian Kolbe.* Translated by Cendrine Fontan. San Francisco: Ignatius Press, 1987.

Fukuda Kazuya. "Nan no tame no keikensa ka." *Bungakukai* 53/10 (October 1999): 148–163.

Gabriel, Philip. "Back to the Unfamiliar: The Travel Writing of Murakami Haruki." *Japanese Language and Literature* 36/2 (October 2002): 151–169.

———. "Dream Messengers, Rental Children, and the Infantile: Shimada Masahiko and the Possibilities of the Postmodern." In *Ōe and Beyond: Fiction in Contemporary Japan,* edited by Stephen Snyder and Philip Gabriel, 219–244. Honolulu: University of Hawai'i Press, 1999.

———. *Mad Wives and Island Dreams: Shimao Toshio and the Margins of Japanese Literature.* Honolulu: University of Hawai'i Press, 1999.

Gardavsky, Vitezslav. *God Is Not Yet Dead.* Translated by Vivienne Menkes. Harmondsworth, England: Penguin, 1973.

Geisler, Norman L. *Christian Apologetics.* Grand Rapids, MI: Baker Books, 1976.

Gessel, Van C. "Voices in the Wilderness: Japanese Christian Authors." *Monumenta Nipponica* 37/4 (Winter 1982): 437–457.

Harada Yōichi. "Kaisetsu." In Miura Ayako, *Hyōten,* 2: 365–371. Tokyo: Kadokawa Bunko, 2001.

———. "Kaisetsu." In Miura Ayako, *Zoku hyōten,* 2: 369–375. Tokyo: Kadokawa Bunko, 2000.

Heschel, Abraham J. *The Prophets.* Peabody, MA: Prince Press, 1999.

Ikebuchi Suzue. "*Hyōten* no tsumi o megutte." *Seiki,* no. 194 (July 1967): 59–64.

Jameson, Fredric. *Postmodernism: Or, the Cultural Logic of Late Capitalism.* Durham: Duke University Press, 1991.

Kaga, Otohiko. "Ōe Kenzaburō, Literary Pathfinder." *Japan Echo* 22/1 (Spring 1995). http://www.japanecho.com/

Kaplan, David. E., and Andrew Marshall. *The Cult at the End of the World.* New York: Crown, 1996.

Karatani Kōjin. *The Origins of Modern Japanese Literature.* Translation edited by Brett de Bary. Durham: Duke University Press, 1993.

Katō, Shūichi. "Kawabata and Ōe: From Exoticism to Universality." *Japan Echo* 22/1 (Spring 1995). http://www.japanecho.com/

Kawakami, Chiyoko. "The Unfinished Cartography: Murakami Haruki and the Postmodern Cognitive Map." *Monumenta Nipponica* 57/3 (Autumn 2002): 309–337.

Kawakami, Rin'itsu. "The Nobel Prize and Ōe's Response." *Japan Echo* 22/1 (Spring 1995). http://www.japanecho.com/

Kawamura Sō. *"Moeagaru midori no ki* sanbu saku: Amubigyuasu na sekai." *Kokubungaku kaishaku to kyōzai no kenkyū* 42/3 (February 1997): 154–160.

Kubota Gyōichi. *Kindai Nihon bungaku to kirisutosha sakka.* Osaka: Izumi Shoin, 1992.

———. "Miura Ayako no joseikan." *Kokubungaku kaishaku to kanshō* 63/11 (November 1998): 35–40.

Kuroko Kazuo. "Miura Ayako no shizenkan." *Kokubungaku kaishaku to kanshō* 63/11 (November 1998): 29–34.

Lacocque, André, and Pierre-Emmanuel Lacocque. *Jonah: A Psycho-Religious Approach to the Prophet.* Columbia: University of South Carolina Press, 1990.

Lewis, C. S. *Miracles.* New York: Touchstone, 1996.

Lifton, Robert Jay. *Destroying the World to Save It: Aum Shinrikyo, Apocalyptic Violence, and the New Global Terrorism.* New York: Henry Holt, 1999.

Limburg, James. *Jonah: A Commentary.* Louisville, KY: Westminster/John Knox Press, 1993.

Lorit, Sergius C. *The Last Days of Maximilian Kolbe.* New York: New City Press, 1988.

Mariani, Paul. "Maximilian Kolbe Poland, 1941." In *Martyrs: Contemporary Writers on Modern Lives of Faith,* edited by Susan Bergman, 216–233. San Francisco: HarperSanFrancisco, 1996.

McFarland, H. Neill. *The Rush Hour of the Gods: A Study of New Religious Movements in Japan.* New York: Harper & Row, 1970.

McHale, Brian. *Constructing Postmodernism.* New York: Routledge, 1992.

———. *Postmodernist Fiction.* New York: Methuen, 1987.

Meier, John P. *A Marginal Jew: Rethinking the Historical Jesus.* Vol. 2, *Mentor, Message, and Miracles.* New York: Doubleday, 1994.

Metraux, Daniel A. *Aum Shinrikyō and Japanese Youth.* New York: University Press of America, 1999.

———. *Aum Shinrikyō's Impact on Japanese Society.* Lewiston, NY: Edwin Mellen Press, 2000.

Miura Ayako. *Freezing Point.* Translated by Hiromu Shimizu and John Terry. Wilmington, DE: Dawn Press, 1986.

———. *Hikari aru uchi ni.* Tokyo: Shinchō Bunko, 1996.

———. *Hyōten.* Tokyo: Kadokawa Bunko, 2001.

———. *"Hyōten" o tabi suru.* Sapporo: Hokkaidō Shimbunsha, 2004.

———. *Shiokari Pass.* Translated by Bill and Sheila Fearnehough. Tokyo: Charles E. Tuttle, 1974.

———. *Shiokari tōge.* Tokyo: Shinchō Bunko, 1998.

———. *Zoku hyōten.* Tokyo: Kadokawa Bunko, 2000.

Moseley, Caroline. "Start from the Personal." www.princeton.edu/pr/pwb/97/
0303/0303-oe.html. Reprinted from the *Princeton Weekly Bulletin*, March 3,
1997. Last accessed October 10, 2002.

Murakami Haruki. *After the Quake.* Translated by Jay Rubin. New York: Knopf,
2002.

———. *Afutādāku.* Tokyo: Kōdansha, 2004.

———. *Andāguraundo.* Tokyo: Kōdansha, 1997.

———. *The Elephant Vanishes.* Translated by Alfred Birnbaum and Jay Rubin.
New York: Knopf, 1993.

———. "Gūzen no tabibito." *Shinchō* (March 2005): 6–22.

———. *Hardboiled Wonderland and the End of the World.* Translated by Alfred
Birnbaum. Tokyo: Kodansha International, 1991.

———. *Henkyō, Kinkyō.* Tokyo: Shinchōsha, 1998.

———. "Hunting Knife." Translated by Philip Gabriel. *New Yorker* (November
17, 2003), 140–149.

———. *Kafka on the Shore.* Translated by Philip Gabriel. New York: Knopf,
2005.

———. *Kami no kodomotachi wa mina odoru.* Tokyo: Shinchōsha, 2000.

———. *Kokkyō no minami, taiyō no nishi.* Tokyo: Kōdansha, 1992.

———. "Man-Eating Cats." Translated by Philip Gabriel. *New Yorker* (December 4, 2000), 84–94.

———. *Murakami Haruki zensakuhin: 1979–1989.* Tokyo: Kōdansha, 1990–
1991.

———. *South of the Border, West of the Sun.* Translated by Philip Gabriel. New
York: Vintage, 1999.

———. *Sputnik Sweetheart.* Translated by Philip Gabriel. New York: Vintage,
2001.

———. *Sputoniku no koibito.* Tokyo: Kōdansha, 1999.

———. *Umibe no Kafuka.* Tokyo: Kōdansha, 2002.

———. "*Umibe no Kafuka* o kataru." Interview with Murakami in *Bungakukai*
57/4 (April 2003): 10–42.

———. *Underground.* Translated by Alfred Birnbaum and Philip Gabriel. New
York: Vintage, 2000.

———. *Yakusoku sareta basho de.* Tokyo: Bungei shunjū, 1998.

Myers, Jacob M. *The Layman's Bible Commentary.* Vol. 14. Atlanta: John Knox
Press, 1959.

Napier, Susan. "Ōe Kenzaburō and the Search for the Sublime at the End of the
Twentieth Century." In *Ōe and Beyond: Fiction in Contemporary Japan,*
edited by Stephen Snyder and Philip Gabriel, 11–35. Honolulu: University
of Hawai'i Press, 1999.

Nathan, John. "Ōe Kenzaburō: Mapping the Land of Dreams." *Japan Quarterly*
42/1 (January–March 1995): 89–97.

Nonomiya Noriko. "*Shiokari tōge.*" *Kokubungaku kaishaku to kanshō* 63/11 (November 1998): 65–69.

Nouwen, Henri J. M. *Reaching Out: The Three Movements of the Spiritual Life.* New York: Doubleday, 1995.

Numano Mitsuyoshi. "Tamashii no koto o suru basho to shite no shōsetsu." *Bungakukai* 53/10 (October 1999): 136–146.

O'Connor, Flannery. *Mystery and Manners.* New York: Noonday Press, 1995.

Ōe Kenzaburō. "An Attempt at Self-Discovery in the Mythic Universe of the Novel." *World Literature Today* 76/1 (Winter 2002): 7–18.

———. *Chūgaeri.* Tokyo: Kōdansha, 1999.

———. *An Echo of Heaven.* Translated by Margaret Mitsutani. Tokyo: Kodansha International, 2000.

———. *Jinsei no shinseki.* Tokyo: Shinchō Bunko, 1989.

———. *Ōinaru hi ni.* Tokyo: Shinchōsha, 1995.

———. *Somersault.* Translated by Philip Gabriel. New York: Grove Press, 2003.

———. *Sukui nushi ga nagurareru made.* Tokyo: Shinchōsha, 1993.

———. *Yureugoku.* Tokyo: Shinchōsha, 1994.

Okuno Masamoto. "*Chūgaeri* o yomu." *Kirisuto bungaku kenkyū* 17 (2000): 46–53.

Ono Kōsei. "Ōe Kenzaburō *Chūgaeri* ni okeru R. S. Tomasu." *Kirisuto bungaku kenkyū* 17 (2000): 54–64.

Ozaki Hokki. "*Hyōten.*" *Asahi Jyānaru* 9/9 (February 1967), 35–40.

———. *Hyōten* būmu wa naze okita ka." *Nihon* 9/6 (June 1966): 177–182.

Ozaki Mariko. "Ōe Kenzaburō no *Chūgaeri*=Tenkō." *Chūō kōron* 114/8 (August 1999): 282–289.

Person, Raymond F., Jr. *In Conversation with Jonah: Conversation Analysis, Literary Criticism, and the Book of Jonah.* Sheffield, England: Sheffield Academic Press, 1996.

Petersen, Gwenn Boardman. *The Moon in the Water: Understanding Tanizaki, Kawabata, and Mishima.* Honolulu: University of Hawai'i Press, 1979.

Phillips, D. Z. *R. S. Thomas: Poet of the Hidden God.* London: Macmillan, 1986.

Reader, Ian. *Religious Violence in Contemporary Japan: The Case of Aum Shinrikyo.* Honolulu: University of Hawai'i Press, 2000.

Royal, Robert. *The Catholic Martyrs of the Twentieth Century.* New York: Crossroad, 2000.

Rubin, Jay. *Haruki Murakami and the Music of Words.* London: Harvill Press, 2002.

Sako Junichirō. "Kaisetsu." *Gendai Nihon kirisutokyō bungaku zenshū* 7: 271–291. Tokyo: Kyōbunkan, 1973.

Scholem, Gershom. *Sabbatai Sevi: The Mystical Messiah, 1626–1676.* Princeton: Princeton University Press, 1973.

Seki Shigeru. "Miura Ayako to kirisutokyō." *Kokubungaku kaishaku to kanshō* 63/11 (November 1998): 23–28.

Shepherd, Elaine. *R. S. Thomas: Conceding an Absence: Images of God Explored.* New York: St. Martin's Press, 1996.

Shimao Toshio. "Dōshite shōsetsu o watakushi wa kaku ka." In *Shimao Toshio zenshū,* 261–266. Tokyo: Shōbunsha, 1986.

———. *"The Sting of Death" and Other Stories by Shimao Toshio.* Translated by Kathryn Sparling. Ann Arbor: Center for Japanese Studies, The University of Michigan, 1985.

Snyder, Stephen, and Philip Gabriel, eds. *Ōe and Beyond: Fiction in Contemporary Japan.* Honolulu: University of Hawai'i Press, 1999.

Sono Ayako. *Kiseki.* Tokyo: Bunshun Bunko, 1977.

———. *No Reason for Murder.* Translated by Edward Putzar. New York: ICG Muse, 2003.

———. "Ochiba no koe." *Gendai Nihon kirisutokyō bungaku zenshū* 7: 127–141. Tokyo: Kyōbunkan, 1973.

———. *Watcher on the Shore.* Translated by Edward Putzar. Tokyo: Kodansha International, 1990.

Starrs, Roy. *An Artless Art: The Zen Aesthetic of Shiga Naoya: A Critical Study with Selected Translations.* London: Curzon, 1998.

Stott, John R. W. *The Message of Ephesians: God's New Society.* Leicester, England: InterVarsity Press, 1979.

Strecher, Matthew Carl. *Dances with Sheep: The Quest for Identity in the Fiction of Murakami Haruki.* Ann Arbor: Center for Japanese Studies, The University of Michigan, 2002.

Thomas, M. Wynn, ed. *The Page's Drift: R. S. Thomas at Eighty.* Mid Glamorgan: Seren Books, 1993.

Thomas, R. S. *Between Here and Now.* London: Macmillan, 1981.

———. *Collected Poems.* London: J. M. Dent, 1993.

———. *Selected Prose.* Edited by Sandra Anstey. Mid Glamorgan: Poetry Wales Press, 1983.

Tomioka Kōichirō. "*Jinsei no Shinseki:* kyūzai no imeiji." *Kokubungaku kaishaku to kyōzai no kenkyū* 42/3 (February 1997): 134–139.

Varley, Paul. *Japanese Culture.* 4th ed. Honolulu: University of Hawai'i Press, 2000.

Vawter, Bruce C. M. *Job and Jonah: Questioning the Hidden God.* New York: Paulist Press, 1983.

Wakasa Tadao. "Genzai no bungaku—*Shiokari tōge.*" *Seiki,* no. 413 (October 1984): 75–85.

Warren, Carol A. B. *Madwives: Schizophrenic Women in the 1950s.* New Brunswick, NJ: Rutgers University Press, 1987.

Williams, Mark B. *Endō Shūsaku: A Literature of Reconciliation.* London: Rout-
    ledge, 1999.
———. "Shadows of the Former Self: Images of Christianity in Contemporary
    Japanese Literature." Ph.D. diss., University of California at Berkeley, 1991.
Yamaji Aizan. 1906. *Essays on the Modern Japanese Church: Christianity in Meiji
    Japan.* Translated by Graham Squires. Ann Arbor: Center for Japanese Stud-
    ies, The University of Michigan, 1999.
Yamamoto Kaoru. "Miura Ayako *Hyōten* no Yōko." *Kokubungaku kaishaku to
    kanshō* 41/11 (September 1976): 146–147.
Yancey, Philip. *What's So Amazing about Grace?* Grand Rapids, MI: Zondervan,
    2002.

Index

About the Author

Philip Gabriel received his Ph.D. from Cornell University in 1993 and is professor of Japanese literature at the University of Arizona and head of the Department of East Asian Studies. Gabriel is the author of *Mad Wives and Island Dreams: Shimao Toshio and the Margins of Japanese Literature* and co-editor of the anthology *Ōe and Beyond: Fiction in Contemporary Japan*. He has translated novels by Kuroi Senji, Shimada Masahiko, Yoshimura Akira, Ōe Kenzaburō, and Haruki Murakami, including the *New York Times* best-seller *Kafka on the Shore*. His translations of Murakami's short stories have appeared in the *New Yorker, Harper's, The Paris Review*, and elsewhere. He is the recipient of the Japan-U.S. Friendship Commission Prize for his translation of Kuroi's *Life in the Cul-de-Sac*, and the Sasakawa Prize for his co-translation of Murakami's *Underground*.